FOR HENRY WEREWOLF, THE BOY WITH THE BIGGEST HEART.
MATT

FOR CATHERINE, THE BEST WIFE A HE COULD HAVE.
CHRISTIAN

IMAGE COMICS, INC.

Robert Kirkman – Chief Operating Officer
Erik Larsen – Chief Financial Officer
Todd McFarlane – President
Marc Silvestri – Chief Executive Officer
Jim Valentino – Vice-President

Eric Stephenson – Publisher
Corey Murphy – Director of Sales
Jeff Boison – Director of Publishing Planning & Book Trade Sales
Jeremy Sullivan – Director of Digital Sales
Kat Salazar – Director of PR & Marketing
Emily Miller – Director of Operations
Branwyn Bigglestone – Senior Accounts Manager
Sarah Mello – Accounts Manager
Drew Gill – Art Director
Jonathan Chan – Production Manager
Meredith Wallace – Print Manager
Briah Skelly – Publicity Assistant
Sasha Head – Sales & Marketing Production Designer
Randy Okamura – Digital Production Designer
David Brothers – Branding Manager
Ally Power – Content Manager
Addison Duke – Production Artist
Vincent Kukua – Production Artist
Tricia Ramos – Production Artist
Jeff Stang – Direct Market Sales Representative
Emilio Bautista – Digital Sales Associate
Leanna Counter – Accounting Assistant
Chloe Ramos-Peterson – Administrative Assistant
IMAGECOMICS.COM

Ψ-C

VOL 2 - SONS OF THE WOLF
STORY - MATT FRACTION
ART & COLORS - CHRISTIAN WARD

LETTERING - CHRIS ELIOPOULOS
FLATS - DEE CUNNIFFE

EDITOR - LAUREN SANKOVITCH

DESIGN - CHRISTIAN WARD & DREW GILL

ODY-C CREATED BY MATT FRACTION AND CHRISTIAN WARD

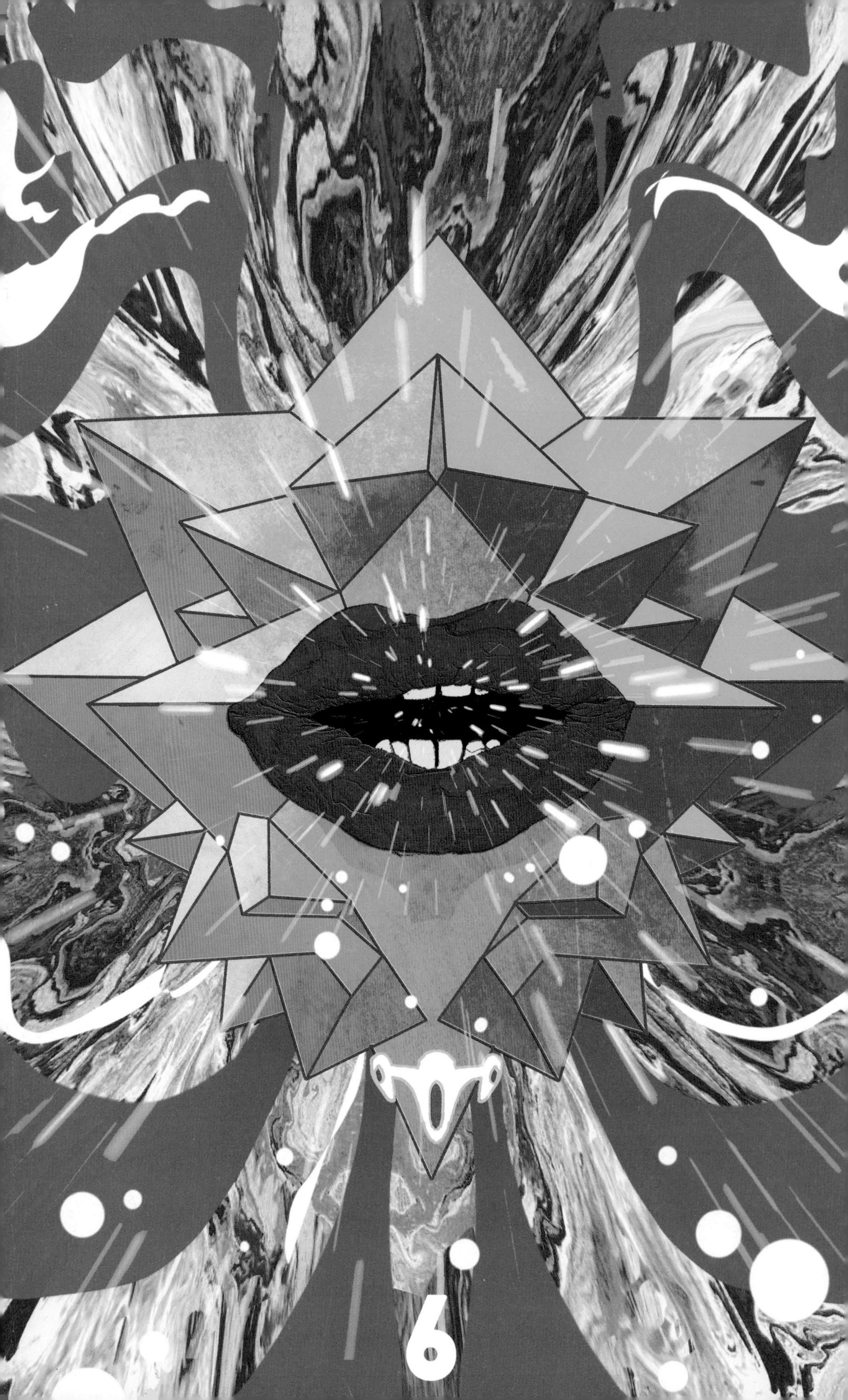
6

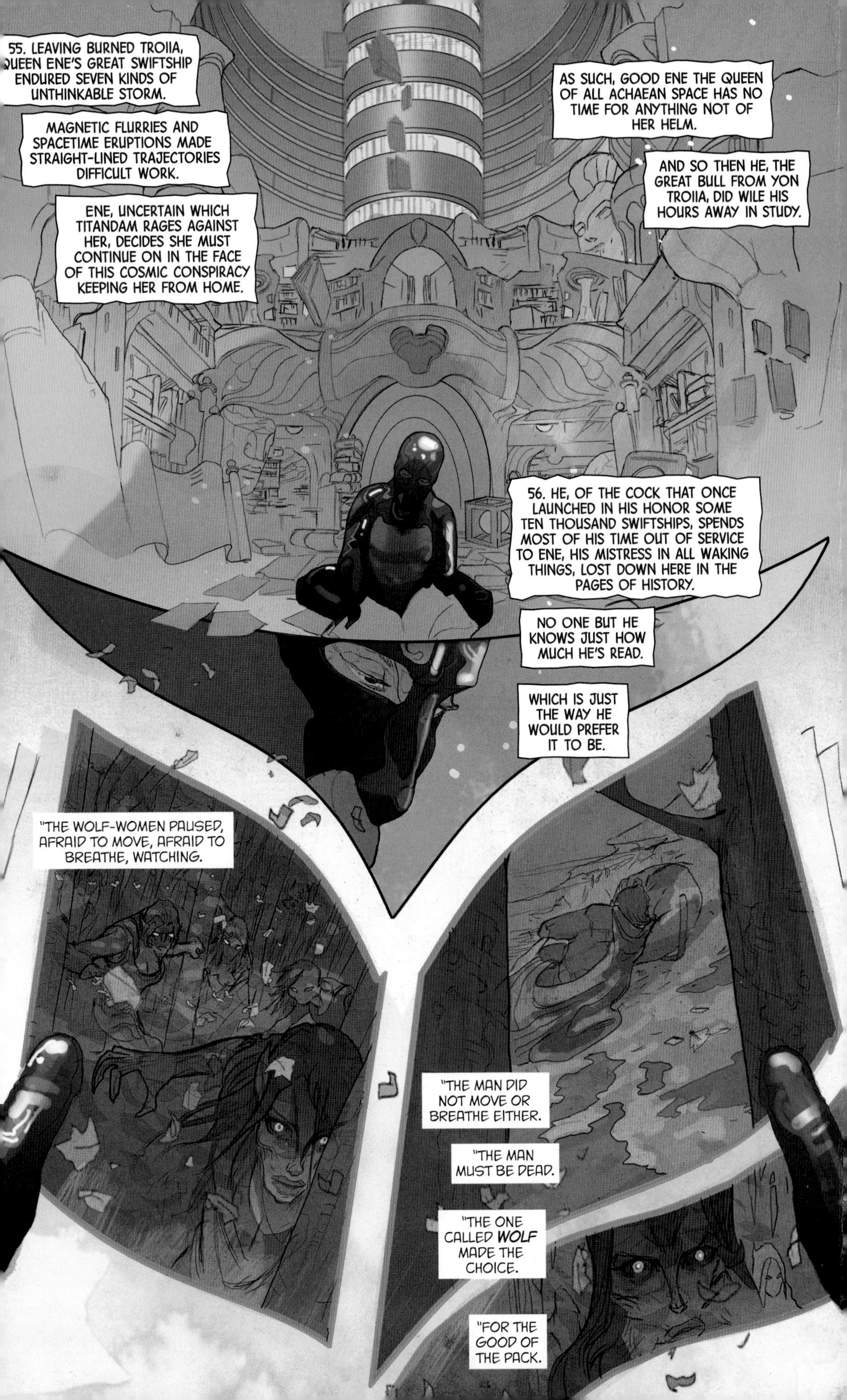
55. LEAVING BURNED TROIIA, QUEEN ENE'S GREAT SWIFTSHIP ENDURED SEVEN KINDS OF UNTHINKABLE STORM.
MAGNETIC FLURRIES AND SPACETIME ERUPTIONS MADE STRAIGHT-LINED TRAJECTORIES DIFFICULT WORK.
ENE, UNCERTAIN WHICH TITANDAM RAGES AGAINST HER, DECIDES SHE MUST CONTINUE ON IN THE FACE OF THIS COSMIC CONSPIRACY KEEPING HER FROM HOME.
AS SUCH, GOOD ENE THE QUEEN OF ALL ACHAEAN SPACE HAS NO TIME FOR ANYTHING NOT OF HER HELM.
AND SO THEN HE, THE GREAT BULL FROM YON TROIIA, DID WILE HIS HOURS AWAY IN STUDY.
56. HE, OF THE COCK THAT ONCE LAUNCHED IN HIS HONOR SOME TEN THOUSAND SWIFTSHIPS, SPENDS MOST OF HIS TIME OUT OF SERVICE TO ENE, HIS MISTRESS IN ALL WAKING THINGS, LOST DOWN HERE IN THE PAGES OF HISTORY.
NO ONE BUT HE KNOWS JUST HOW MUCH HE'S READ.
WHICH IS JUST THE WAY HE WOULD PREFER IT TO BE.
"THE WOLF-WOMEN PAUSED, AFRAID TO MOVE, AFRAID TO BREATHE, WATCHING.
"THE MAN DID NOT MOVE OR BREATHE EITHER.
"THE MAN MUST BE DEAD.
"THE ONE CALLED *WOLF* MADE THE CHOICE.
"FOR THE GOOD OF THE PACK.

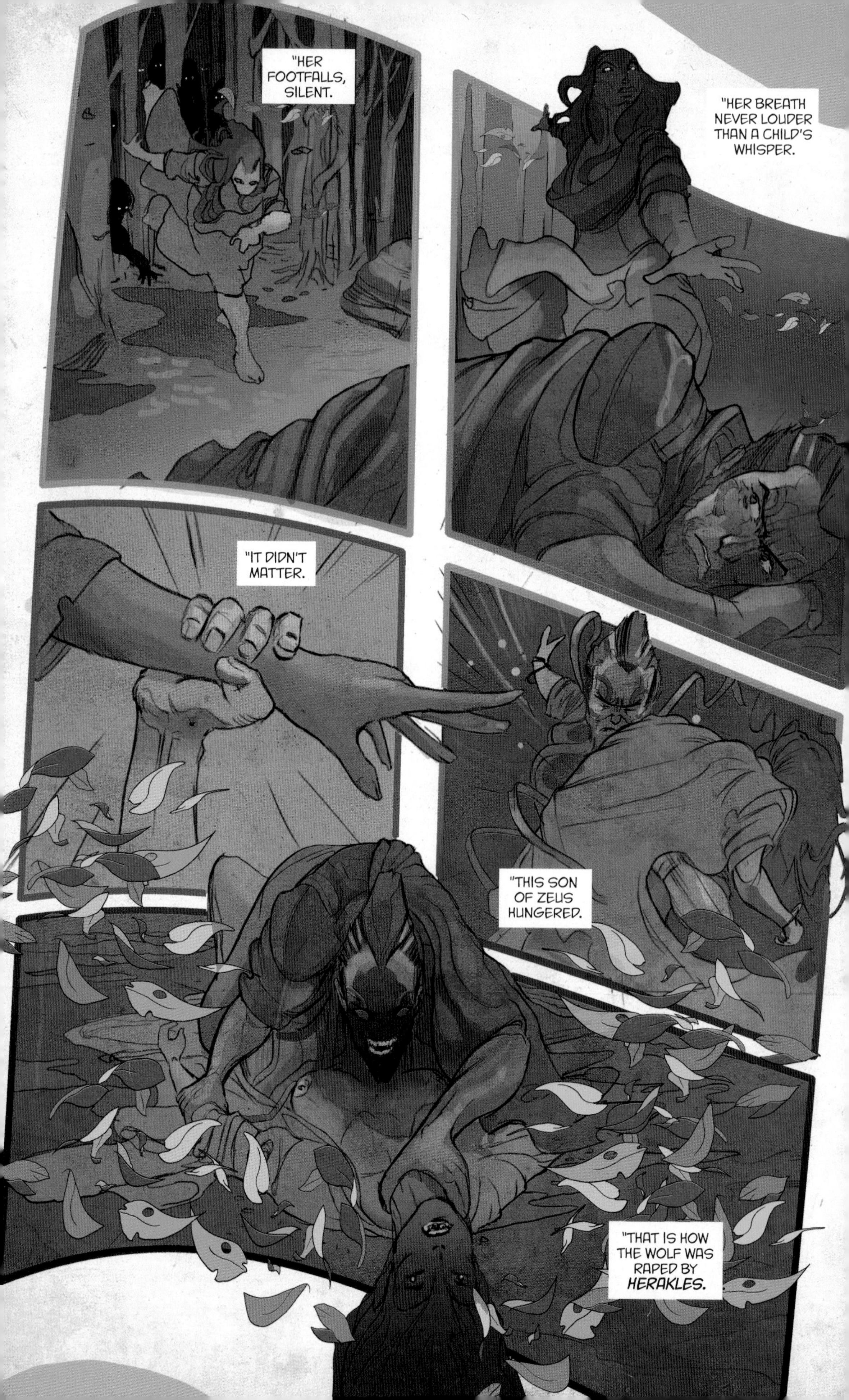
"HER FOOTFALLS, SILENT.
"HER BREATH NEVER LOUDER THAN A CHILD'S WHISPER.
"IT DIDN'T MATTER.
"THIS SON OF ZEUS HUNGERED.
"THAT IS HOW THE WOLF WAS RAPED BY HERAKLES.

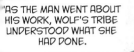

"AS THE MAN WENT ABOUT HIS WORK, WOLF'S TRIBE UNDERSTOOD WHAT SHE HAD DONE.

"AND, GRATEFUL TO HER, THEY DISAPPEARED ONCE MORE INTO THE NIGHT.

"WHEN HE WAS DONE THIS SON OF ZEUS SAT NEAR HER AND RAMBLED THE WAY MEN DO ONCE SPENT.

"NOT WANTING TO BE STRUCK IN THE FACE ONCE MORE (FOR IF WOLF SURVIVED THE NIGHT SHE STILL HAD A LIVING TO EARN) THE BAD-WOMAN-OF-THE-WOODS LISTENED.

"HE TOLD STORIES ABOUT HIS OWN GREATNESS, ABOUT HIS WORKS, HIS GREAT *LABORS*.

"SHE LISTENED UNTIL SHE COULD STOMACH NO MORE. AND THEN SHE BEGAN:

'And the worst farmer ever to till the land, called A-LE-TUDA...

'Who prayed on an ascendant star beneath the only thing growing on his land he had not yet killed...

'I am told, sire, a story of the whore-goddess Inanna...

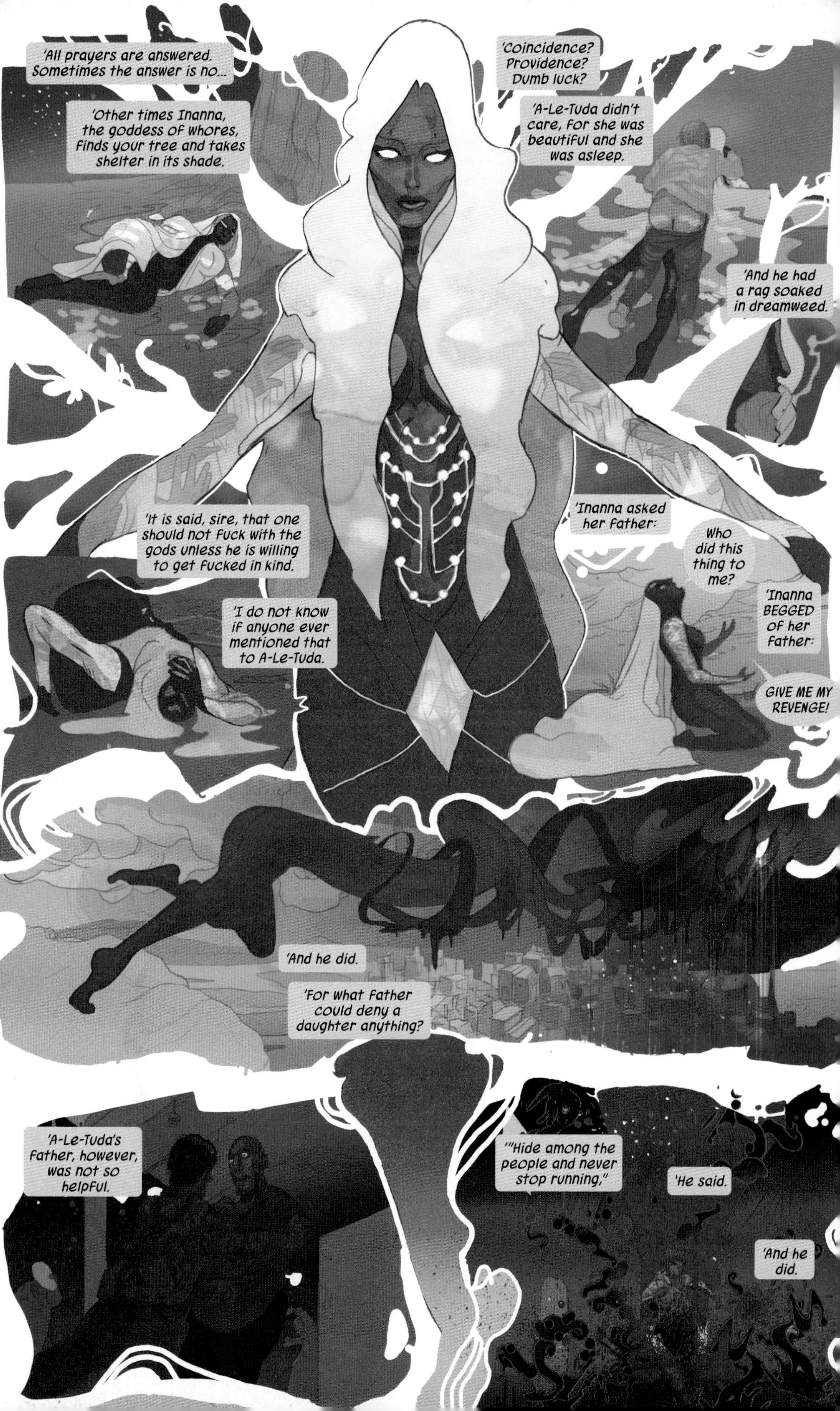
'All prayers are answered. Sometimes the answer is no...
'Other times Inanna, the goddess of whores, finds your tree and takes shelter in its shade.
'Coincidence? Providence? Dumb luck?
'A-Le-Tuda didn't care, for she was beautiful and she was asleep.
'And he had a rag soaked in dreamweed.
'It is said, sire, that one should not fuck with the gods unless he is willing to get fucked in kind.
'I do not know if anyone ever mentioned that to A-Le-Tuda.
'Inanna asked her Father:
Who did this thing to me?
'Inanna BEGGED of her Father:
GIVE ME MY REVENGE!
'And he did.
'For what Father could deny a daughter anything?
'A-Le-Tuda's father, however, was not so helpful.
'"Hide among the people and never stop running,"
'He said.
'And he did.

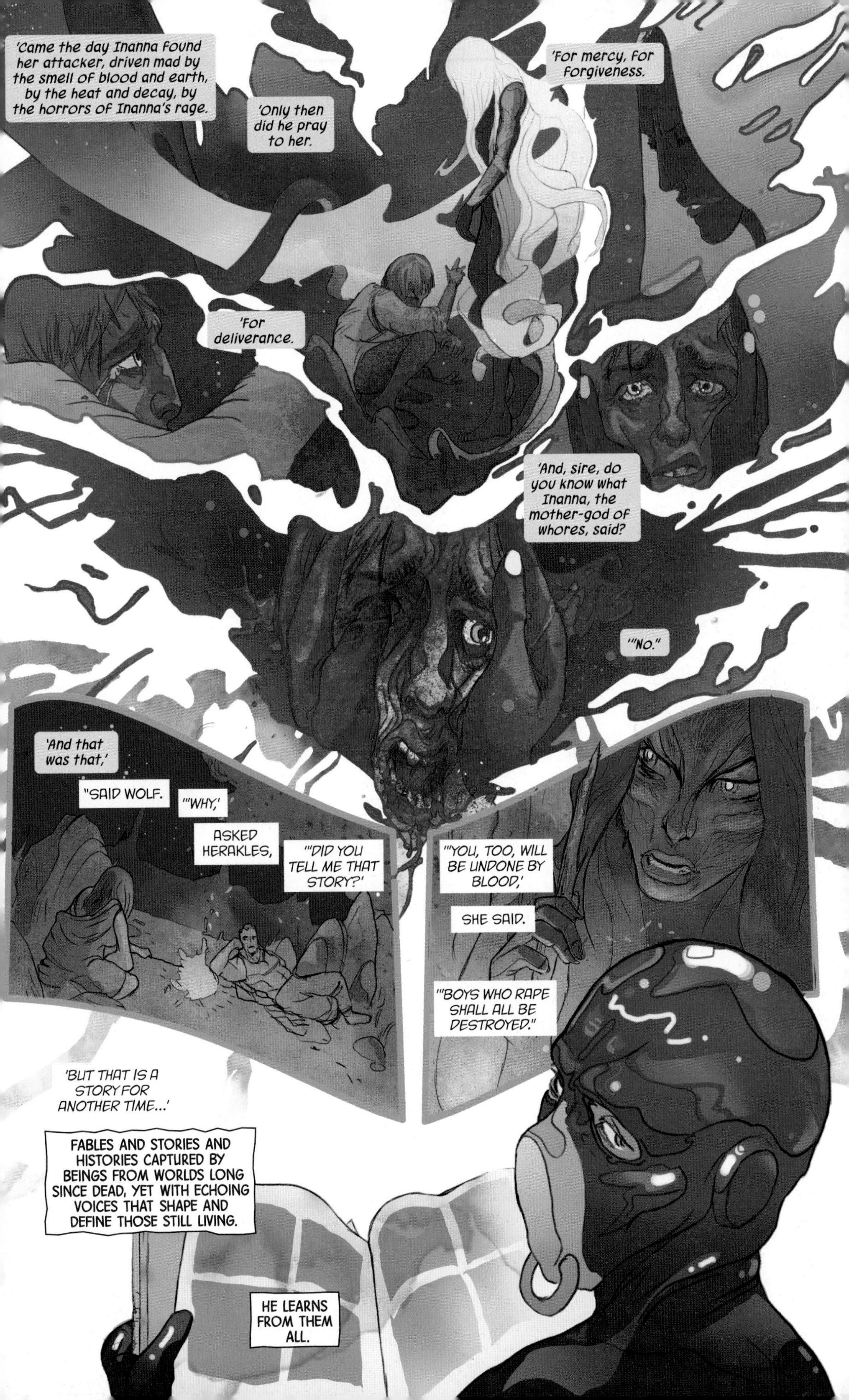
'Came the day Inanna found her attacker, driven mad by the smell of blood and earth, by the heat and decay, by the horrors of Inanna's rage.
'Only then did he pray to her.
'For mercy, for forgiveness.
'For deliverance.
'And, sire, do you know what Inanna, the mother-god of whores, said?
'"No."
'And that was that,'
"SAID WOLF.
'"WHY,'
ASKED HERAKLES,
'"DID YOU TELL ME THAT STORY?'
'"YOU, TOO, WILL BE UNDONE BY BLOOD,'
SHE SAID.
'"BOYS WHO RAPE SHALL ALL BE DESTROYED."
'BUT THAT IS A STORY FOR ANOTHER TIME...'
FABLES AND STORIES AND HISTORIES CAPTURED BY BEINGS FROM WORLDS LONG SINCE DEAD, YET WITH ECHOING VOICES THAT SHAPE AND DEFINE THOSE STILL LIVING.
HE LEARNS FROM THEM ALL.

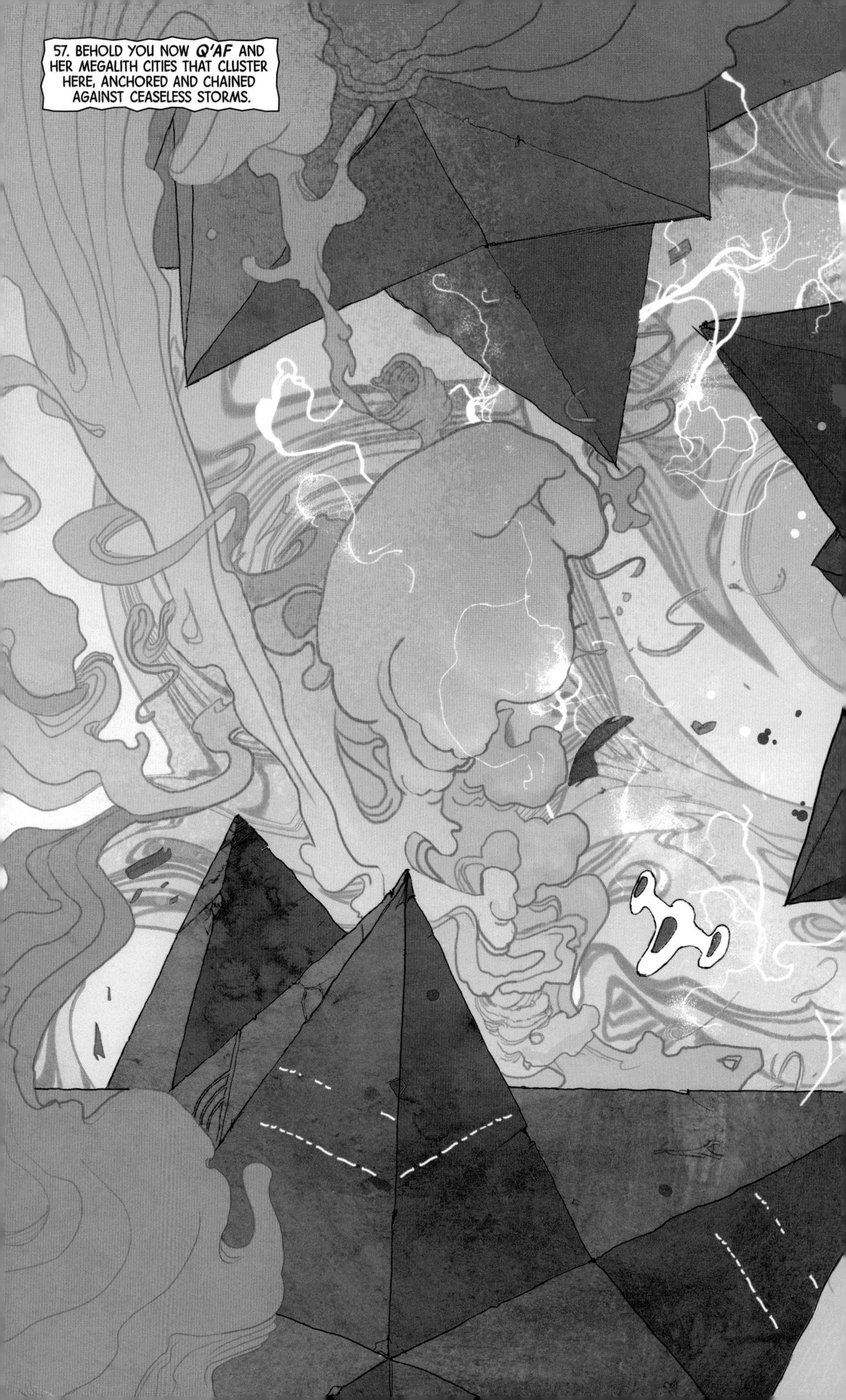
57. BEHOLD YOU NOW Q'AF AND HER MEGALITH CITIES THAT CLUSTER HERE, ANCHORED AND CHAINED AGAINST CEASELESS STORMS.

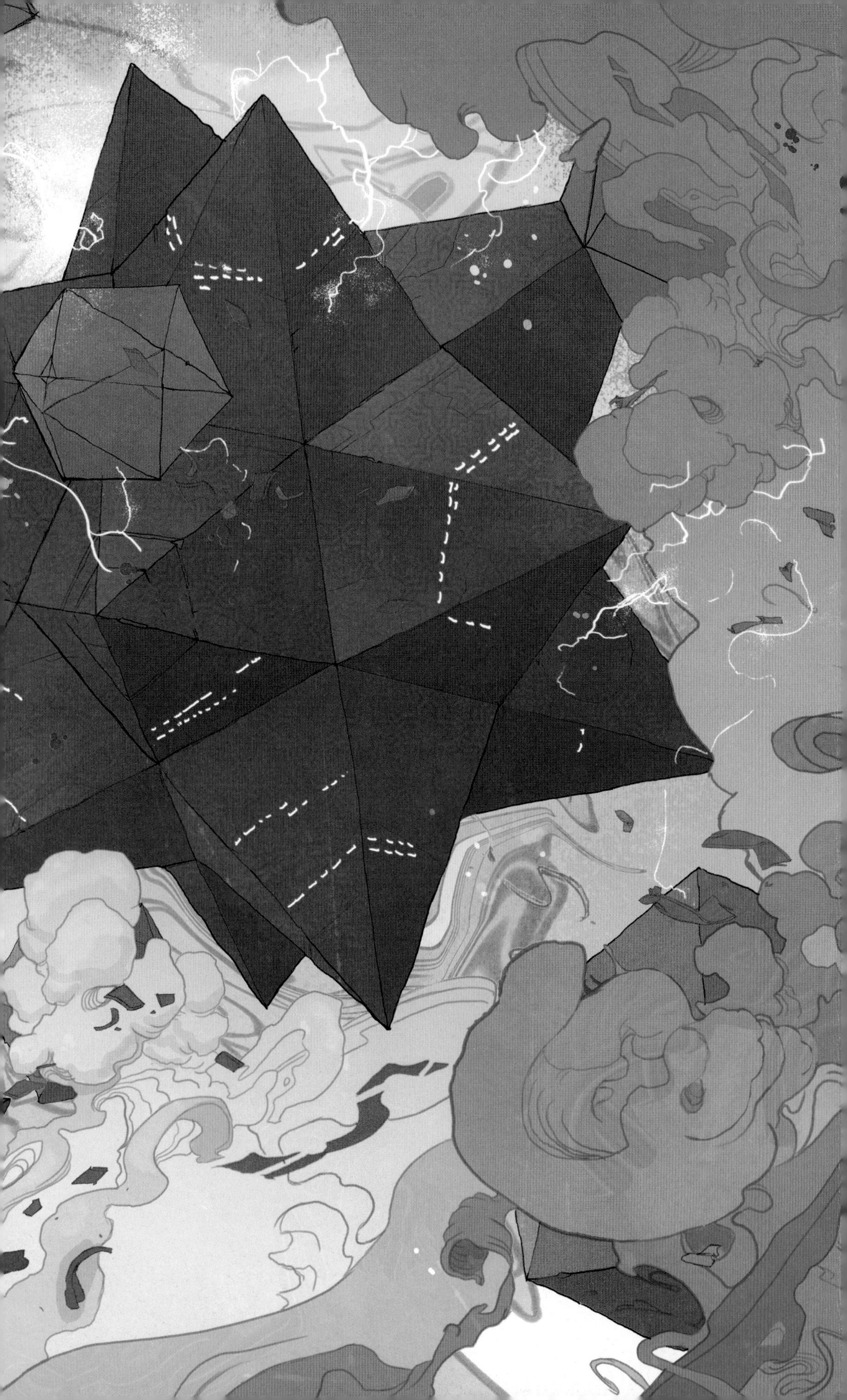

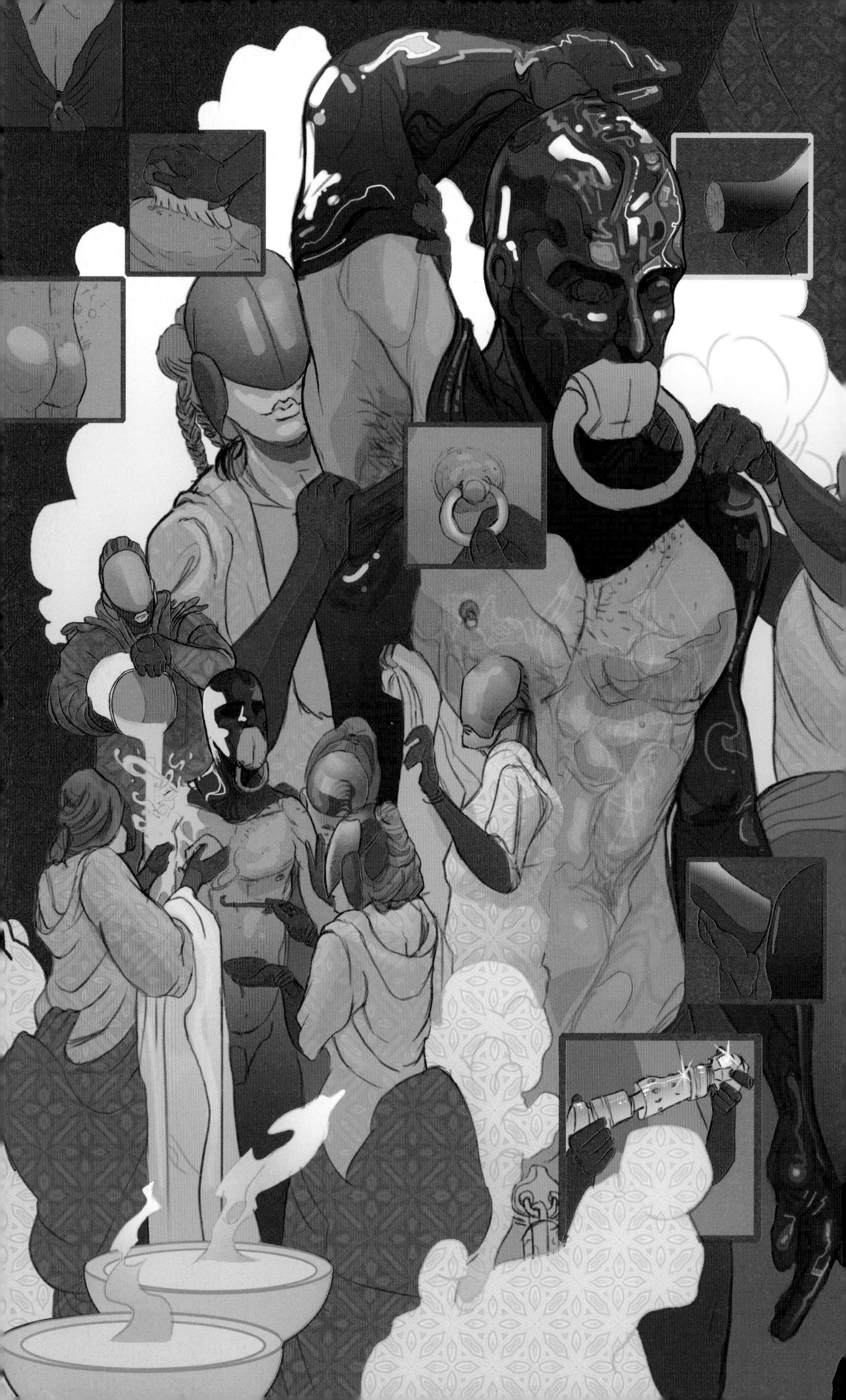

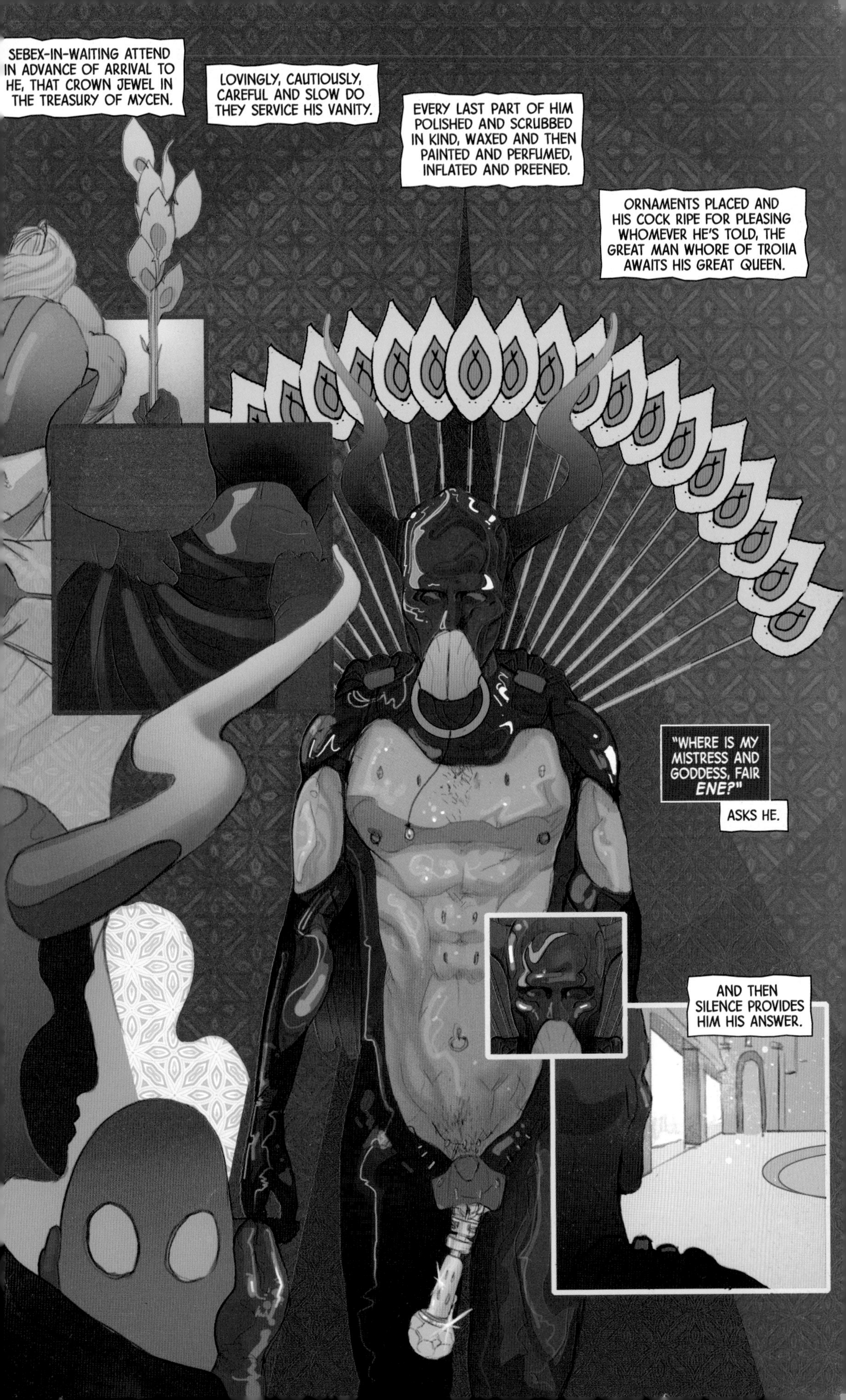
SEBEX-IN-WAITING ATTEND IN ADVANCE OF ARRIVAL TO HE, THAT CROWN JEWEL IN THE TREASURY OF MYCEN.
LOVINGLY, CAUTIOUSLY, CAREFUL AND SLOW DO THEY SERVICE HIS VANITY.
EVERY LAST PART OF HIM POLISHED AND SCRUBBED IN KIND, WAXED AND THEN PAINTED AND PERFUMED, INFLATED AND PREENED.
ORNAMENTS PLACED AND HIS COCK RIPE FOR PLEASING WHOMEVER HE'S TOLD, THE GREAT MAN WHORE OF TROIIA AWAITS HIS GREAT QUEEN.
"WHERE IS MY MISTRESS AND GODDESS, FAIR ENE?"
ASKS HE.
AND THEN SILENCE PROVIDES HIM HIS ANSWER.

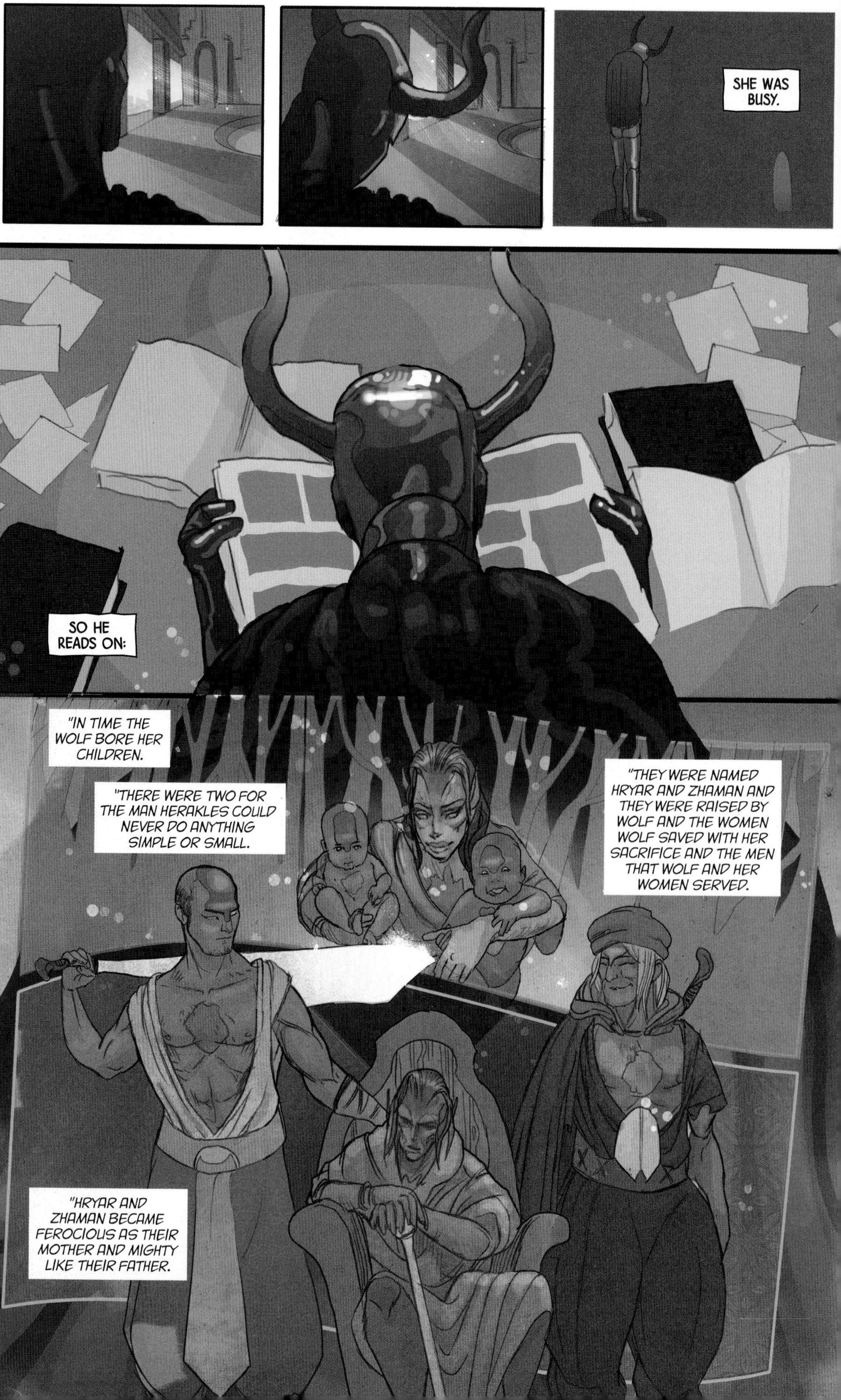
SHE WAS BUSY.
SO HE READS ON:
"IN TIME THE WOLF BORE HER CHILDREN.
"THERE WERE TWO FOR THE MAN HERAKLES COULD NEVER DO ANYTHING SIMPLE OR SMALL.
"THEY WERE NAMED HRYAR AND ZHAMAN AND THEY WERE RAISED BY WOLF AND THE WOMEN WOLF SAVED WITH HER SACRIFICE AND THE MEN THAT WOLF AND HER WOMEN SERVED.
"HRYAR AND ZHAMAN BECAME FEROCIOUS AS THEIR MOTHER AND MIGHTY LIKE THEIR FATHER.

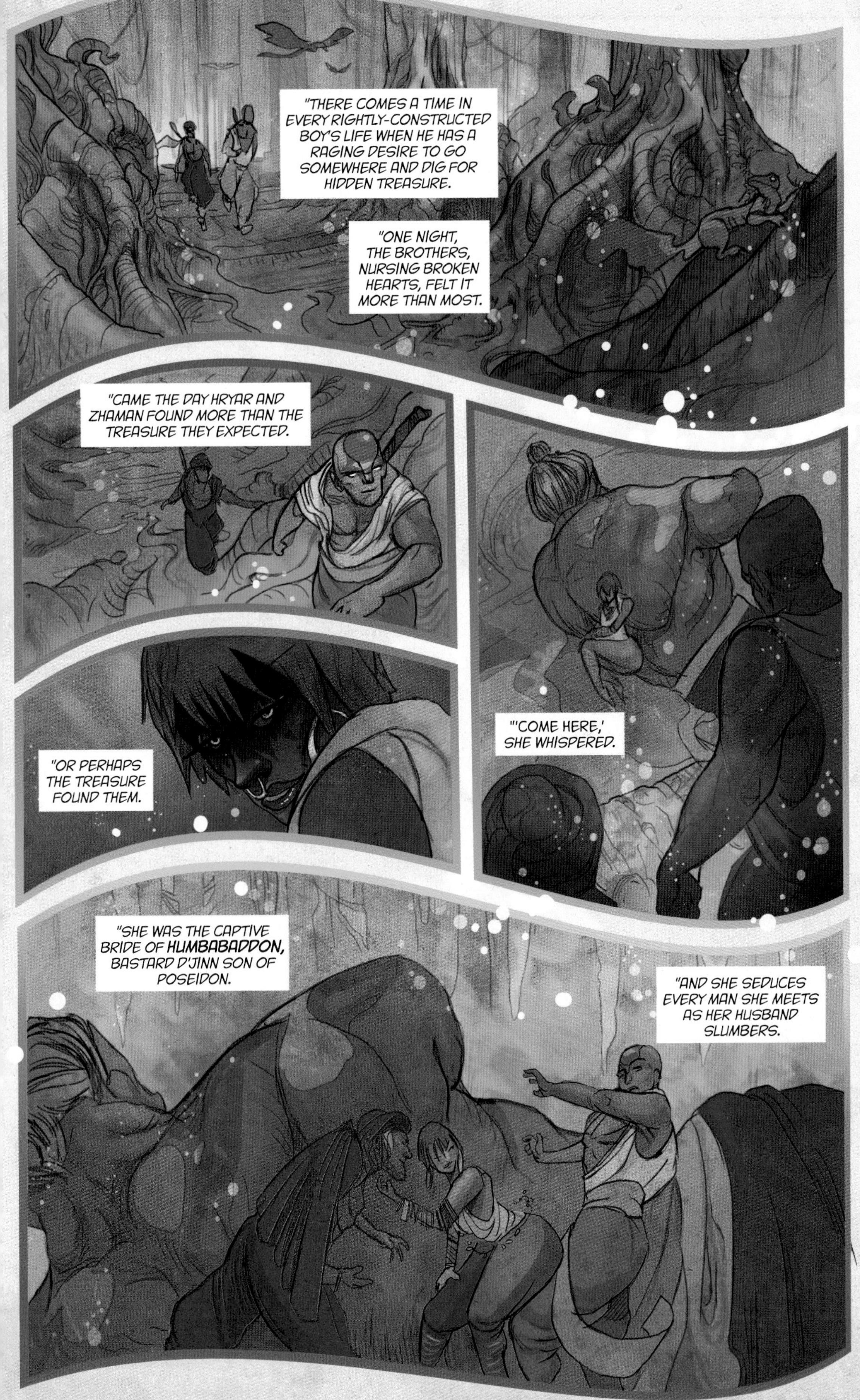
"THERE COMES A TIME IN EVERY RIGHTLY-CONSTRUCTED BOY'S LIFE WHEN HE HAS A RAGING DESIRE TO GO SOMEWHERE AND DIG FOR HIDDEN TREASURE.
"ONE NIGHT, THE BROTHERS, NURSING BROKEN HEARTS, FELT IT MORE THAN MOST.
"CAME THE DAY HRYAR AND ZHAMAN FOUND MORE THAN THE TREASURE THEY EXPECTED.
"OR PERHAPS THE TREASURE FOUND THEM.
"'COME HERE,' SHE WHISPERED.
"SHE WAS THE CAPTIVE BRIDE OF **HUMBABADDON,** BASTARD D'JINN SON OF POSEIDON.
"AND SHE SEDUCES EVERY MAN SHE MEETS AS HER HUSBAND SLUMBERS.

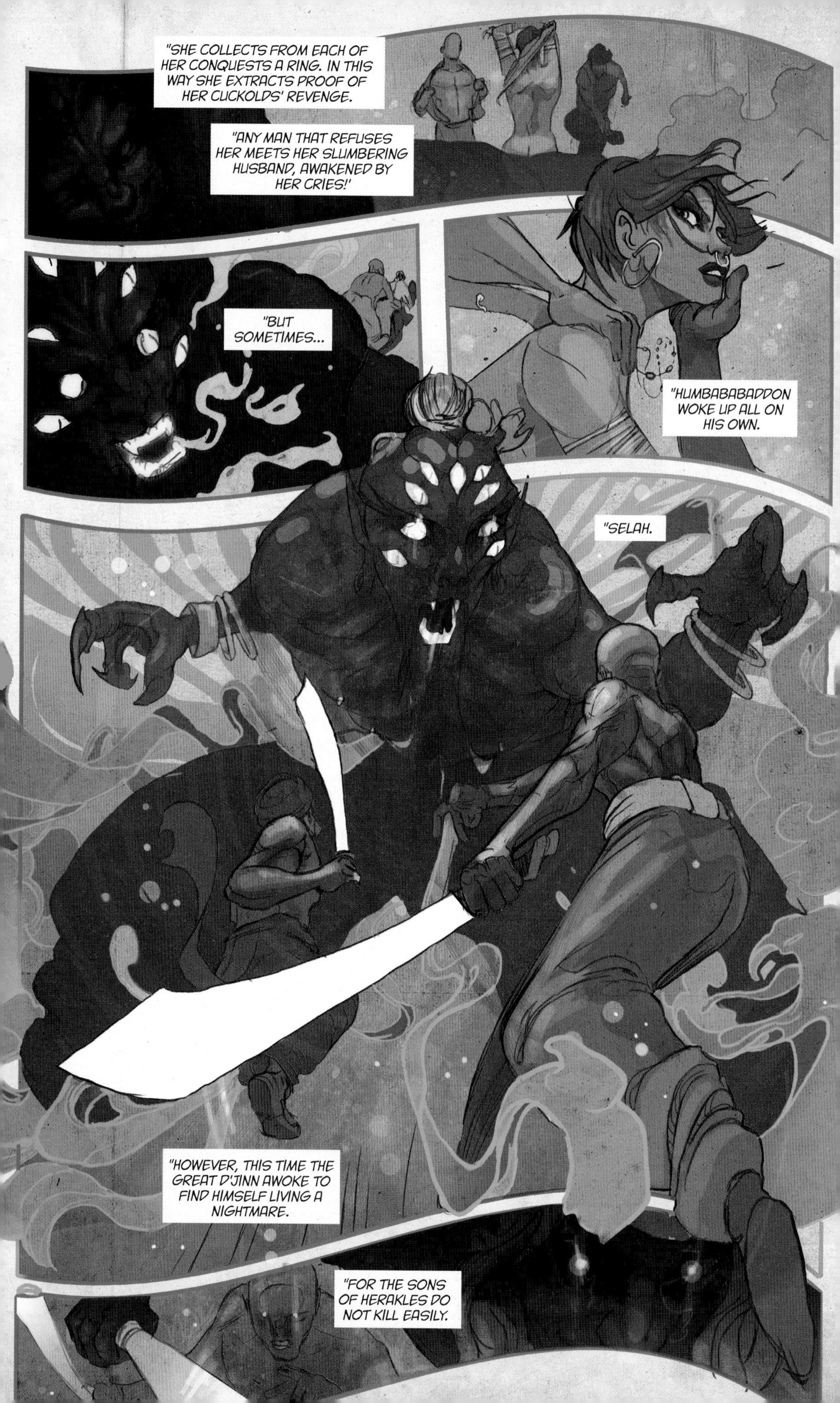
"SHE COLLECTS FROM EACH OF HER CONQUESTS A RING. IN THIS WAY SHE EXTRACTS PROOF OF HER CUCKOLDS' REVENGE.
"ANY MAN THAT REFUSES HER MEETS HER SLUMBERING HUSBAND, AWAKENED BY HER CRIES!"
"BUT SOMETIMES...
"HUMBABABADDON WOKE UP ALL ON HIS OWN.
"SELAH.
"HOWEVER, THIS TIME THE GREAT D'JINN AWOKE TO FIND HIMSELF LIVING A NIGHTMARE.
"FOR THE SONS OF HERAKLES DO NOT KILL EASILY.

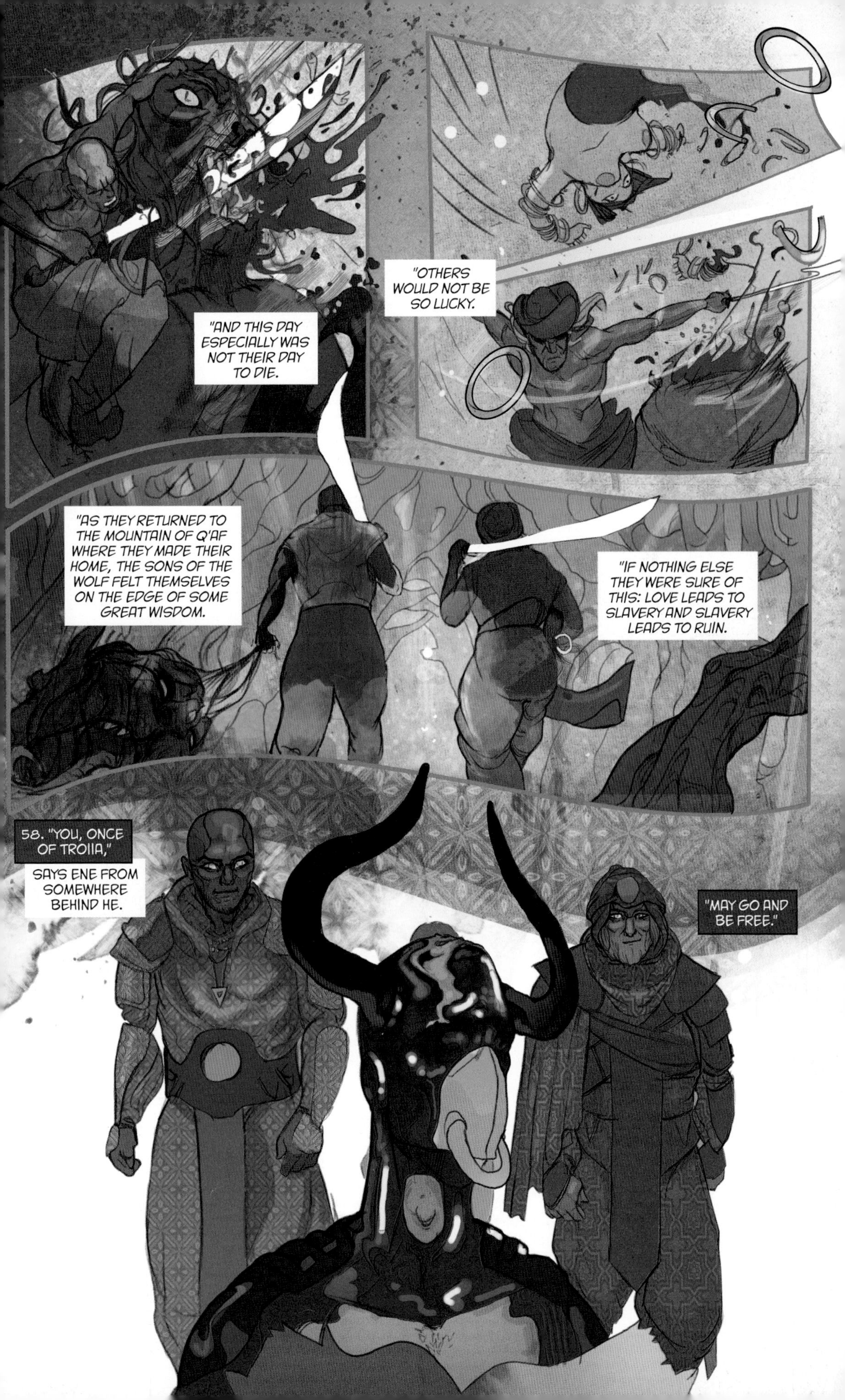
"AND THIS DAY ESPECIALLY WAS NOT THEIR DAY TO DIE.
"OTHERS WOULD NOT BE SO LUCKY.
"AS THEY RETURNED TO THE MOUNTAIN OF Q'AF WHERE THEY MADE THEIR HOME, THE SONS OF THE WOLF FELT THEMSELVES ON THE EDGE OF SOME GREAT WISDOM.
"IF NOTHING ELSE THEY WERE SURE OF THIS: LOVE LEADS TO SLAVERY AND SLAVERY LEADS TO RUIN.
58. "YOU, ONCE OF TROIIA,"
SAYS ENE FROM SOMEWHERE BEHIND HE.
"MAY GO AND BE FREE."

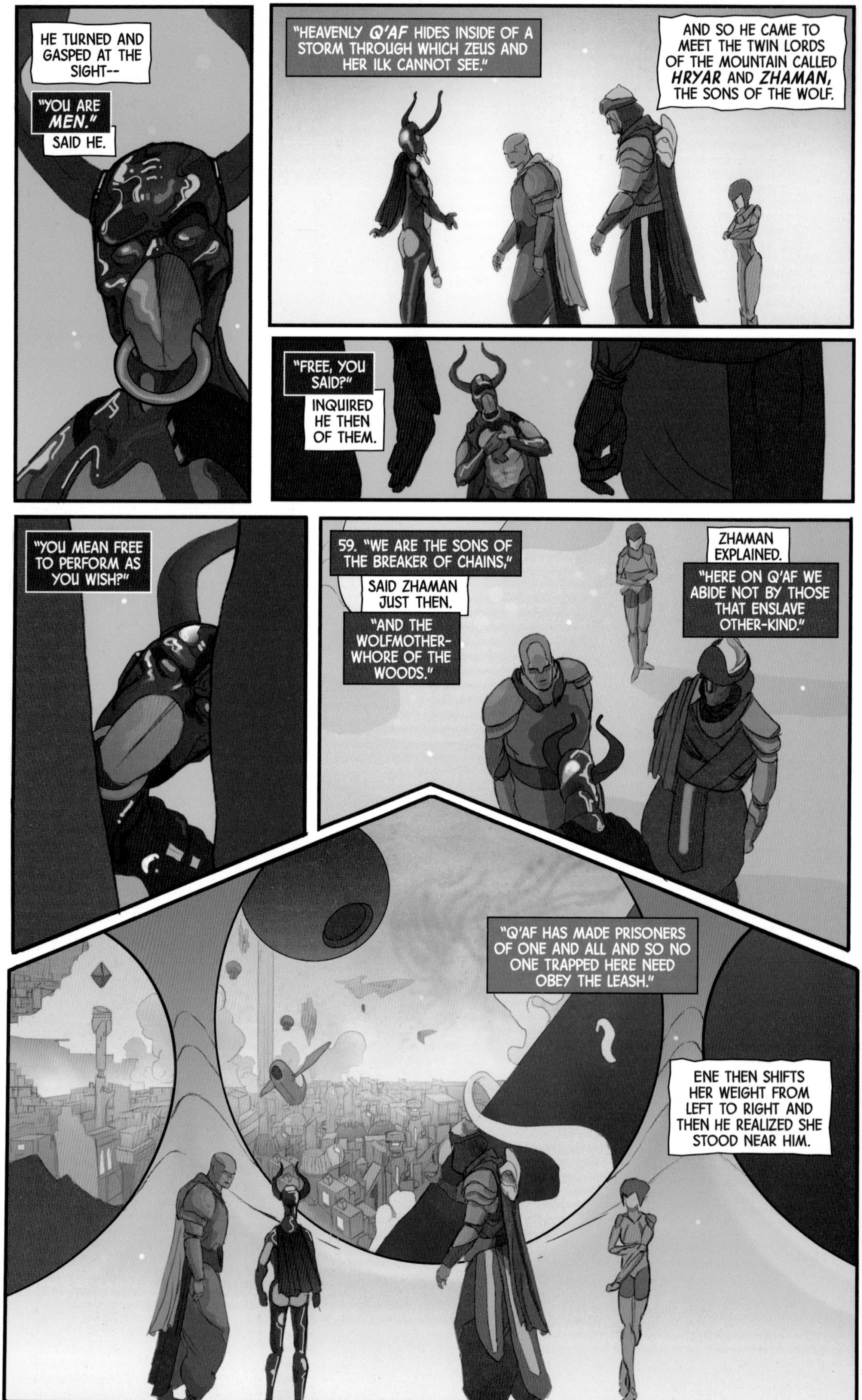
HE TURNED AND GASPED AT THE SIGHT--
"YOU ARE MEN."
SAID HE.
"HEAVENLY Q'AF HIDES INSIDE OF A STORM THROUGH WHICH ZEUS AND HER ILK CANNOT SEE."
AND SO HE CAME TO MEET THE TWIN LORDS OF THE MOUNTAIN CALLED HRYAR AND ZHAMAN, THE SONS OF THE WOLF.
"FREE, YOU SAID?"
INQUIRED HE THEN OF THEM.
"YOU MEAN FREE TO PERFORM AS YOU WISH?"
59. "WE ARE THE SONS OF THE BREAKER OF CHAINS,"
SAID ZHAMAN JUST THEN.
"AND THE WOLFMOTHER-WHORE OF THE WOODS."
ZHAMAN EXPLAINED.
"HERE ON Q'AF WE ABIDE NOT BY THOSE THAT ENSLAVE OTHER-KIND."
"Q'AF HAS MADE PRISONERS OF ONE AND ALL AND SO NO ONE TRAPPED HERE NEED OBEY THE LEASH."
ENE THEN SHIFTS HER WEIGHT FROM LEFT TO RIGHT AND THEN HE REALIZED SHE STOOD NEAR HIM.

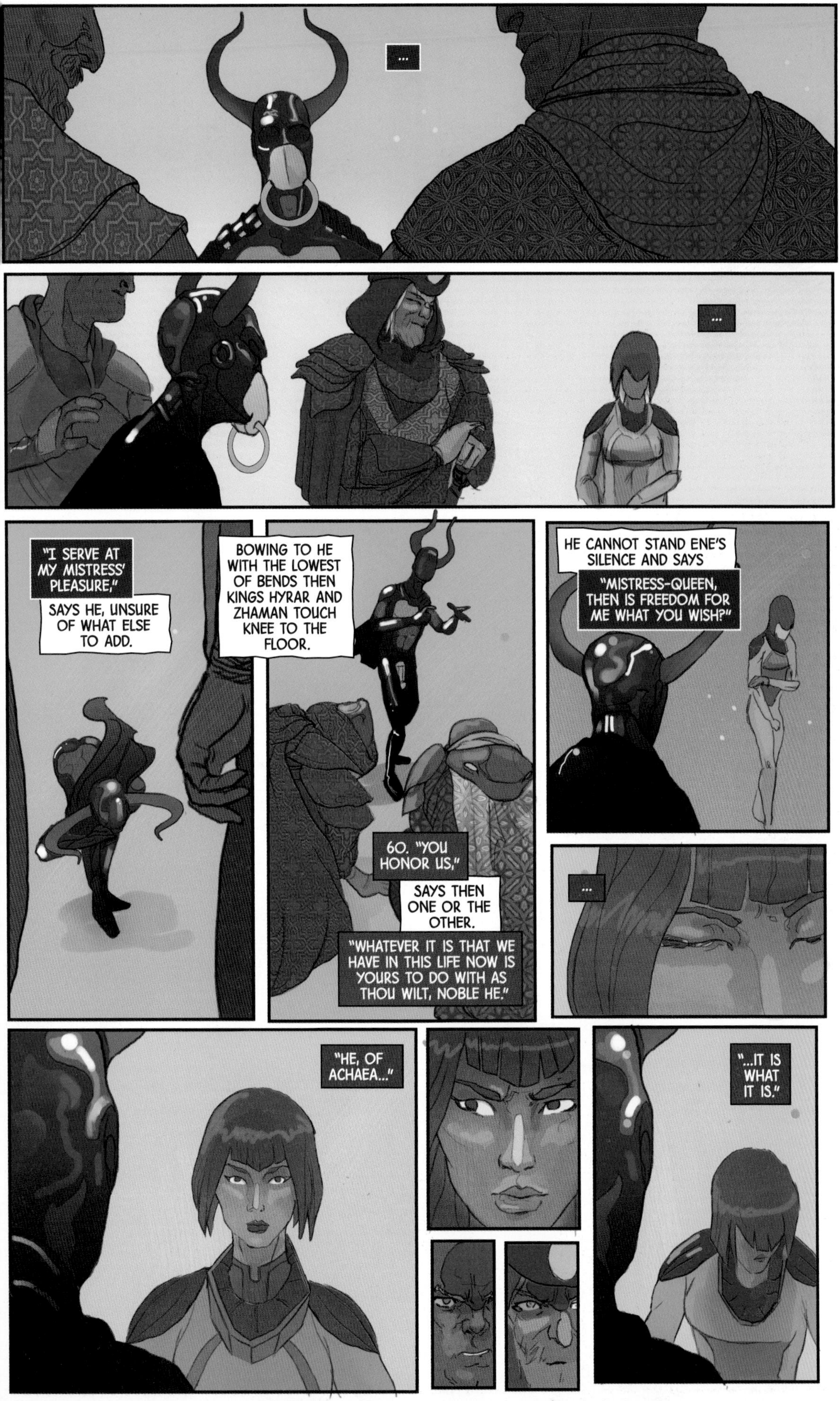
...
...
"I SERVE AT MY MISTRESS' PLEASURE,"
SAYS HE, UNSURE OF WHAT ELSE TO ADD.
BOWING TO HE WITH THE LOWEST OF BENDS THEN KINGS HYRAR AND ZHAMAN TOUCH KNEE TO THE FLOOR.
60. "YOU HONOR US,"
SAYS THEN ONE OR THE OTHER.
"WHATEVER IT IS THAT WE HAVE IN THIS LIFE NOW IS YOURS TO DO WITH AS THOU WILT, NOBLE HE."
HE CANNOT STAND ENE'S SILENCE AND SAYS
"MISTRESS-QUEEN, THEN IS FREEDOM FOR ME WHAT YOU WISH?"
...
"HE, OF ACHAEA..."
"...IT IS WHAT IT IS."

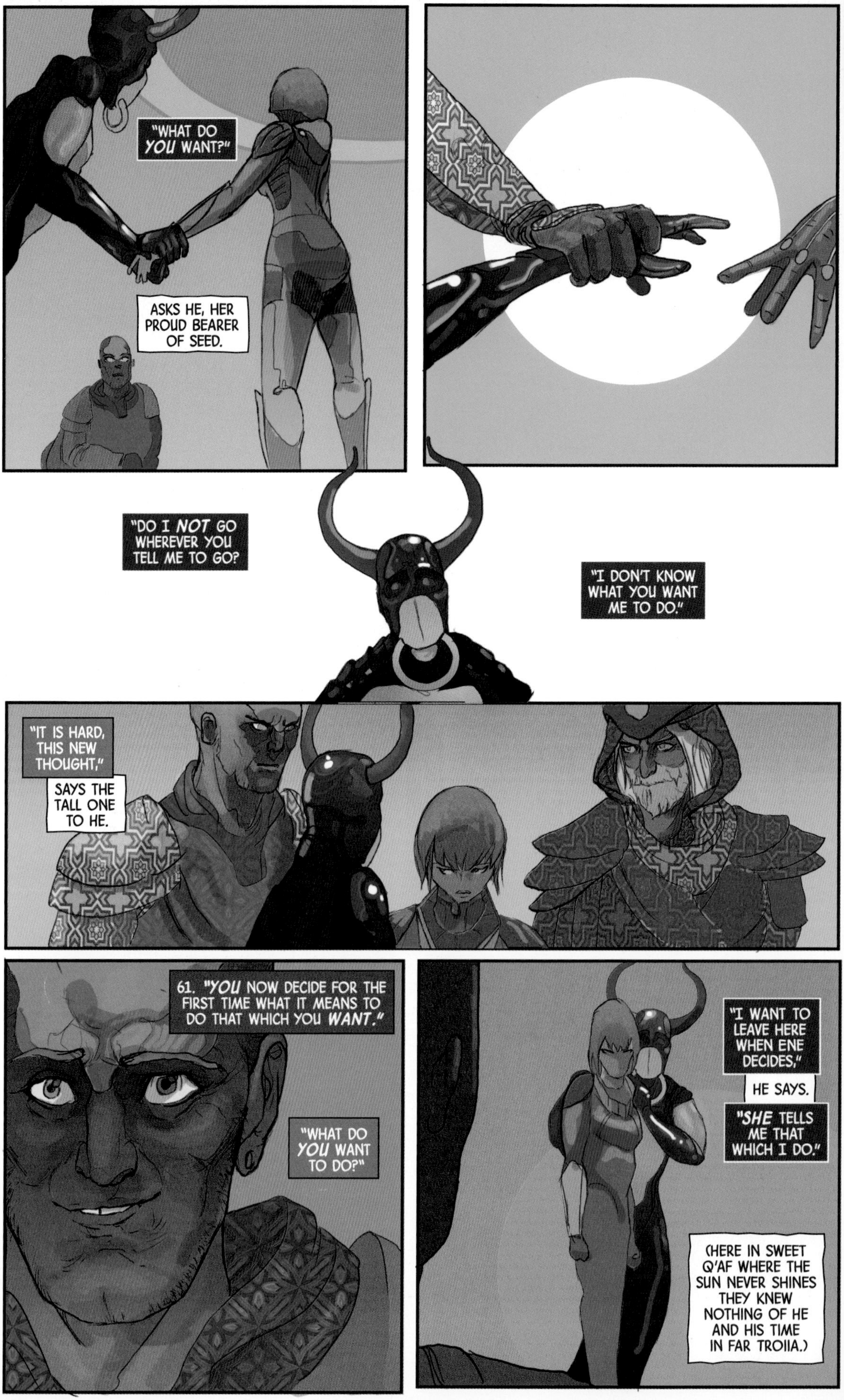
"WHAT DO YOU WANT?"
ASKS HE, HER PROUD BEARER OF SEED.
"DO I NOT GO WHEREVER YOU TELL ME TO GO?
"I DON'T KNOW WHAT YOU WANT ME TO DO."
"IT IS HARD, THIS NEW THOUGHT,"
SAYS THE TALL ONE TO HE.
61. "YOU NOW DECIDE FOR THE FIRST TIME WHAT IT MEANS TO DO THAT WHICH YOU WANT."
"WHAT DO YOU WANT TO DO?"
"I WANT TO LEAVE HERE WHEN ENE DECIDES,"
HE SAYS.
"SHE TELLS ME THAT WHICH I DO."
(HERE IN SWEET Q'AF WHERE THE SUN NEVER SHINES THEY KNEW NOTHING OF HE AND HIS TIME IN FAR TROIIA.)

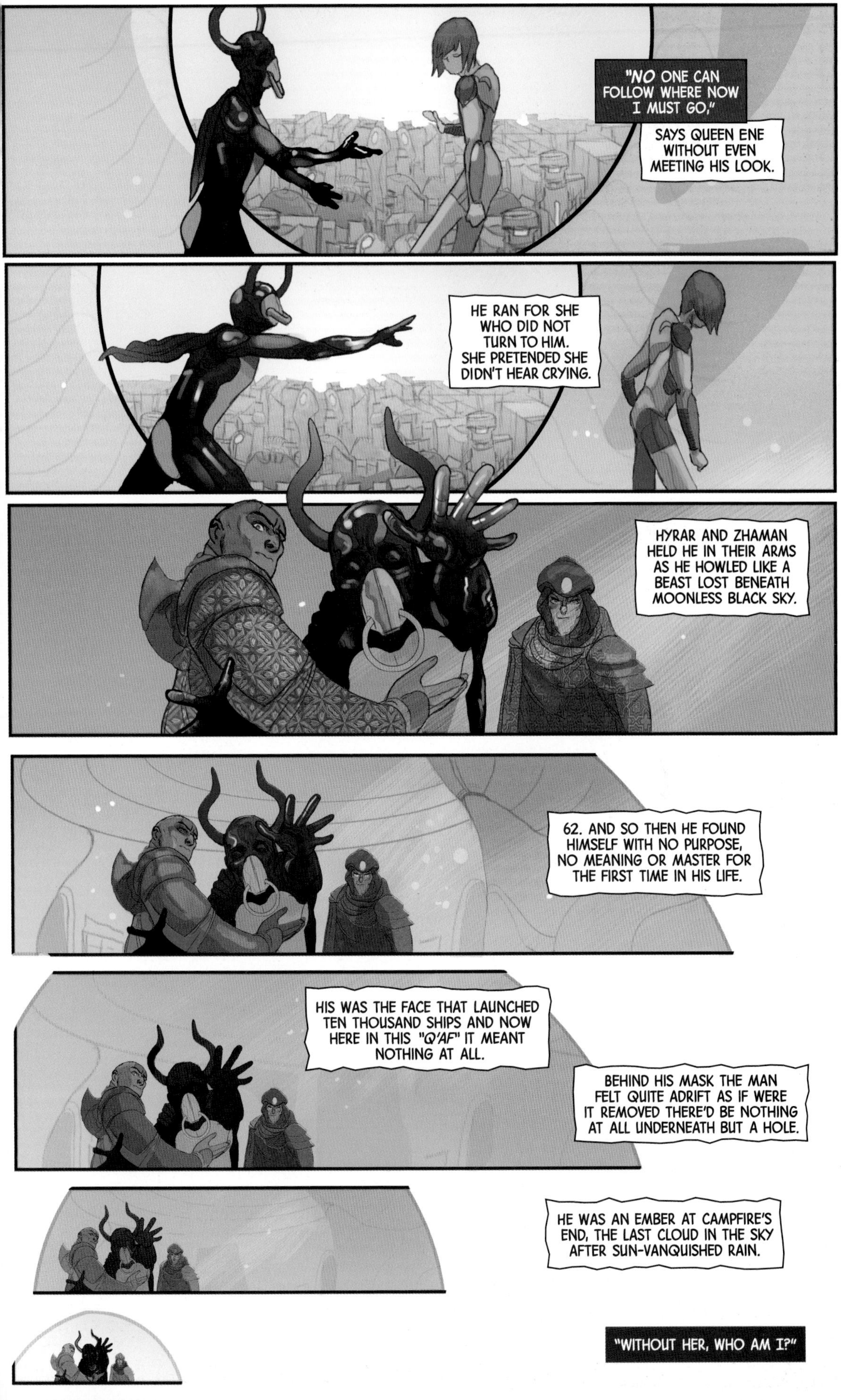
"NO ONE CAN FOLLOW WHERE NOW I MUST GO,"
SAYS QUEEN ENE WITHOUT EVEN MEETING HIS LOOK.
HE RAN FOR SHE WHO DID NOT TURN TO HIM. SHE PRETENDED SHE DIDN'T HEAR CRYING.
HYRAR AND ZHAMAN HELD HE IN THEIR ARMS AS HE HOWLED LIKE A BEAST LOST BENEATH MOONLESS BLACK SKY.
62. AND SO THEN HE FOUND HIMSELF WITH NO PURPOSE, NO MEANING OR MASTER FOR THE FIRST TIME IN HIS LIFE.
HIS WAS THE FACE THAT LAUNCHED TEN THOUSAND SHIPS AND NOW HERE IN THIS "Q'AF" IT MEANT NOTHING AT ALL.
BEHIND HIS MASK THE MAN FELT QUITE ADRIFT AS IF WERE IT REMOVED THERE'D BE NOTHING AT ALL UNDERNEATH BUT A HOLE.
HE WAS AN EMBER AT CAMPFIRE'S END, THE LAST CLOUD IN THE SKY AFTER SUN-VANQUISHED RAIN.
"WITHOUT HER, WHO AM I?"

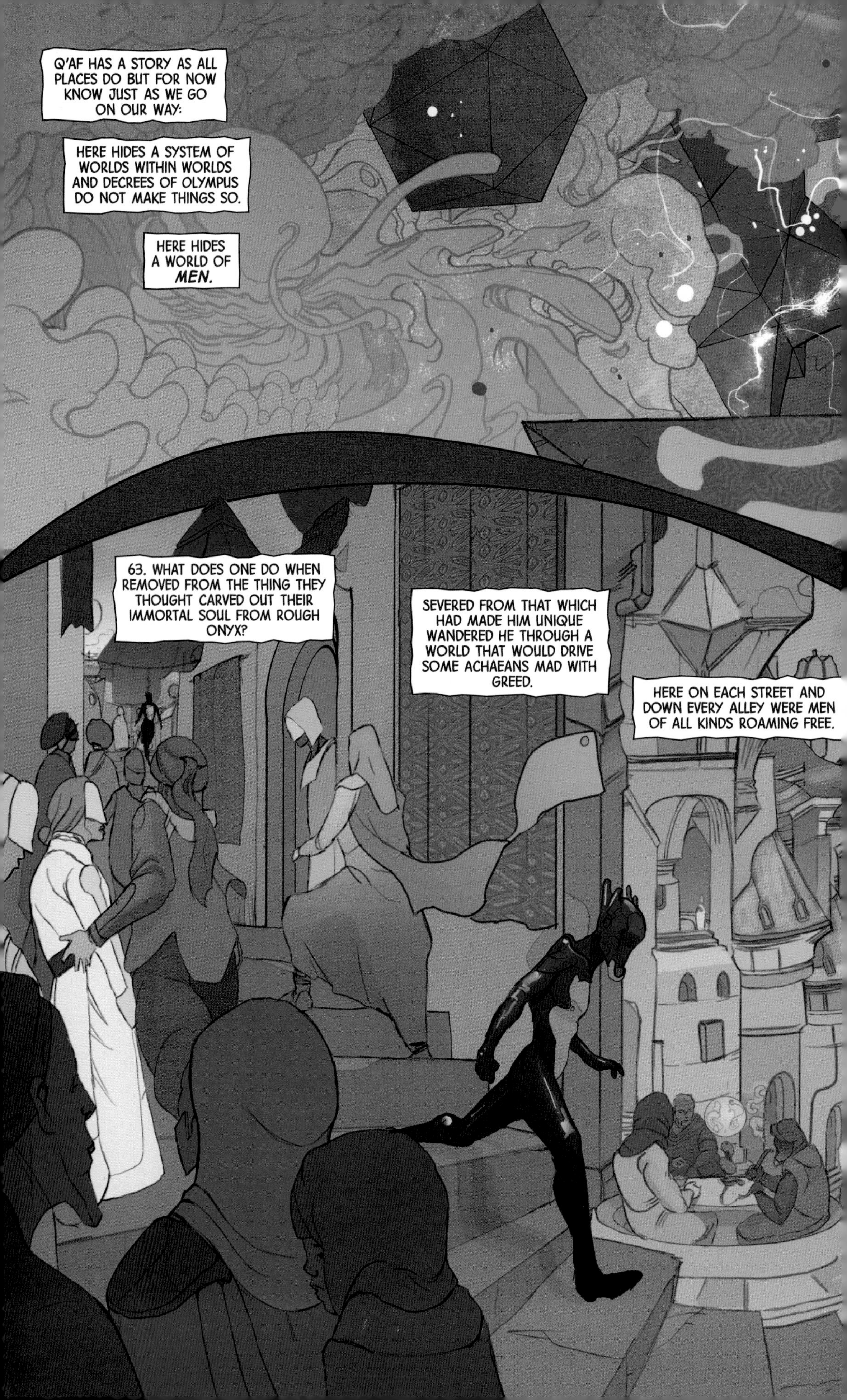
Q'AF HAS A STORY AS ALL PLACES DO BUT FOR NOW KNOW JUST AS WE GO ON OUR WAY:
HERE HIDES A SYSTEM OF WORLDS WITHIN WORLDS AND DECREES OF OLYMPUS DO NOT MAKE THINGS SO.
HERE HIDES A WORLD OF *MEN.*
63. WHAT DOES ONE DO WHEN REMOVED FROM THE THING THEY THOUGHT CARVED OUT THEIR IMMORTAL SOUL FROM ROUGH ONYX?
SEVERED FROM THAT WHICH HAD MADE HIM UNIQUE WANDERED HE THROUGH A WORLD THAT WOULD DRIVE SOME ACHAEANS MAD WITH GREED.
HERE ON EACH STREET AND DOWN EVERY ALLEY WERE MEN OF ALL KINDS ROAMING FREE.

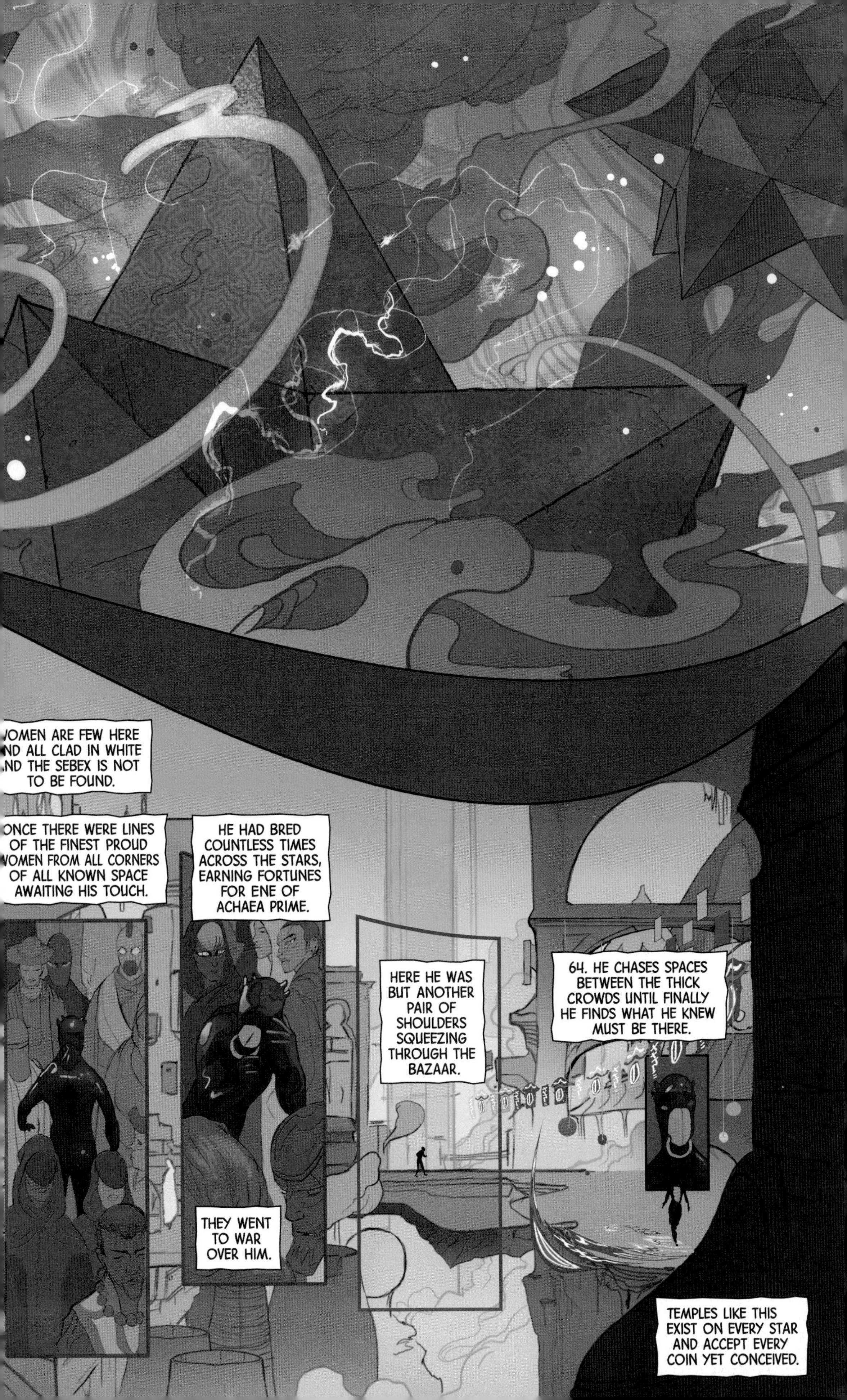

OMEN ARE FEW HERE ND ALL CLAD IN WHITE ND THE SEBEX IS NOT TO BE FOUND.
ONCE THERE WERE LINES OF THE FINEST PROUD OMEN FROM ALL CORNERS OF ALL KNOWN SPACE AWAITING HIS TOUCH.
HE HAD BRED COUNTLESS TIMES ACROSS THE STARS, EARNING FORTUNES FOR ENE OF ACHAEA PRIME.
THEY WENT TO WAR OVER HIM.
HERE HE WAS BUT ANOTHER PAIR OF SHOULDERS SQUEEZING THROUGH THE BAZAAR.
64. HE CHASES SPACES BETWEEN THE THICK CROWDS UNTIL FINALLY HE FINDS WHAT HE KNEW MUST BE THERE.
TEMPLES LIKE THIS EXIST ON EVERY STAR AND ACCEPT EVERY COIN YET CONCEIVED.

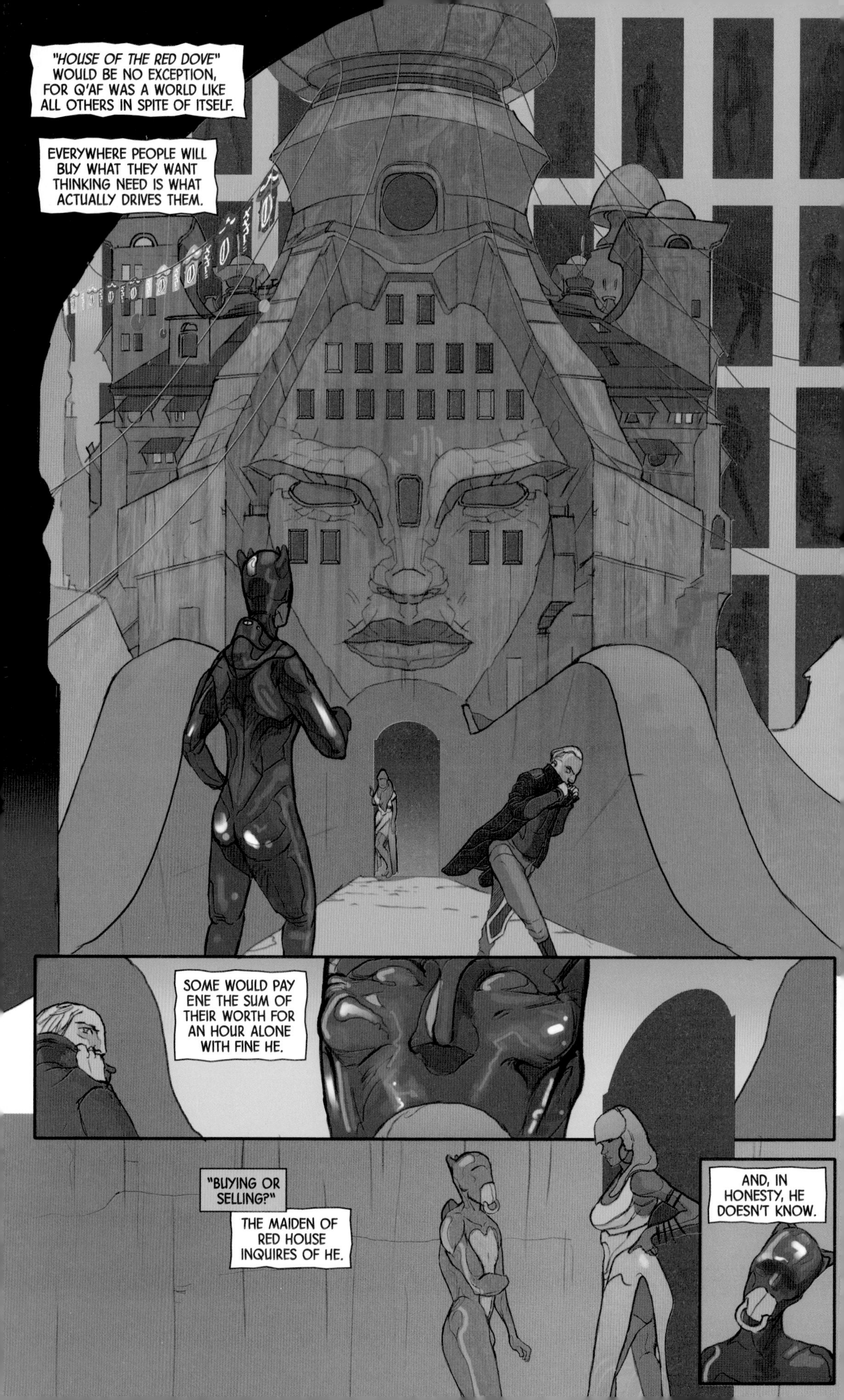
"HOUSE OF THE RED DOVE" WOULD BE NO EXCEPTION, FOR Q'AF WAS A WORLD LIKE ALL OTHERS IN SPITE OF ITSELF.
EVERYWHERE PEOPLE WILL BUY WHAT THEY WANT THINKING NEED IS WHAT ACTUALLY DRIVES THEM.
SOME WOULD PAY ENE THE SUM OF THEIR WORTH FOR AN HOUR ALONE WITH FINE HE.
"BUYING OR SELLING?"
THE MAIDEN OF RED HOUSE INQUIRES OF HE.
AND, IN HONESTY, HE DOESN'T KNOW.

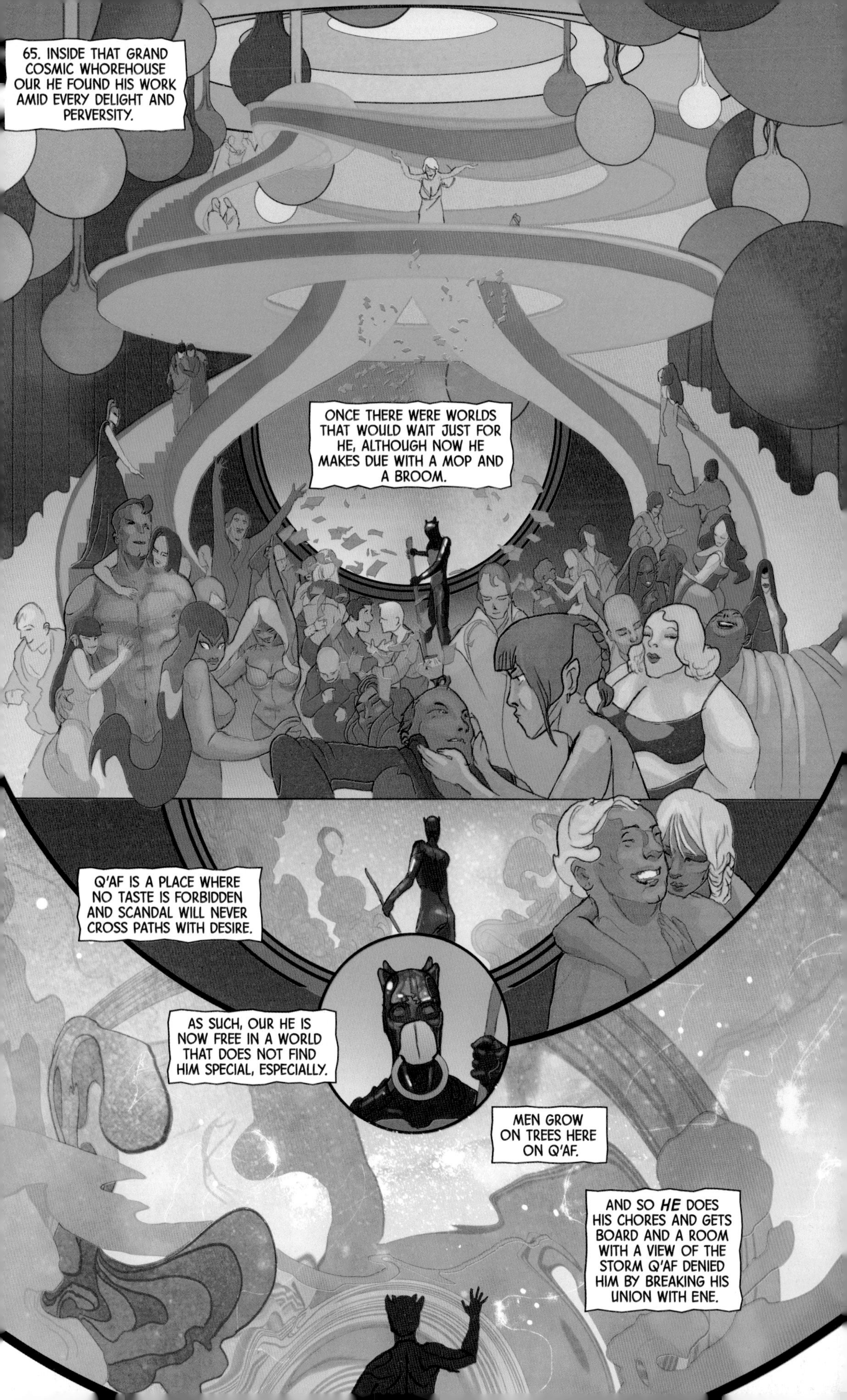
65. INSIDE THAT GRAND COSMIC WHOREHOUSE OUR HE FOUND HIS WORK AMID EVERY DELIGHT AND PERVERSITY.
ONCE THERE WERE WORLDS THAT WOULD WAIT JUST FOR HE, ALTHOUGH NOW HE MAKES DUE WITH A MOP AND A BROOM.
Q'AF IS A PLACE WHERE NO TASTE IS FORBIDDEN AND SCANDAL WILL NEVER CROSS PATHS WITH DESIRE.
AS SUCH, OUR HE IS NOW FREE IN A WORLD THAT DOES NOT FIND HIM SPECIAL, ESPECIALLY.
MEN GROW ON TREES HERE ON Q'AF.
AND SO *HE* DOES HIS CHORES AND GETS BOARD AND A ROOM WITH A VIEW OF THE STORM Q'AF DENIED HIM BY BREAKING HIS UNION WITH ENE.

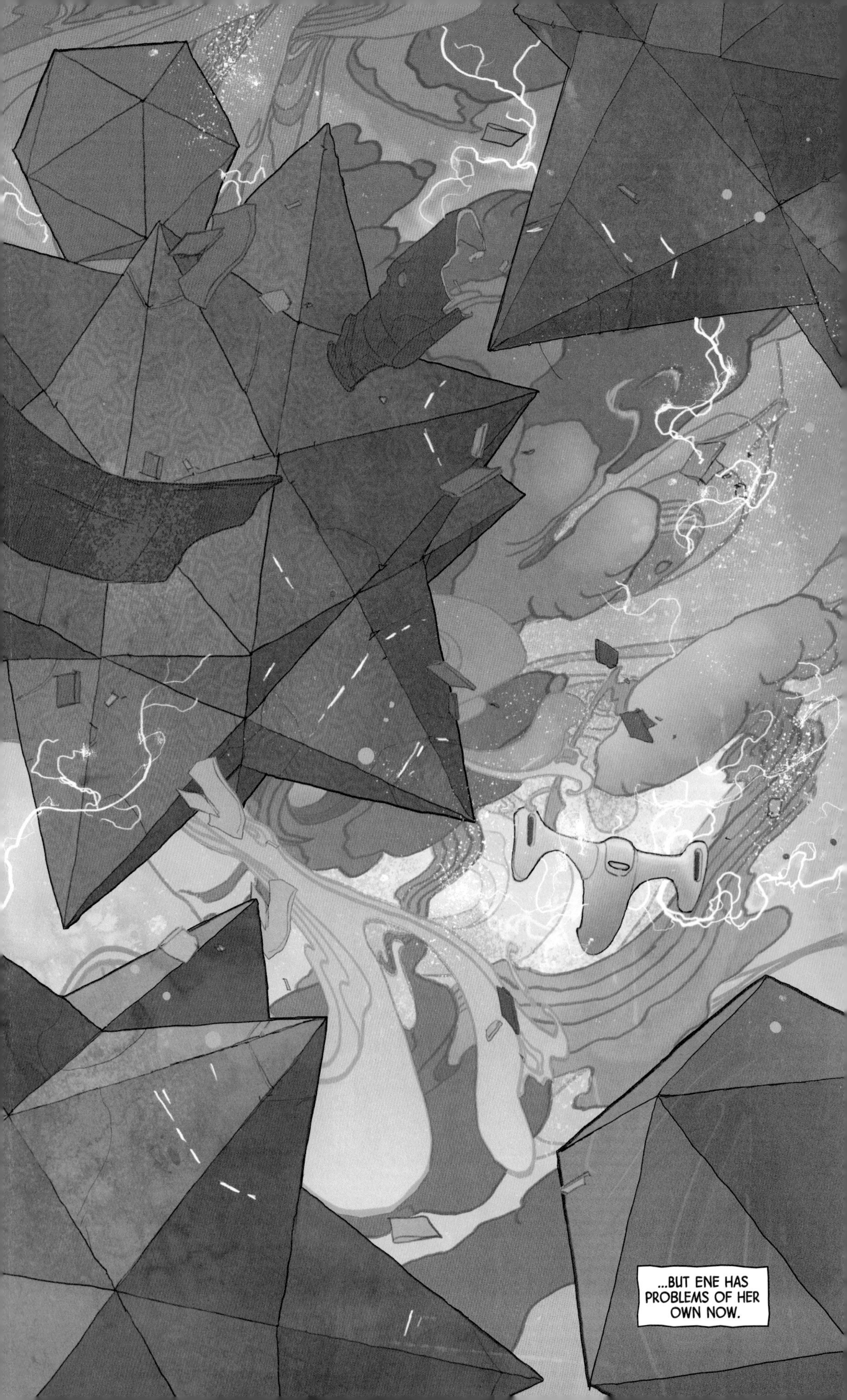
...BUT ENE HAS PROBLEMS OF HER OWN NOW.

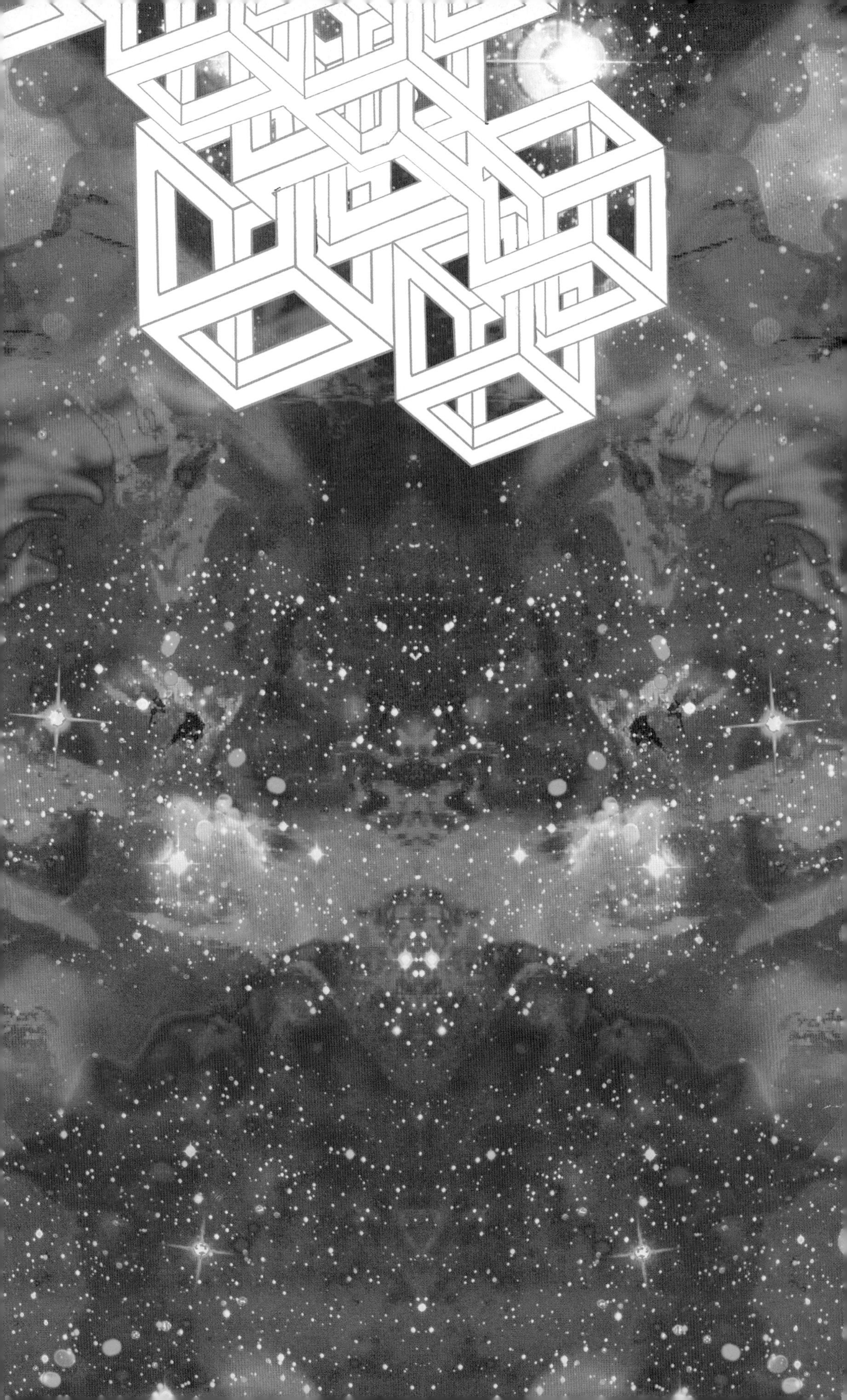

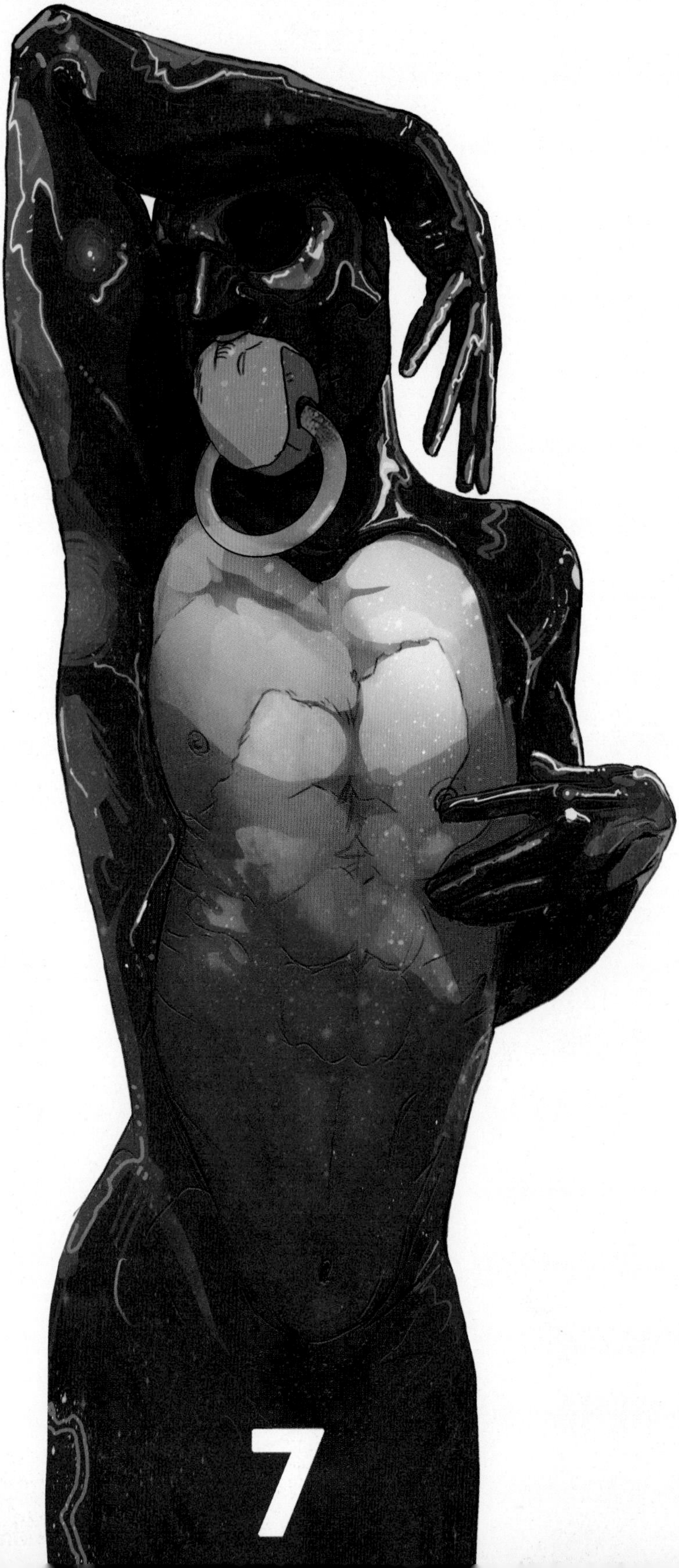
7

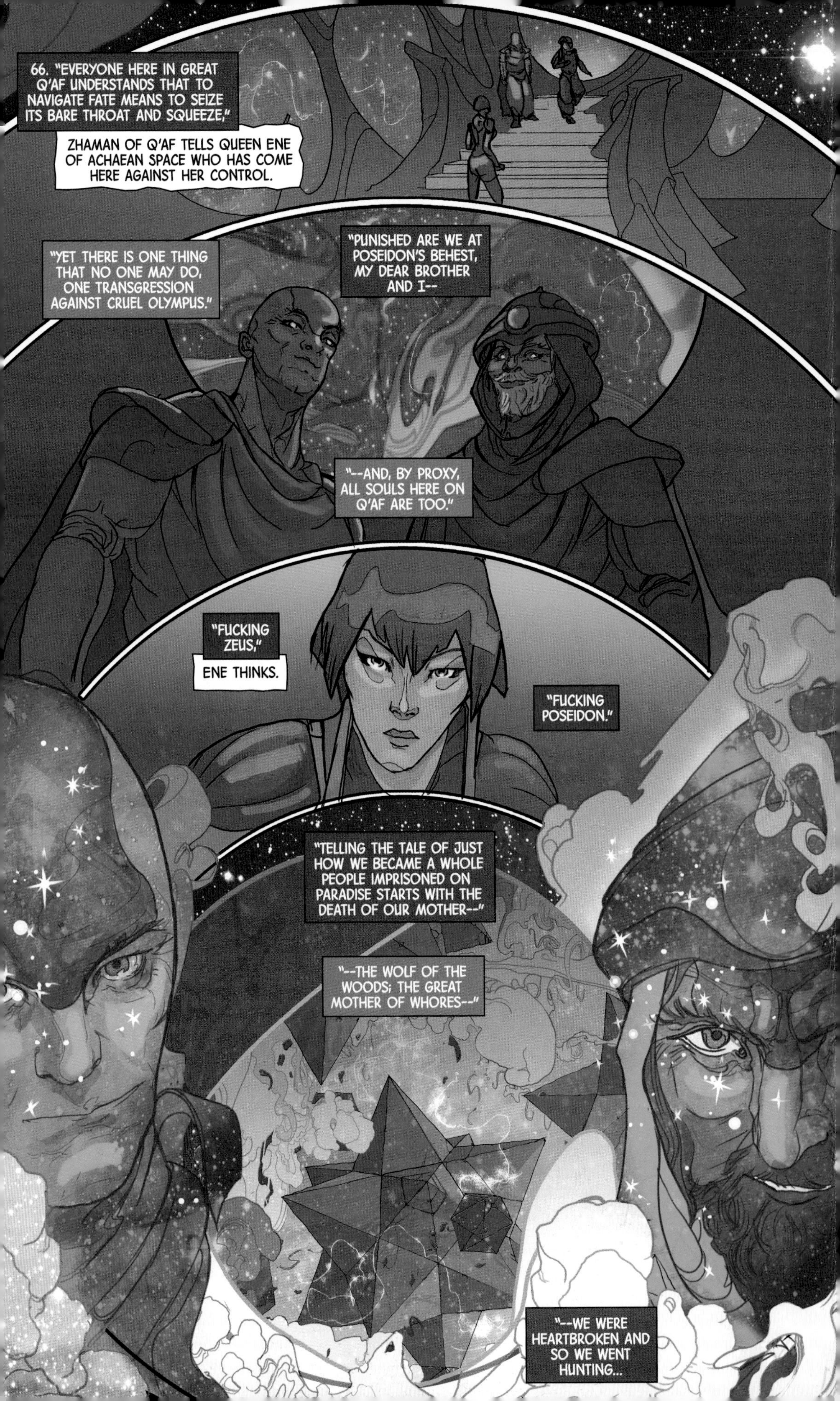

66. "EVERYONE HERE IN GREAT Q'AF UNDERSTANDS THAT TO NAVIGATE FATE MEANS TO SEIZE ITS BARE THROAT AND SQUEEZE,"
ZHAMAN OF Q'AF TELLS QUEEN ENE OF ACHAEAN SPACE WHO HAS COME HERE AGAINST HER CONTROL.
"YET THERE IS ONE THING THAT NO ONE MAY DO, ONE TRANSGRESSION AGAINST CRUEL OLYMPUS."
"PUNISHED ARE WE AT POSEIDON'S BEHEST, MY DEAR BROTHER AND I--
"--AND, BY PROXY, ALL SOULS HERE ON Q'AF ARE TOO."
"FUCKING ZEUS,"
ENE THINKS.
"FUCKING POSEIDON."
"TELLING THE TALE OF JUST HOW WE BECAME A WHOLE PEOPLE IMPRISONED ON PARADISE STARTS WITH THE DEATH OF OUR MOTHER--"
"--THE WOLF OF THE WOODS; THE GREAT MOTHER OF WHORES--"
"--WE WERE HEARTBROKEN AND SO WE WENT HUNTING...

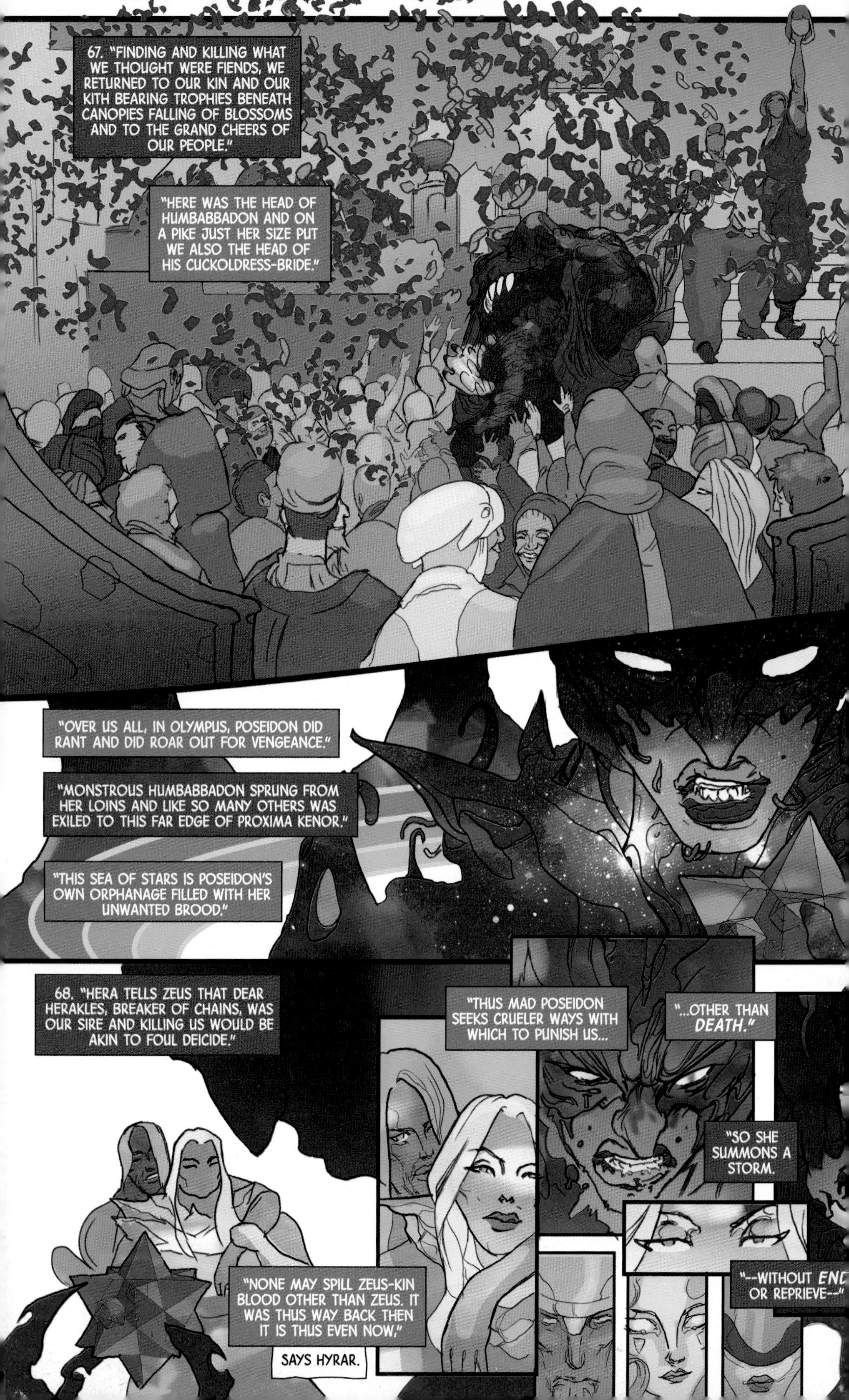
67. "FINDING AND KILLING WHAT WE THOUGHT WERE FIENDS, WE RETURNED TO OUR KIN AND OUR KITH BEARING TROPHIES BENEATH CANOPIES FALLING OF BLOSSOMS AND TO THE GRAND CHEERS OF OUR PEOPLE."
"HERE WAS THE HEAD OF HUMBABBADON AND ON A PIKE JUST HER SIZE PUT WE ALSO THE HEAD OF HIS CUCKOLDRESS-BRIDE."
"OVER US ALL, IN OLYMPUS, POSEIDON DID RANT AND DID ROAR OUT FOR VENGEANCE."
"MONSTROUS HUMBABBADON SPRUNG FROM HER LOINS AND LIKE SO MANY OTHERS WAS EXILED TO THIS FAR EDGE OF PROXIMA KENOR."
"THIS SEA OF STARS IS POSEIDON'S OWN ORPHANAGE FILLED WITH HER UNWANTED BROOD."
68. "HERA TELLS ZEUS THAT DEAR HERAKLES, BREAKER OF CHAINS, WAS OUR SIRE AND KILLING US WOULD BE AKIN TO FOUL DEICIDE."
"NONE MAY SPILL ZEUS-KIN BLOOD OTHER THAN ZEUS. IT WAS THUS WAY BACK THEN IT IS THUS EVEN NOW,"
SAYS HYRAR.
"THUS MAD POSEIDON SEEKS CRUELER WAYS WITH WHICH TO PUNISH US...
"...OTHER THAN *DEATH*."
"SO SHE SUMMONS A STORM.
"--WITHOUT *END* OR REPRIEVE--"

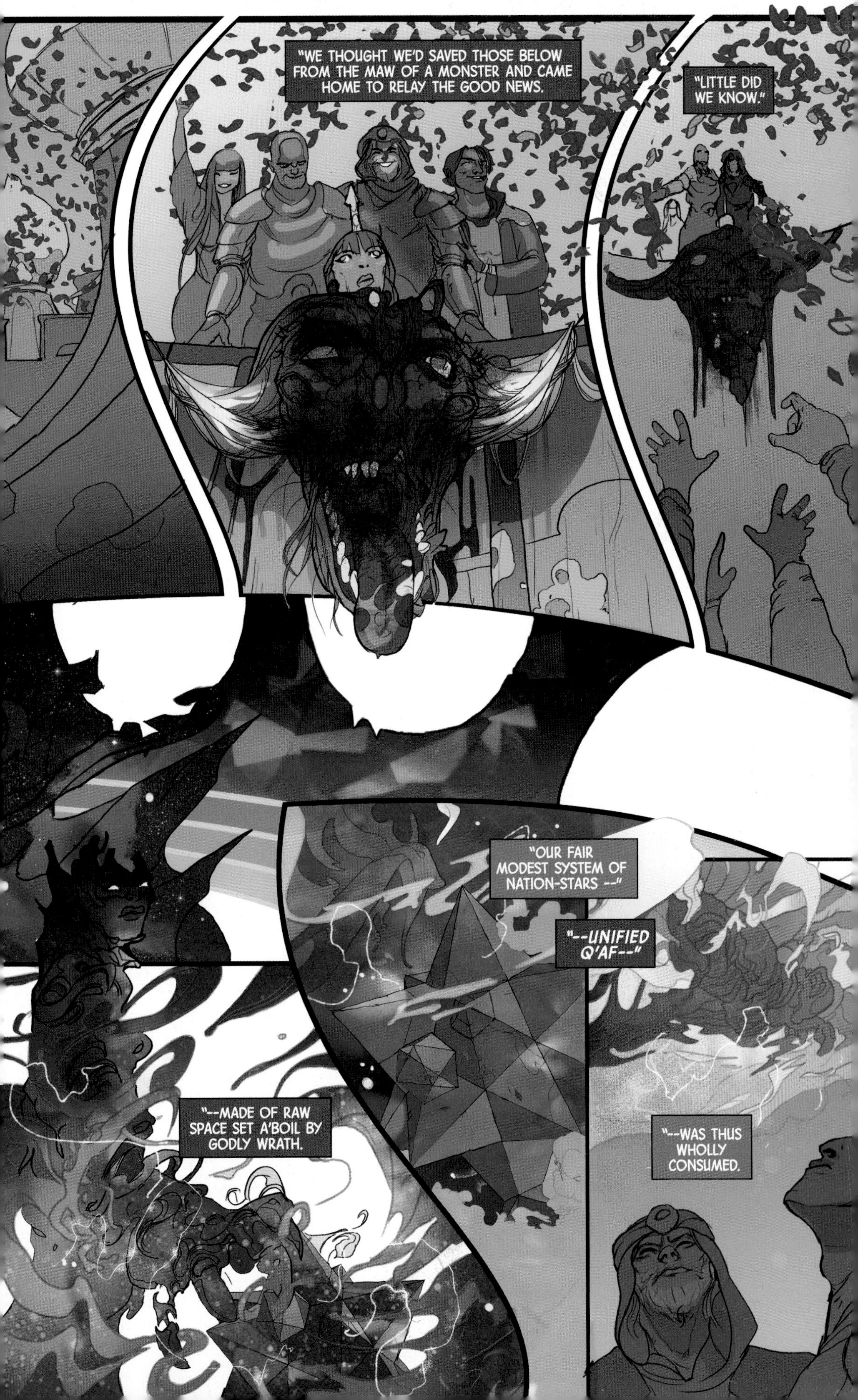
"WE THOUGHT WE'D SAVED THOSE BELOW FROM THE MAW OF A MONSTER AND CAME HOME TO RELAY THE GOOD NEWS.
"LITTLE DID WE KNOW."
"OUR FAIR MODEST SYSTEM OF NATION-STARS --"
"--UNIFIED Q'AF--"
"--MADE OF RAW SPACE SET A'BOIL BY GODLY WRATH.
"--WAS THUS WHOLLY CONSUMED.

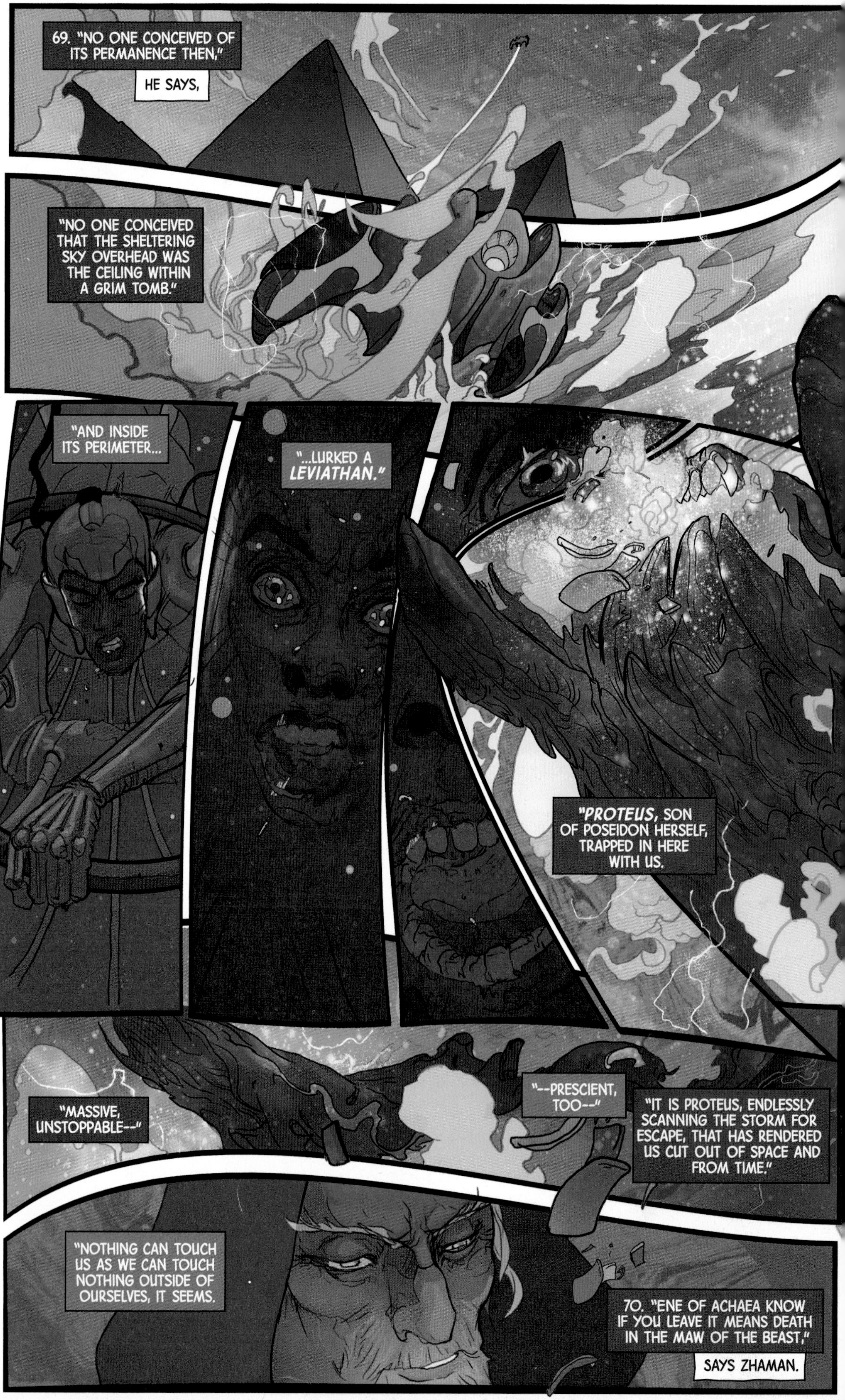
69. "NO ONE CONCEIVED OF ITS PERMANENCE THEN,"
HE SAYS,
"NO ONE CONCEIVED THAT THE SHELTERING SKY OVERHEAD WAS THE CEILING WITHIN A GRIM TOMB."
"AND INSIDE ITS PERIMETER...
"...LURKED A *LEVIATHAN.*"
"*PROTEUS,* SON OF POSEIDON HERSELF, TRAPPED IN HERE WITH US.
"MASSIVE, UNSTOPPABLE--"
"--PRESCIENT, TOO--"
"IT IS PROTEUS, ENDLESSLY SCANNING THE STORM FOR ESCAPE, THAT HAS RENDERED US CUT OUT OF SPACE AND FROM TIME."
"NOTHING CAN TOUCH US AS WE CAN TOUCH NOTHING OUTSIDE OF OURSELVES, IT SEEMS.
70. "ENE OF ACHAEA KNOW IF YOU LEAVE IT MEANS DEATH IN THE MAW OF THE BEAST,"
SAYS ZHAMAN.

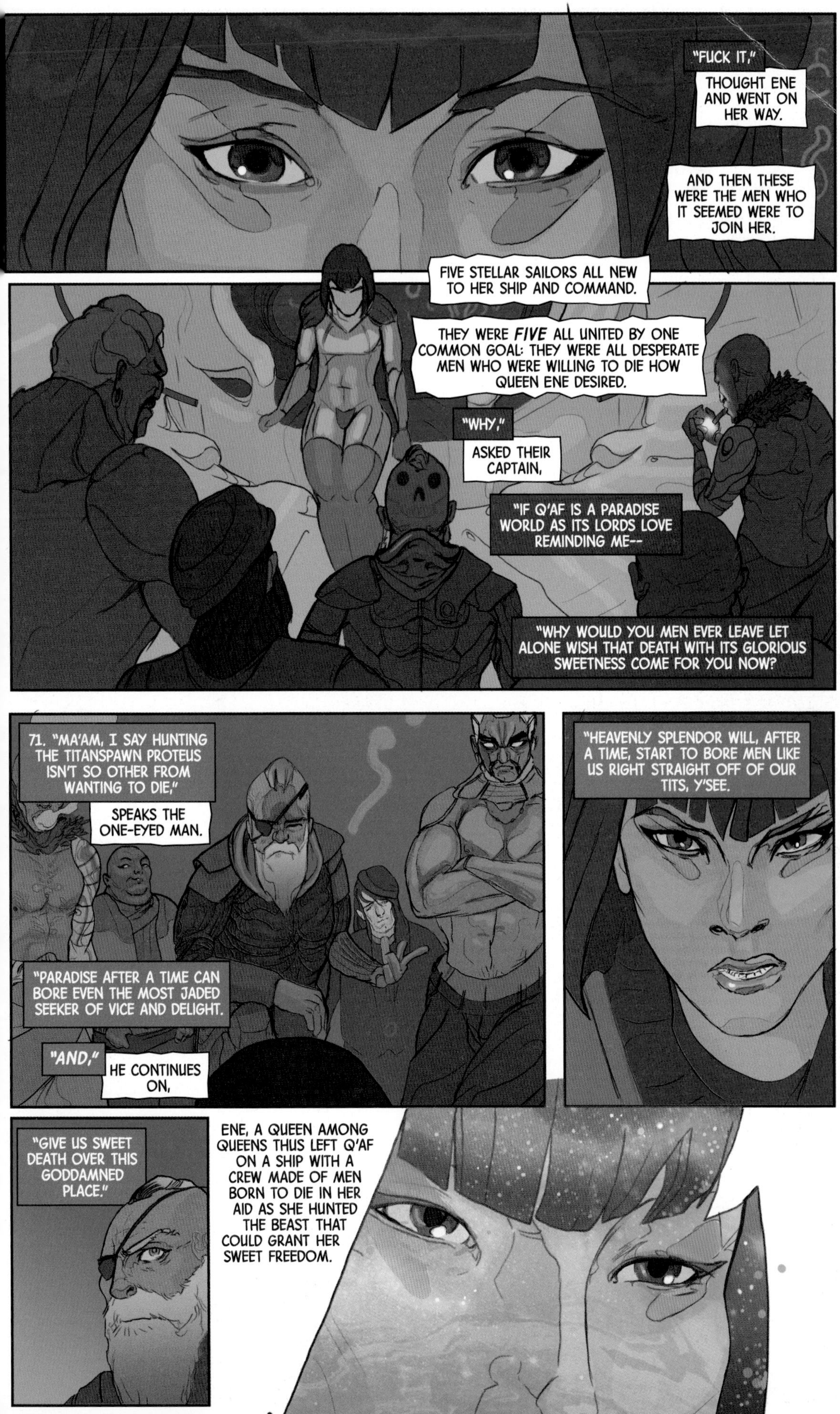
"FUCK IT,"
THOUGHT ENE AND WENT ON HER WAY.
AND THEN THESE WERE THE MEN WHO IT SEEMED WERE TO JOIN HER.
FIVE STELLAR SAILORS ALL NEW TO HER SHIP AND COMMAND.
THEY WERE *FIVE* ALL UNITED BY ONE COMMON GOAL: THEY WERE ALL DESPERATE MEN WHO WERE WILLING TO DIE HOW QUEEN ENE DESIRED.
"WHY,"
ASKED THEIR CAPTAIN,
"IF Q'AF IS A PARADISE WORLD AS ITS LORDS LOVE REMINDING ME--
"WHY WOULD YOU MEN EVER LEAVE LET ALONE WISH THAT DEATH WITH ITS GLORIOUS SWEETNESS COME FOR YOU NOW?
71. "MA'AM, I SAY HUNTING THE TITANSPAWN PROTEUS ISN'T SO OTHER FROM WANTING TO DIE,"
SPEAKS THE ONE-EYED MAN.
"PARADISE AFTER A TIME CAN BORE EVEN THE MOST JADED SEEKER OF VICE AND DELIGHT.
"AND,"
HE CONTINUES ON,
"HEAVENLY SPLENDOR WILL, AFTER A TIME, START TO BORE MEN LIKE US RIGHT STRAIGHT OFF OF OUR TITS, Y'SEE.
"GIVE US SWEET DEATH OVER THIS GODDAMNED PLACE."
ENE, A QUEEN AMONG QUEENS THUS LEFT Q'AF ON A SHIP WITH A CREW MADE OF MEN BORN TO DIE IN HER AID AS SHE HUNTED THE BEAST THAT COULD GRANT HER SWEET FREEDOM.

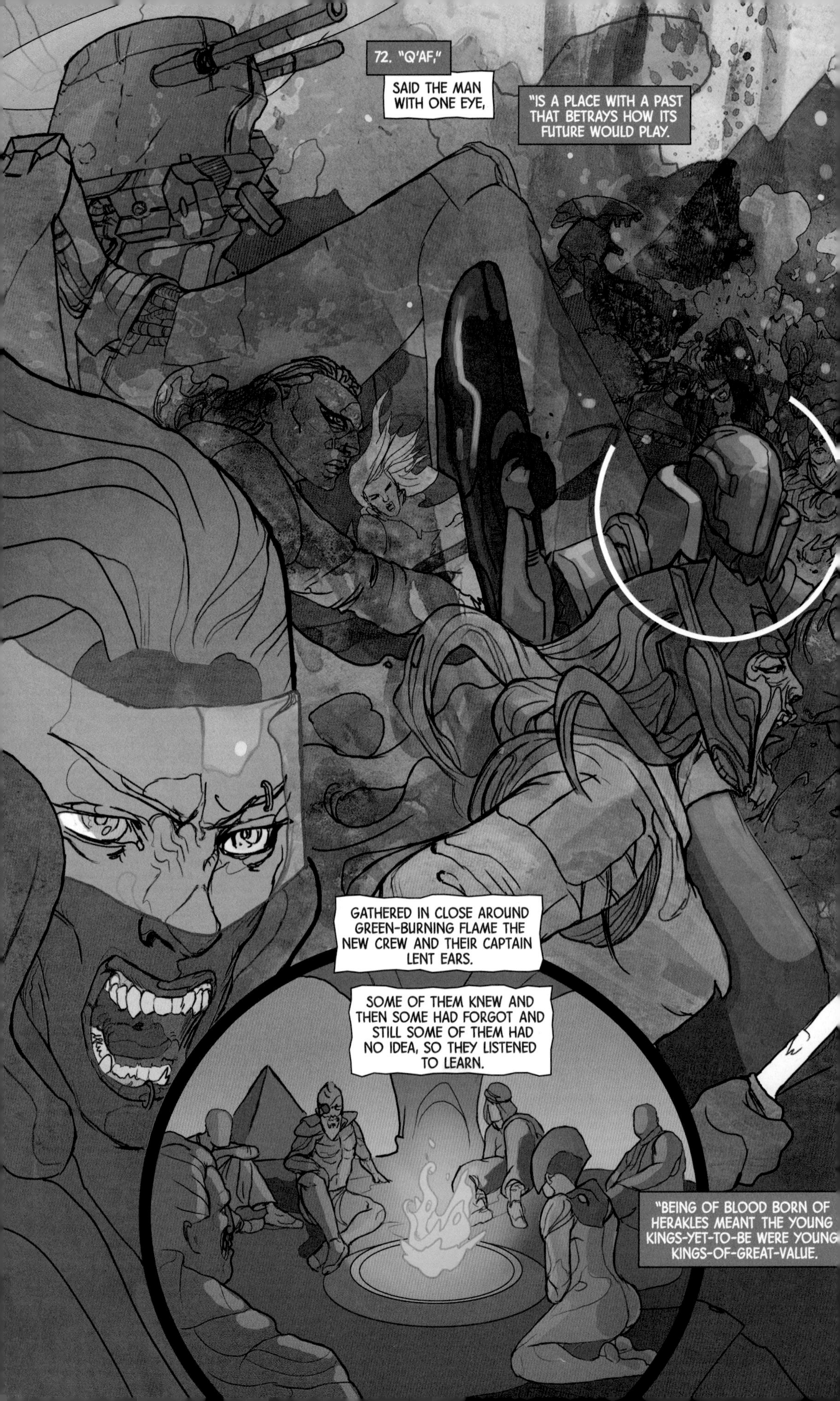
72. "Q'AF,"
SAID THE MAN WITH ONE EYE,
"IS A PLACE WITH A PAST THAT BETRAYS HOW ITS FUTURE WOULD PLAY.
GATHERED IN CLOSE AROUND GREEN-BURNING FLAME THE NEW CREW AND THEIR CAPTAIN LENT EARS.
SOME OF THEM KNEW AND THEN SOME HAD FORGOT AND STILL SOME OF THEM HAD NO IDEA, SO THEY LISTENED TO LEARN.
"BEING OF BLOOD BORN OF HERAKLES MEANT THE YOUNG KINGS-YET-TO-BE WERE YOUNG KINGS-OF-GREAT-VALUE.

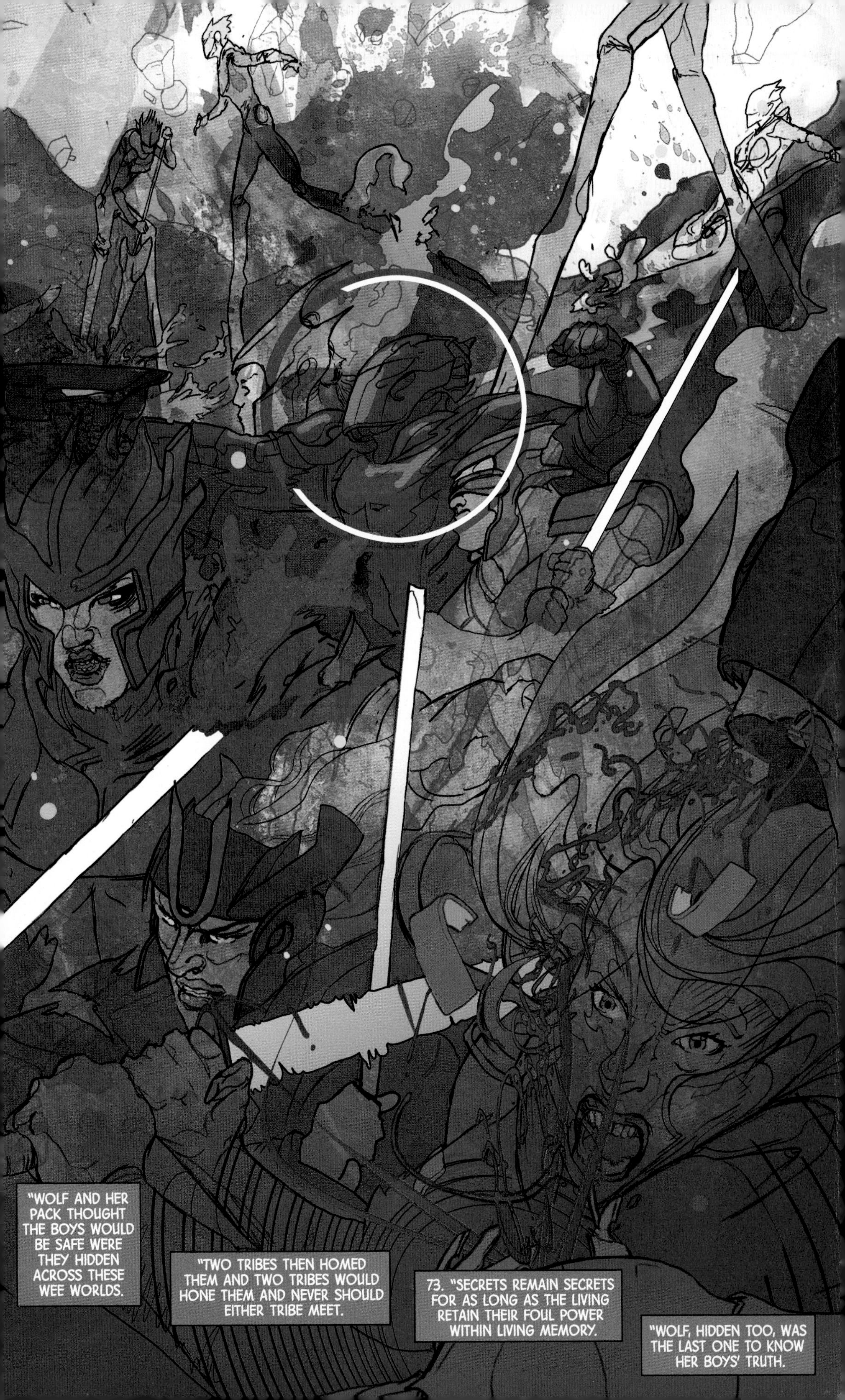
"WOLF AND HER PACK THOUGHT THE BOYS WOULD BE SAFE WERE THEY HIDDEN ACROSS THESE WEE WORLDS.
"TWO TRIBES THEN HOMED THEM AND TWO TRIBES WOULD HONE THEM AND NEVER SHOULD EITHER TRIBE MEET.
73. "SECRETS REMAIN SECRETS FOR AS LONG AS THE LIVING RETAIN THEIR FOUL POWER WITHIN LIVING MEMORY.
"WOLF, HIDDEN TOO, WAS THE LAST ONE TO KNOW HER BOYS' TRUTH.

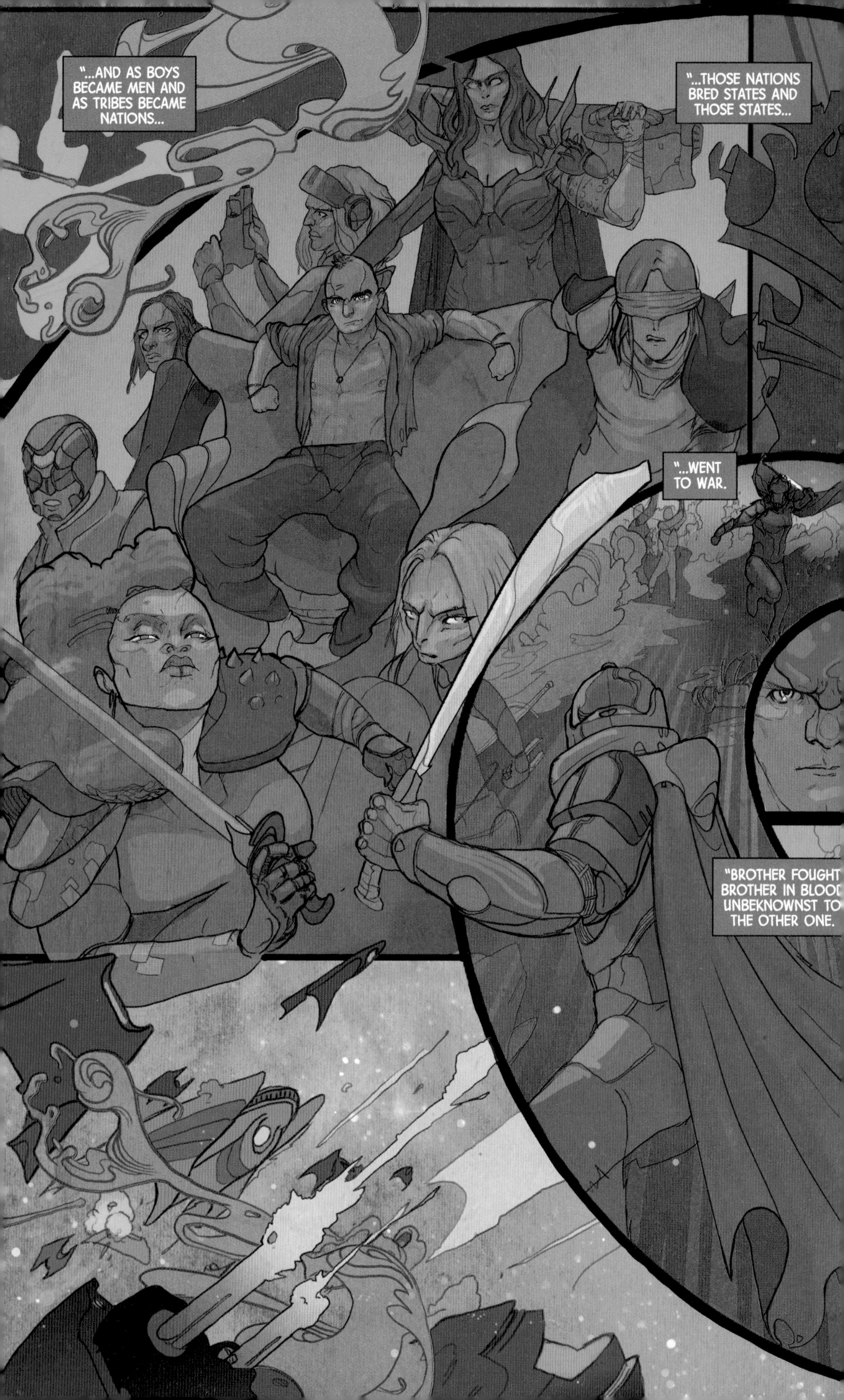
"...AND AS BOYS BECAME MEN AND AS TRIBES BECAME NATIONS...
"...THOSE NATIONS BRED STATES AND THOSE STATES...
"...WENT TO WAR.
"BROTHER FOUGHT BROTHER IN BLOOD UNBEKNOWNST TO THE OTHER ONE.

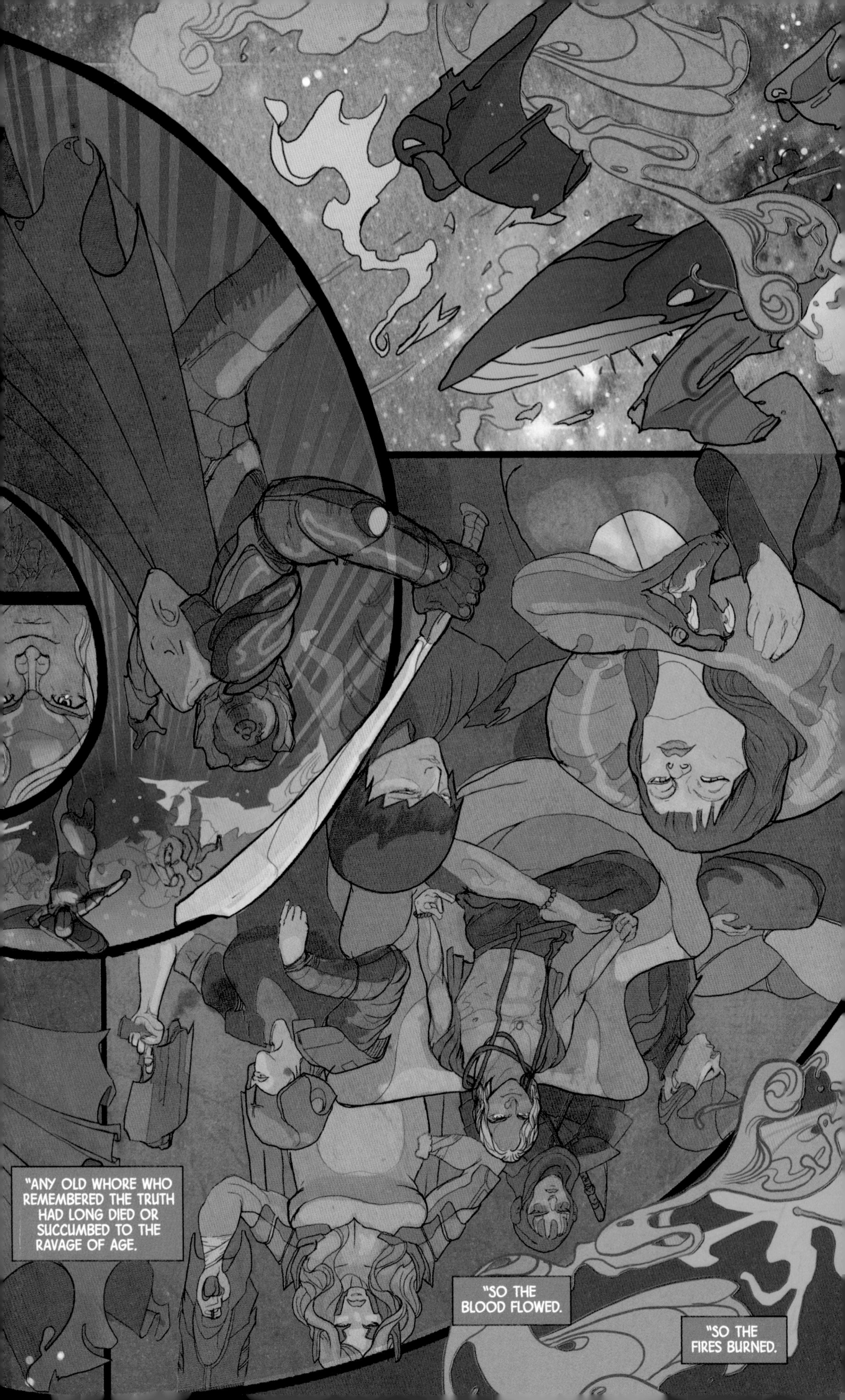
"ANY OLD WHORE WHO REMEMBERED THE TRUTH HAD LONG DIED OR SUCCUMBED TO THE RAVAGE OF AGE.
"SO THE BLOOD FLOWED.
"SO THE FIRES BURNED.

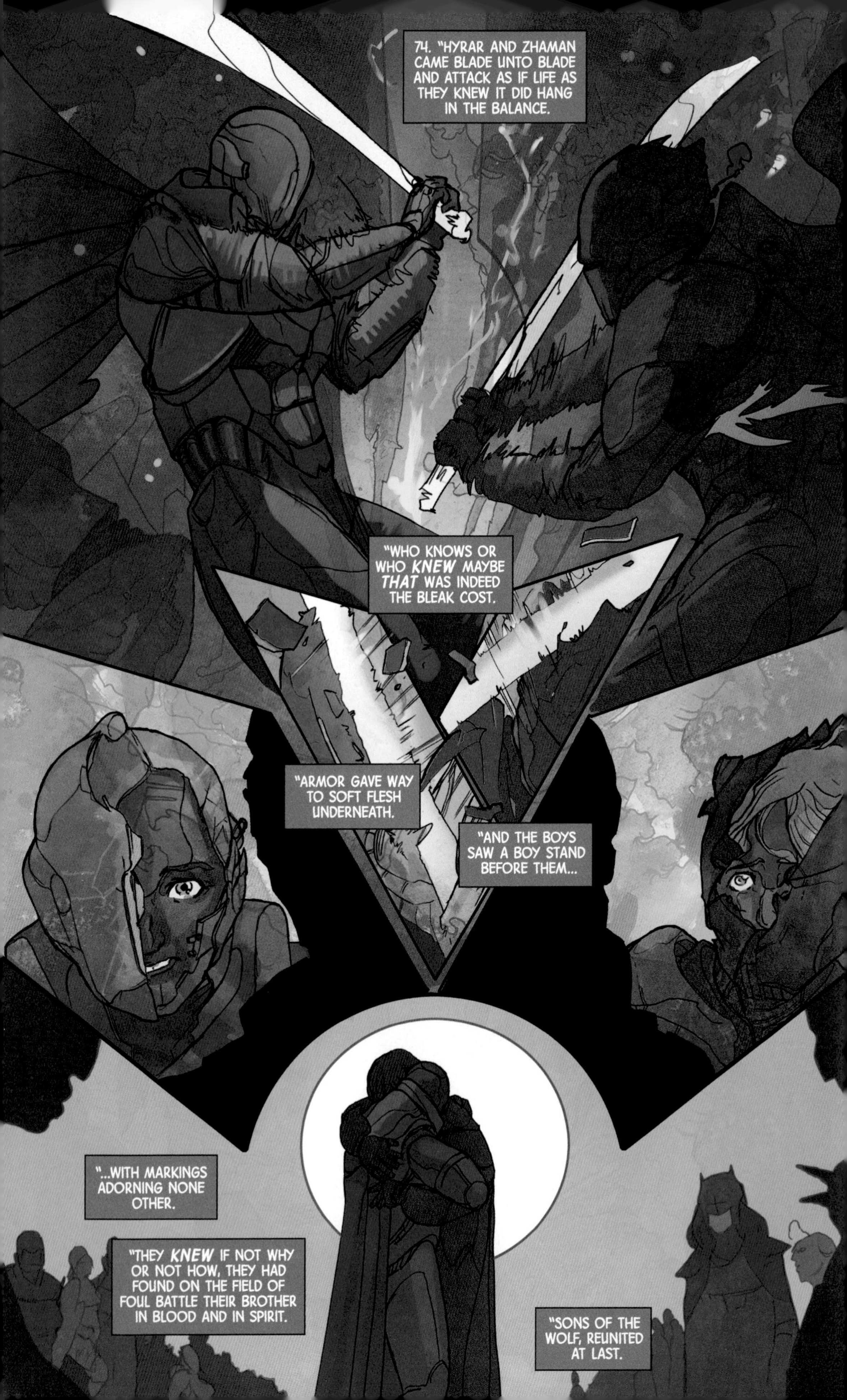
74. "HYRAR AND ZHAMAN CAME BLADE UNTO BLADE AND ATTACK AS IF LIFE AS THEY KNEW IT DID HANG IN THE BALANCE.
"WHO KNOWS OR WHO KNEW MAYBE THAT WAS INDEED THE BLEAK COST.
"ARMOR GAVE WAY TO SOFT FLESH UNDERNEATH.
"AND THE BOYS SAW A BOY STAND BEFORE THEM...
"...WITH MARKINGS ADORNING NONE OTHER.
"THEY KNEW IF NOT WHY OR NOT HOW, THEY HAD FOUND ON THE FIELD OF FOUL BATTLE THEIR BROTHER IN BLOOD AND IN SPIRIT.
"SONS OF THE WOLF, REUNITED AT LAST.

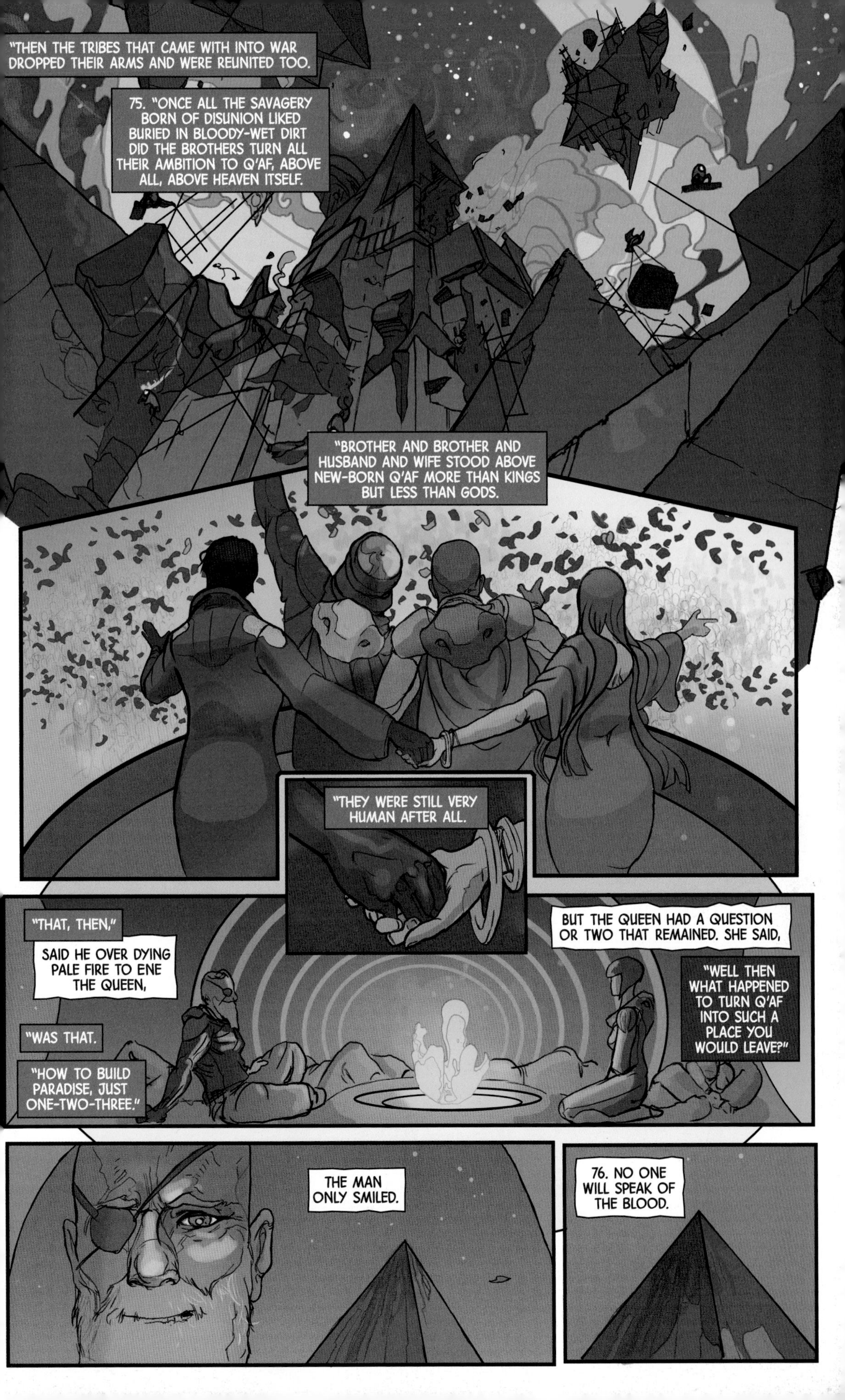
"THEN THE TRIBES THAT CAME WITH INTO WAR DROPPED THEIR ARMS AND WERE REUNITED TOO.
75. "ONCE ALL THE SAVAGERY BORN OF DISUNION LIKED BURIED IN BLOODY-WET DIRT DID THE BROTHERS TURN ALL THEIR AMBITION TO Q'AF, ABOVE ALL, ABOVE HEAVEN ITSELF.
"BROTHER AND BROTHER AND HUSBAND AND WIFE STOOD ABOVE NEW-BORN Q'AF MORE THAN KINGS BUT LESS THAN GODS.
"THEY WERE STILL VERY HUMAN AFTER ALL.
"THAT, THEN,"
SAID HE OVER DYING PALE FIRE TO ENE THE QUEEN,
"WAS THAT.
"HOW TO BUILD PARADISE, JUST ONE-TWO-THREE."
BUT THE QUEEN HAD A QUESTION OR TWO THAT REMAINED. SHE SAID,
"WELL THEN WHAT HAPPENED TO TURN Q'AF INTO SUCH A PLACE YOU WOULD LEAVE?"
THE MAN ONLY SMILED.
76. NO ONE WILL SPEAK OF THE BLOOD.

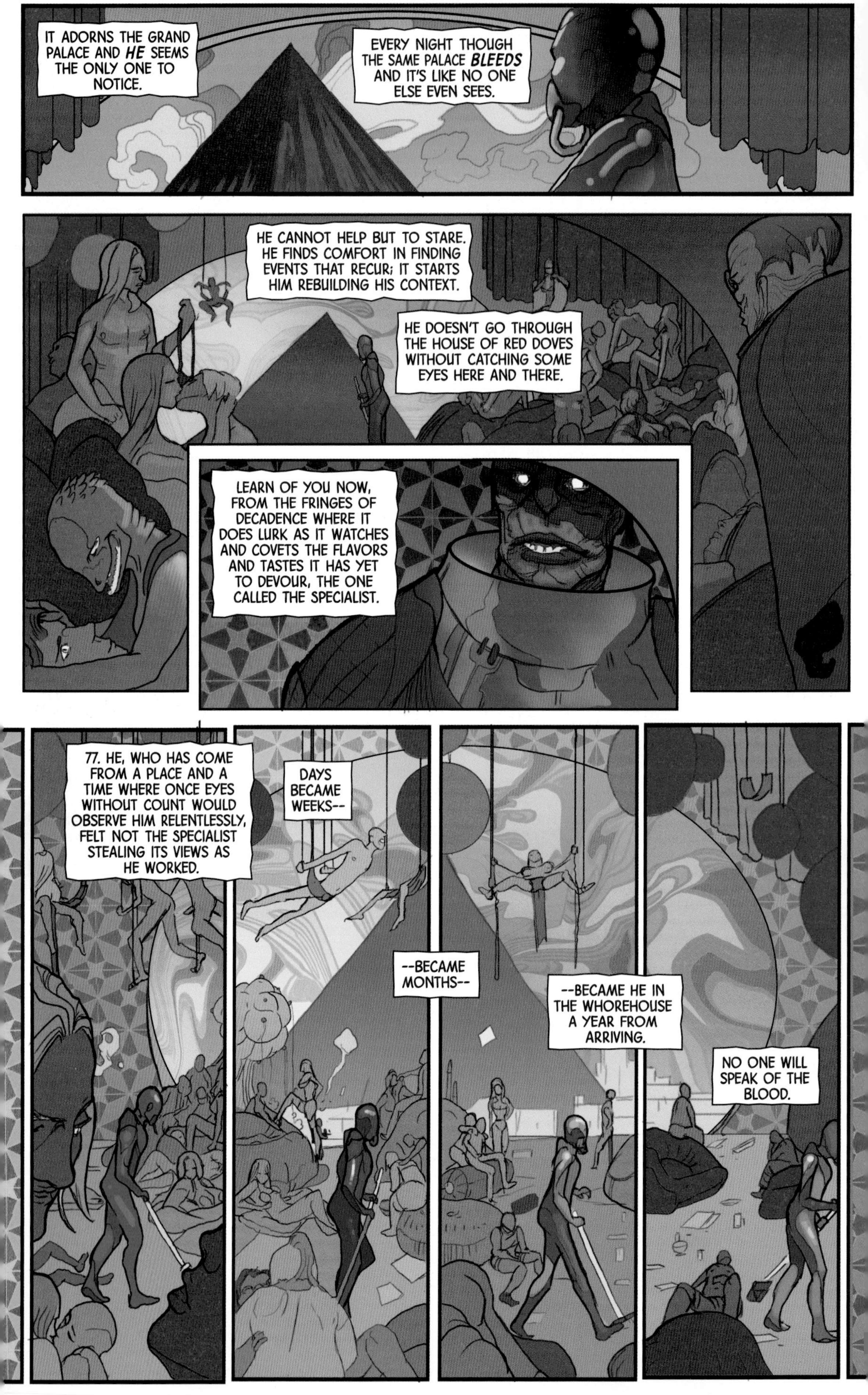
IT ADORNS THE GRAND PALACE AND *HE* SEEMS THE ONLY ONE TO NOTICE.
EVERY NIGHT THOUGH THE SAME PALACE ***BLEEDS*** AND IT'S LIKE NO ONE ELSE EVEN SEES.
HE CANNOT HELP BUT TO STARE. HE FINDS COMFORT IN FINDING EVENTS THAT RECUR; IT STARTS HIM REBUILDING HIS CONTEXT.
HE DOESN'T GO THROUGH THE HOUSE OF RED DOVES WITHOUT CATCHING SOME EYES HERE AND THERE.
LEARN OF YOU NOW, FROM THE FRINGES OF DECADENCE WHERE IT DOES LURK AS IT WATCHES AND COVETS THE FLAVORS AND TASTES IT HAS YET TO DEVOUR, THE ONE CALLED THE SPECIALIST.
77. HE, WHO HAS COME FROM A PLACE AND A TIME WHERE ONCE EYES WITHOUT COUNT WOULD OBSERVE HIM RELENTLESSLY, FELT NOT THE SPECIALIST STEALING ITS VIEWS AS HE WORKED.
DAYS BECAME WEEKS--
--BECAME MONTHS--
--BECAME HE IN THE WHOREHOUSE A YEAR FROM ARRIVING.
NO ONE WILL SPEAK OF THE BLOOD.

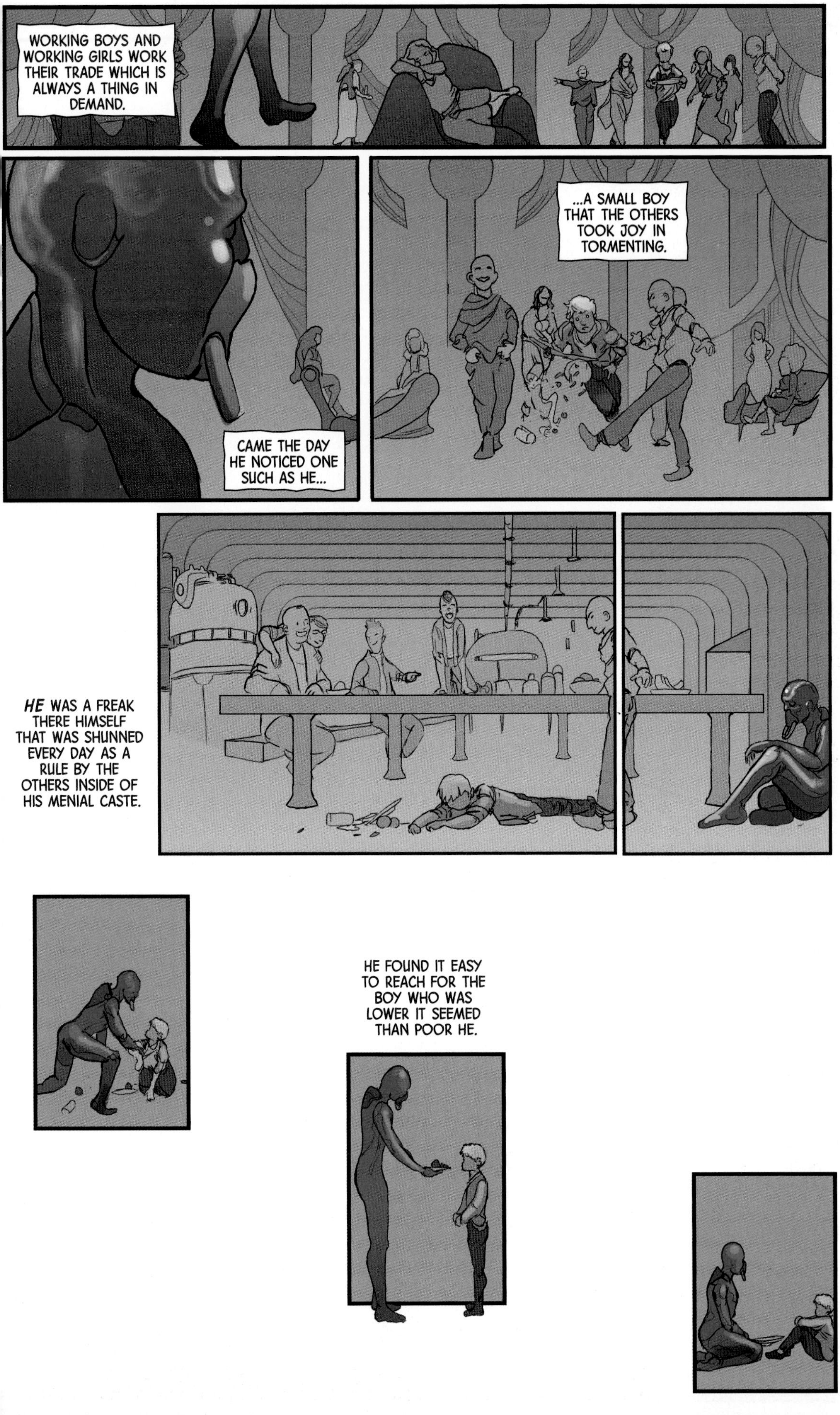
WORKING BOYS AND WORKING GIRLS WORK THEIR TRADE WHICH IS ALWAYS A THING IN DEMAND.
CAME THE DAY HE NOTICED ONE SUCH AS HE...
...A SMALL BOY THAT THE OTHERS TOOK JOY IN TORMENTING.
HE WAS A FREAK THERE HIMSELF THAT WAS SHUNNED EVERY DAY AS A RULE BY THE OTHERS INSIDE OF HIS MENIAL CASTE.
HE FOUND IT EASY TO REACH FOR THE BOY WHO WAS LOWER IT SEEMED THAN POOR HE.

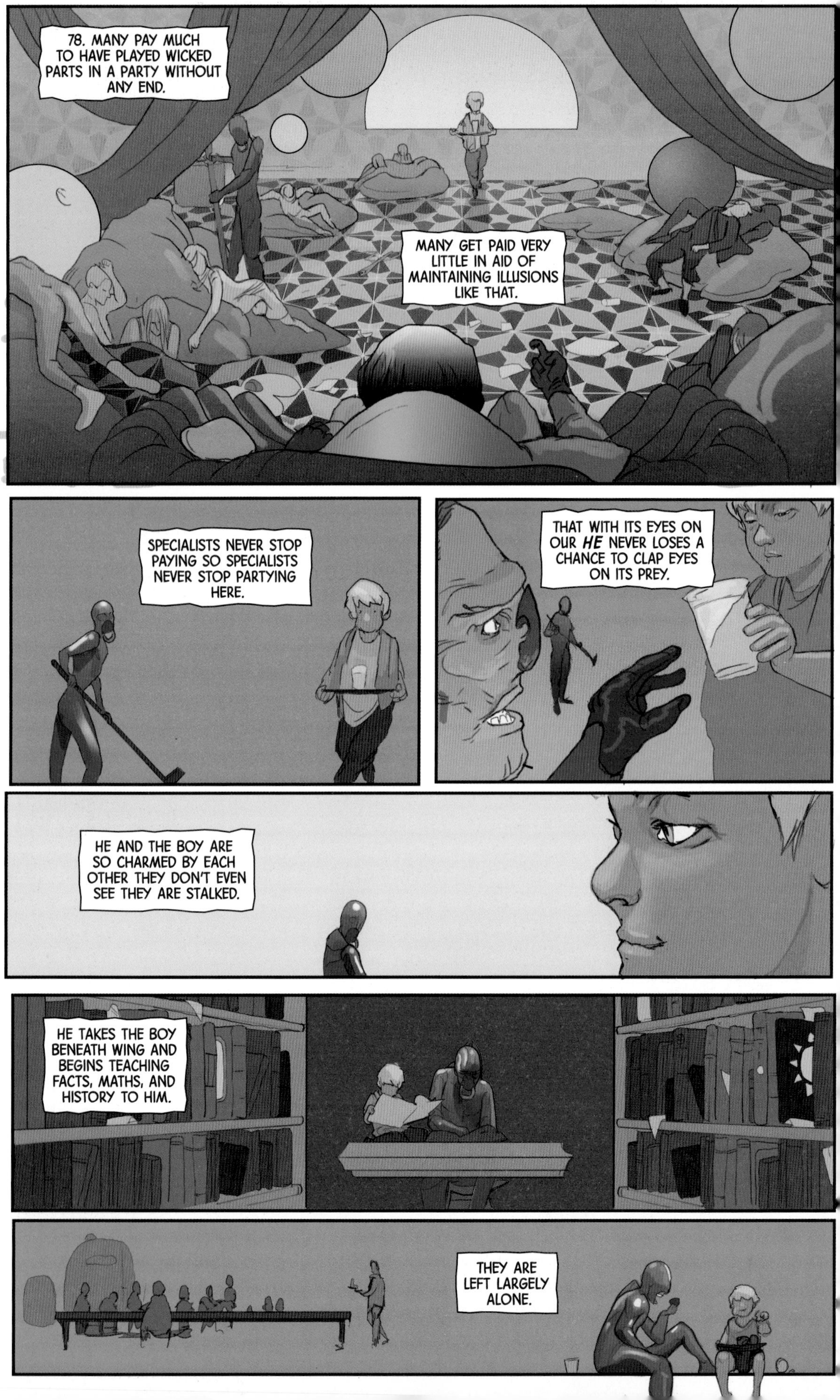
78. MANY PAY MUCH TO HAVE PLAYED WICKED PARTS IN A PARTY WITHOUT ANY END.
MANY GET PAID VERY LITTLE IN AID OF MAINTAINING ILLUSIONS LIKE THAT.
SPECIALISTS NEVER STOP PAYING SO SPECIALISTS NEVER STOP PARTYING HERE.
THAT WITH ITS EYES ON OUR *HE* NEVER LOSES A CHANCE TO CLAP EYES ON ITS PREY.
HE AND THE BOY ARE SO CHARMED BY EACH OTHER THEY DON'T EVEN SEE THEY ARE STALKED.
HE TAKES THE BOY BENEATH WING AND BEGINS TEACHING FACTS, MATHS, AND HISTORY TO HIM.
THEY ARE LEFT LARGELY ALONE.

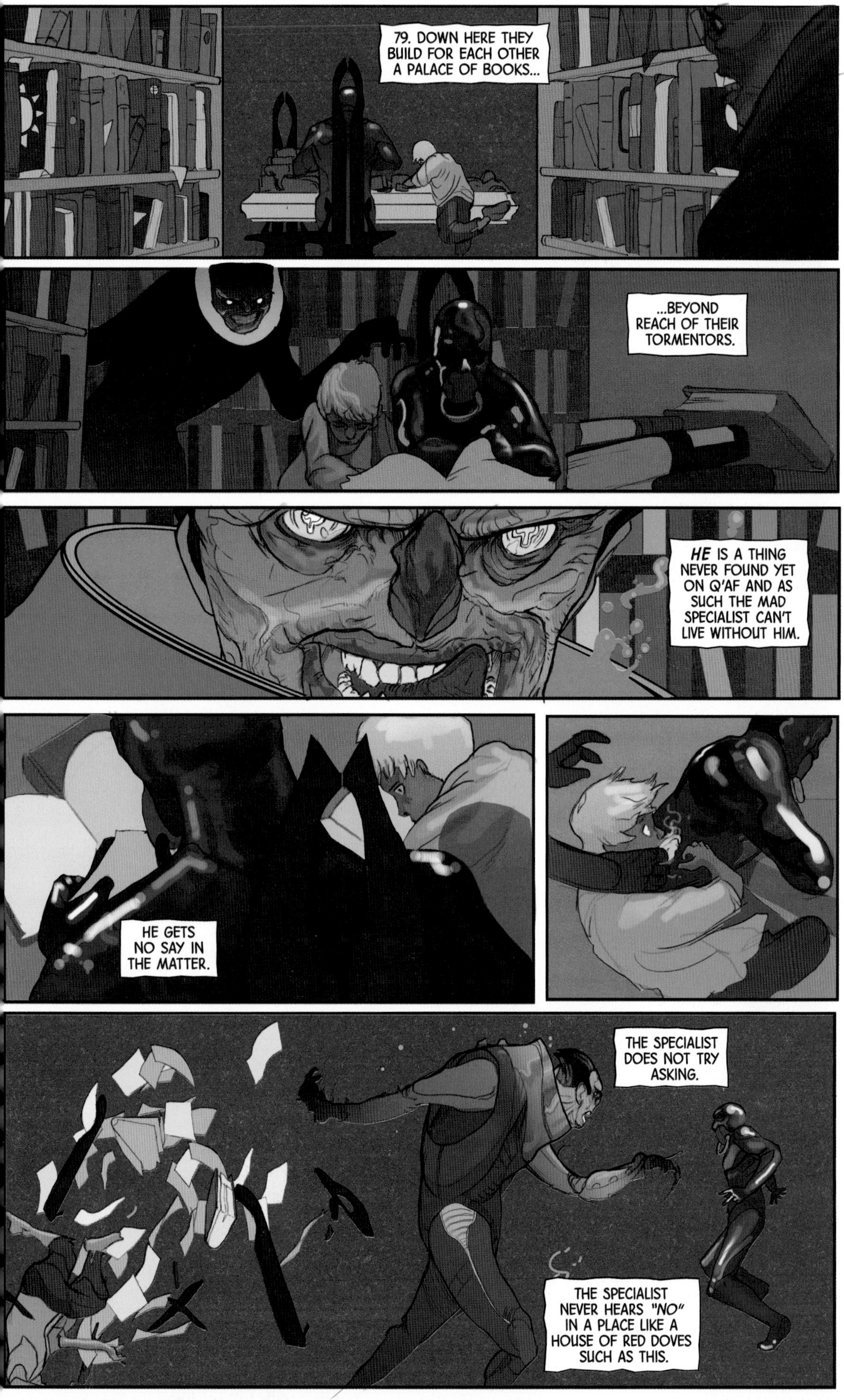
79. DOWN HERE THEY BUILD FOR EACH OTHER A PALACE OF BOOKS...
...BEYOND REACH OF THEIR TORMENTORS.
HE IS A THING NEVER FOUND YET ON Q'AF AND AS SUCH THE MAD SPECIALIST CAN'T LIVE WITHOUT HIM.
HE GETS NO SAY IN THE MATTER.
THE SPECIALIST DOES NOT TRY ASKING.
THE SPECIALIST NEVER HEARS "NO" IN A PLACE LIKE A HOUSE OF RED DOVES SUCH AS THIS.

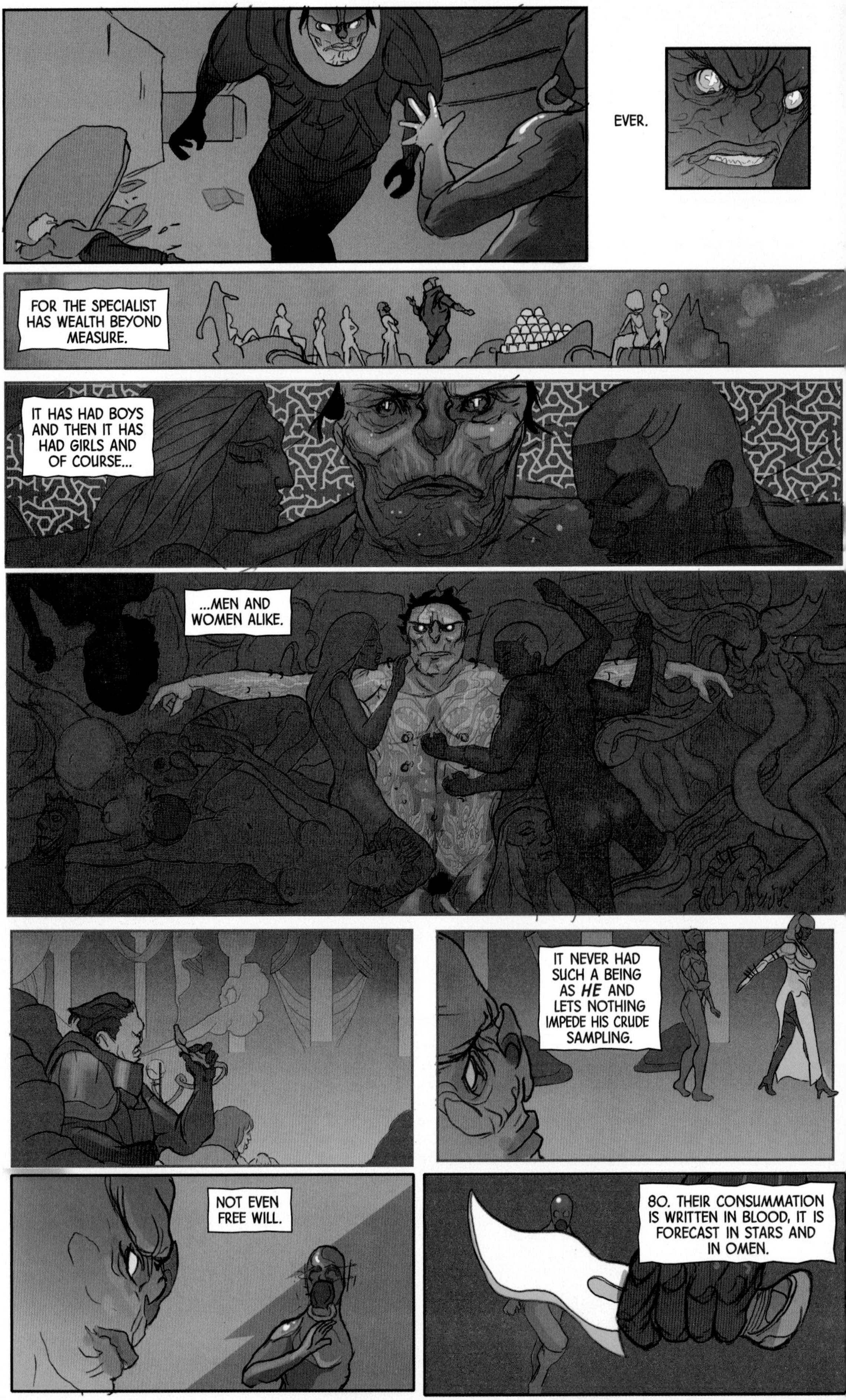
EVER.
FOR THE SPECIALIST HAS WEALTH BEYOND MEASURE.
IT HAS HAD BOYS AND THEN IT HAS HAD GIRLS AND OF COURSE...
...MEN AND WOMEN ALIKE.
IT NEVER HAD SUCH A BEING AS *HE* AND LETS NOTHING IMPEDE HIS CRUDE SAMPLING.
NOT EVEN FREE WILL.
80. THEIR CONSUMMATION IS WRITTEN IN BLOOD, IT IS FORECAST IN STARS AND IN OMEN.

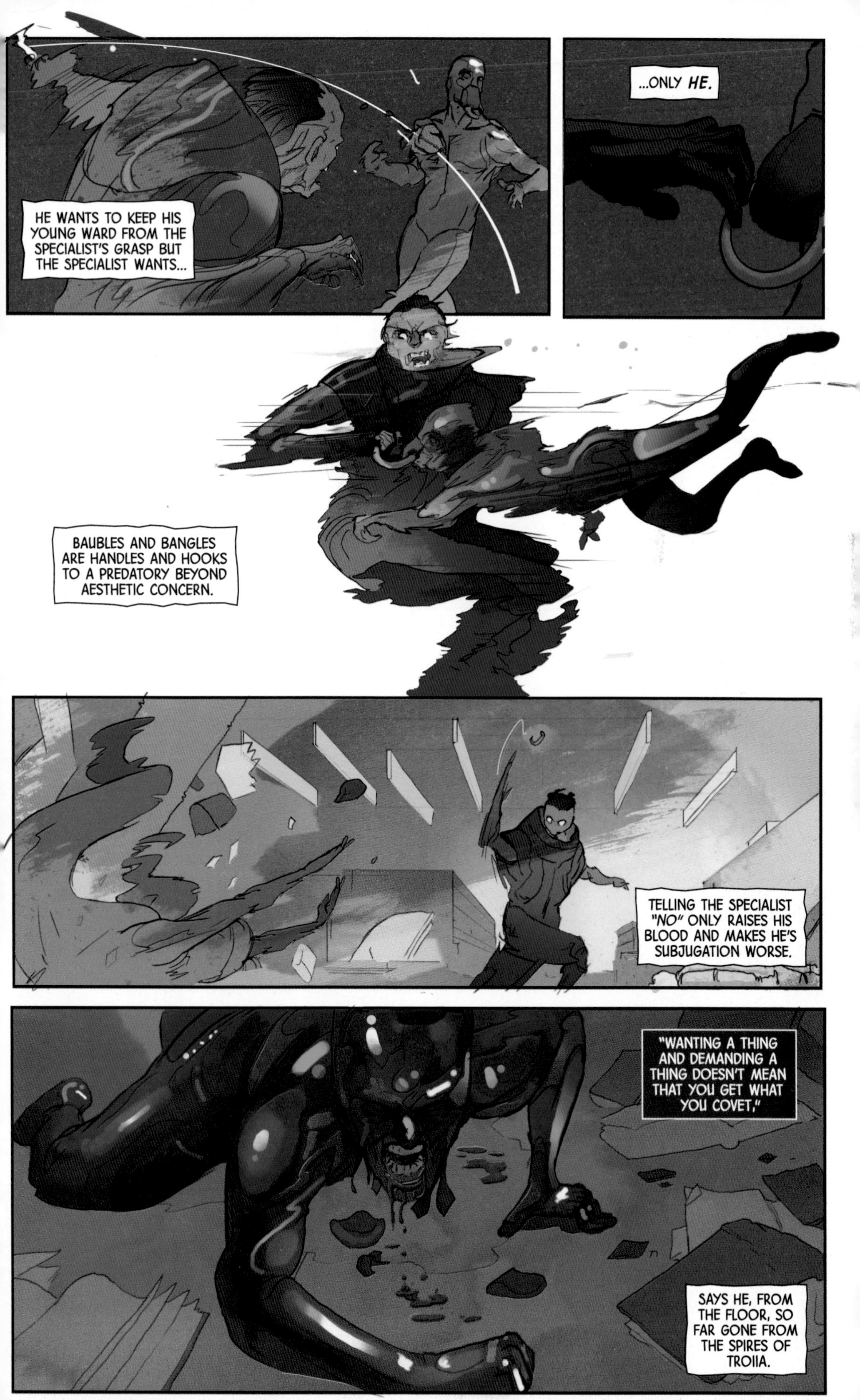
HE WANTS TO KEEP HIS YOUNG WARD FROM THE SPECIALIST'S GRASP BUT THE SPECIALIST WANTS...
...ONLY HE.
BAUBLES AND BANGLES ARE HANDLES AND HOOKS TO A PREDATORY BEYOND AESTHETIC CONCERN.
TELLING THE SPECIALIST "NO" ONLY RAISES HIS BLOOD AND MAKES HE'S SUBJUGATION WORSE.
"WANTING A THING AND DEMANDING A THING DOESN'T MEAN THAT YOU GET WHAT YOU COVET,"
SAYS HE, FROM THE FLOOR, SO FAR GONE FROM THE SPIRES OF TROIIA.

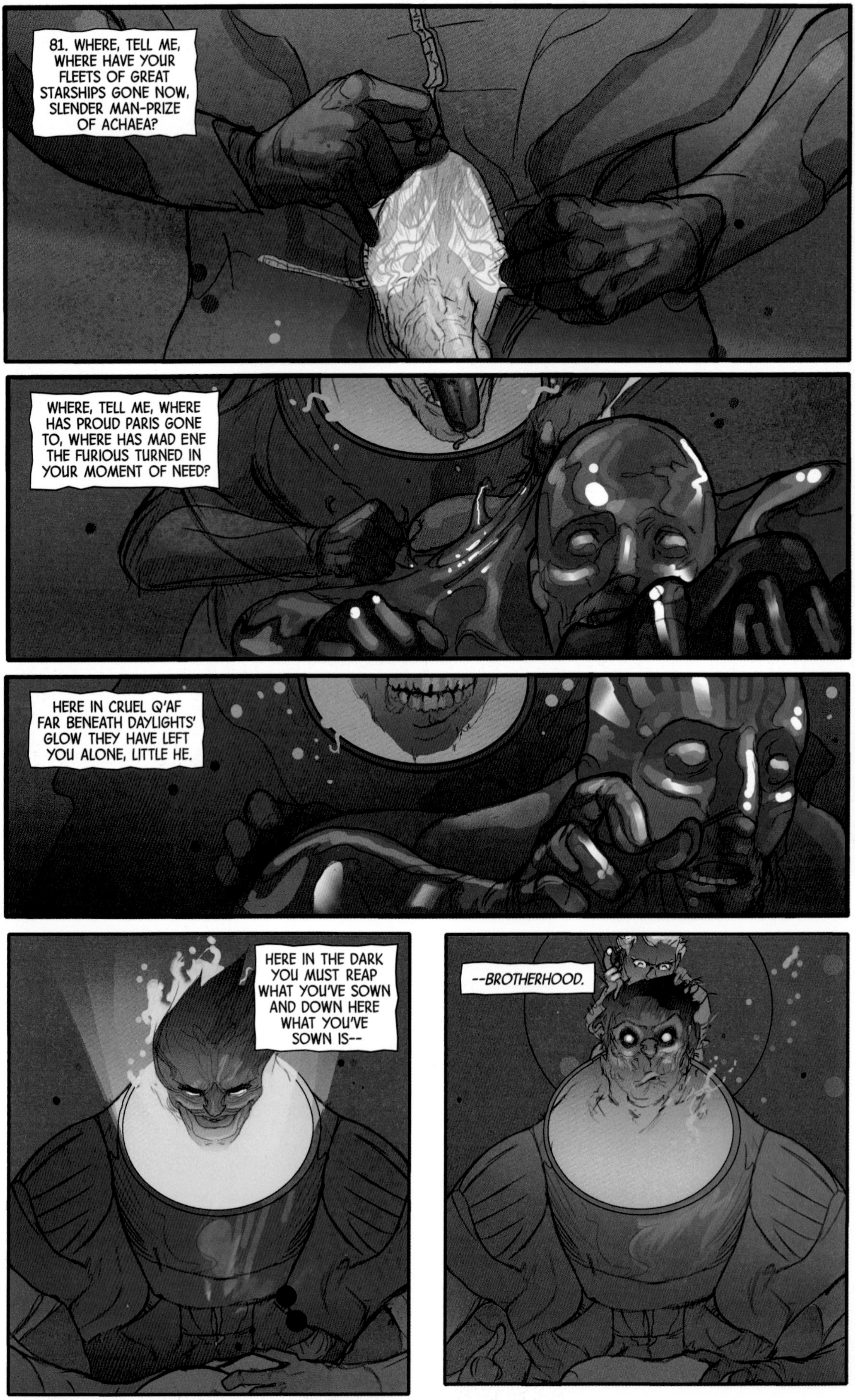
81. WHERE, TELL ME, WHERE HAVE YOUR FLEETS OF GREAT STARSHIPS GONE NOW, SLENDER MAN-PRIZE OF ACHAEA?
WHERE, TELL ME, WHERE HAS PROUD PARIS GONE TO, WHERE HAS MAD ENE THE FURIOUS TURNED IN YOUR MOMENT OF NEED?
HERE IN CRUEL Q'AF FAR BENEATH DAYLIGHTS' GLOW THEY HAVE LEFT YOU ALONE, LITTLE HE.
HERE IN THE DARK YOU MUST REAP WHAT YOU'VE SOWN AND DOWN HERE WHAT YOU'VE SOWN IS--
--BROTHERHOOD.

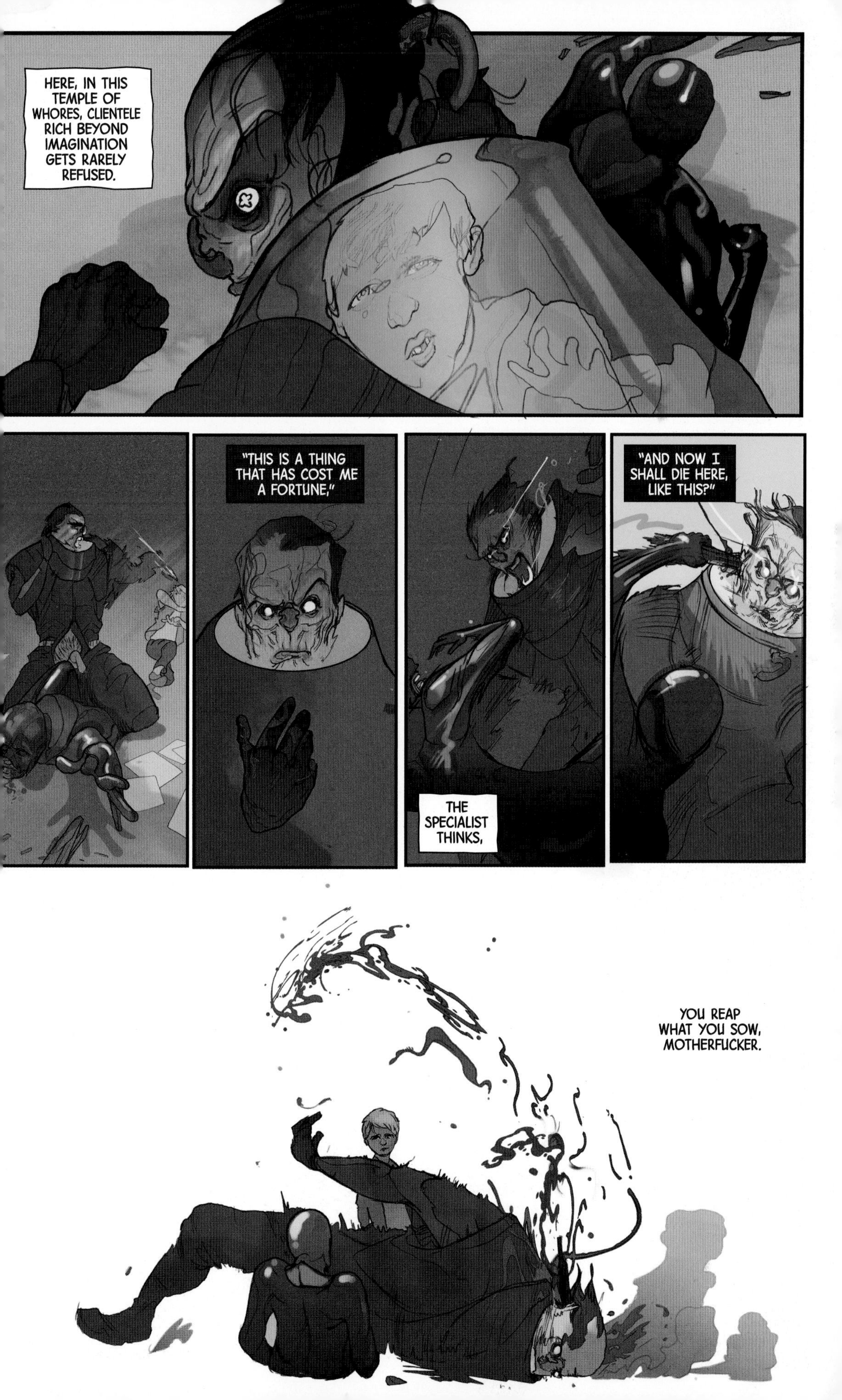
HERE, IN THIS TEMPLE OF WHORES, CLIENTELE RICH BEYOND IMAGINATION GETS RARELY REFUSED.
"THIS IS A THING THAT HAS COST ME A FORTUNE,"
THE SPECIALIST THINKS,
"AND NOW I SHALL DIE HERE, LIKE THIS?"
YOU REAP WHAT YOU SOW, MOTHERFUCKER.

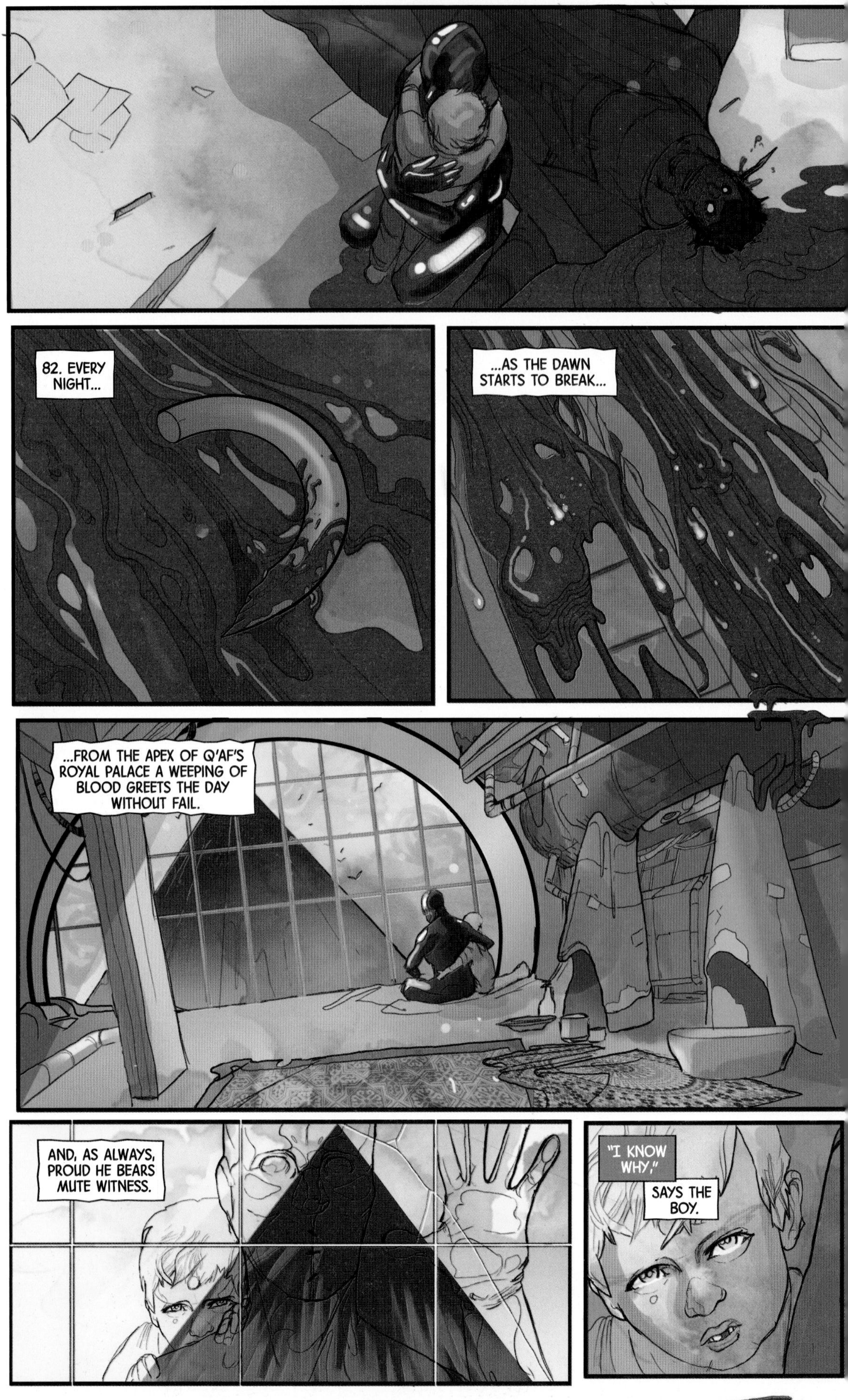
82. EVERY NIGHT...
...AS THE DAWN STARTS TO BREAK...
...FROM THE APEX OF Q'AF'S ROYAL PALACE A WEEPING OF BLOOD GREETS THE DAY WITHOUT FAIL.
AND, AS ALWAYS, PROUD HE BEARS MUTE WITNESS.
"I KNOW WHY,"
SAYS THE BOY.

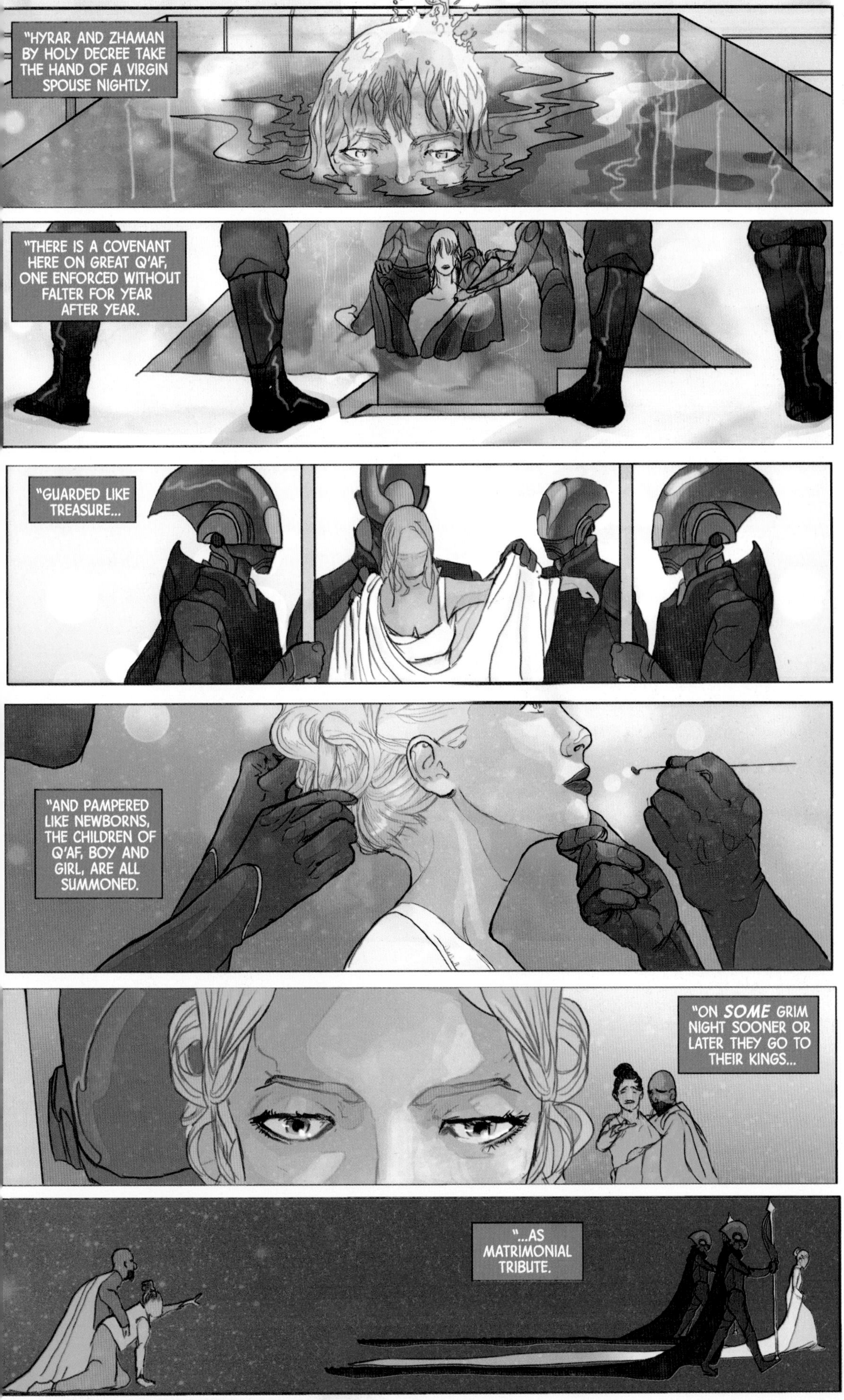
"HYRAR AND ZHAMAN BY HOLY DECREE TAKE THE HAND OF A VIRGIN SPOUSE NIGHTLY.
"THERE IS A COVENANT HERE ON GREAT Q'AF, ONE ENFORCED WITHOUT FALTER FOR YEAR AFTER YEAR.
"GUARDED LIKE TREASURE...
"AND PAMPERED LIKE NEWBORNS, THE CHILDREN OF Q'AF, BOY AND GIRL, ARE ALL SUMMONED.
"ON *SOME* GRIM NIGHT SOONER OR LATER THEY GO TO THEIR KINGS...
"...AS MATRIMONIAL TRIBUTE.

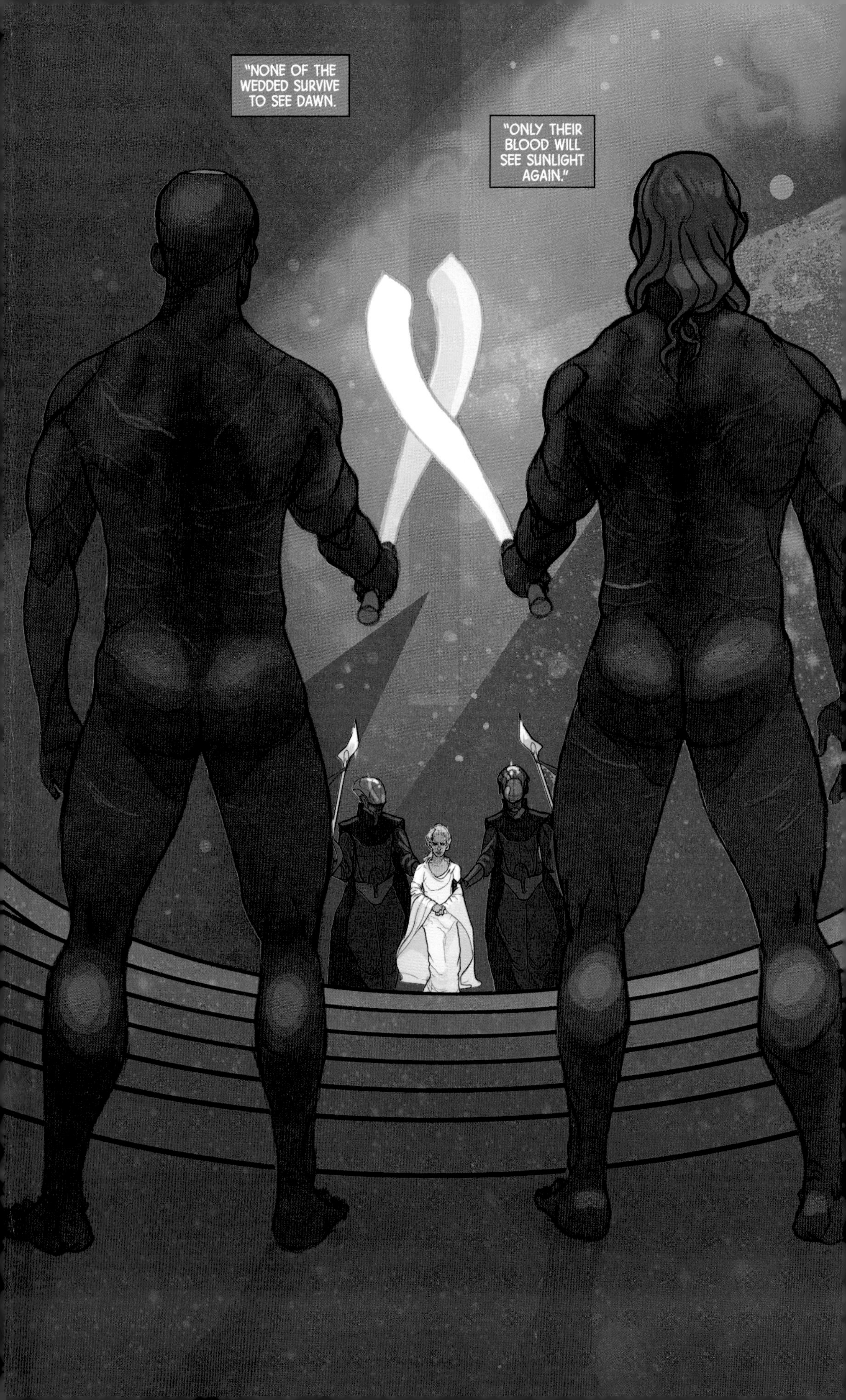
"NONE OF THE WEDDED SURVIVE TO SEE DAWN.
"ONLY THEIR BLOOD WILL SEE SUNLIGHT AGAIN."

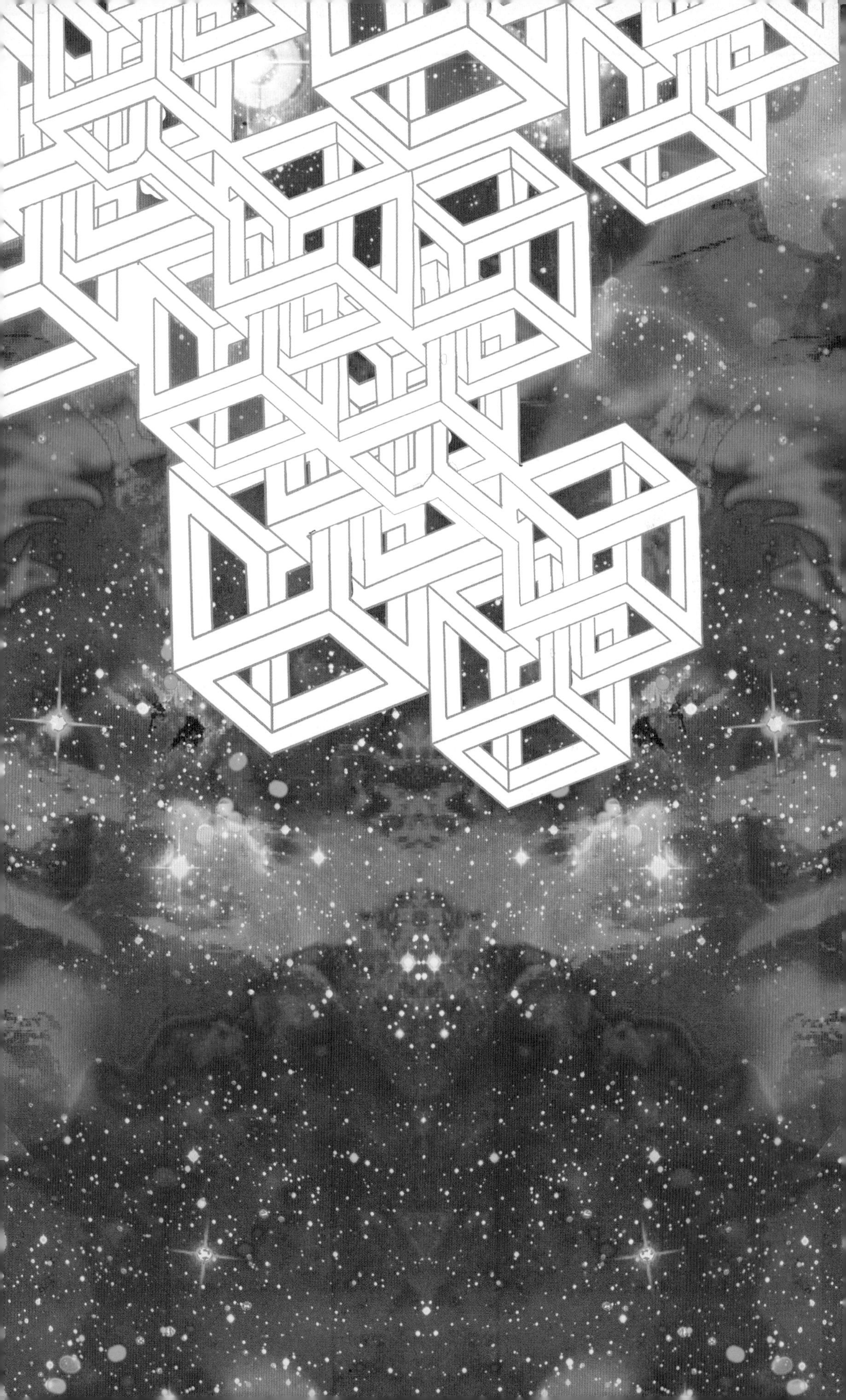

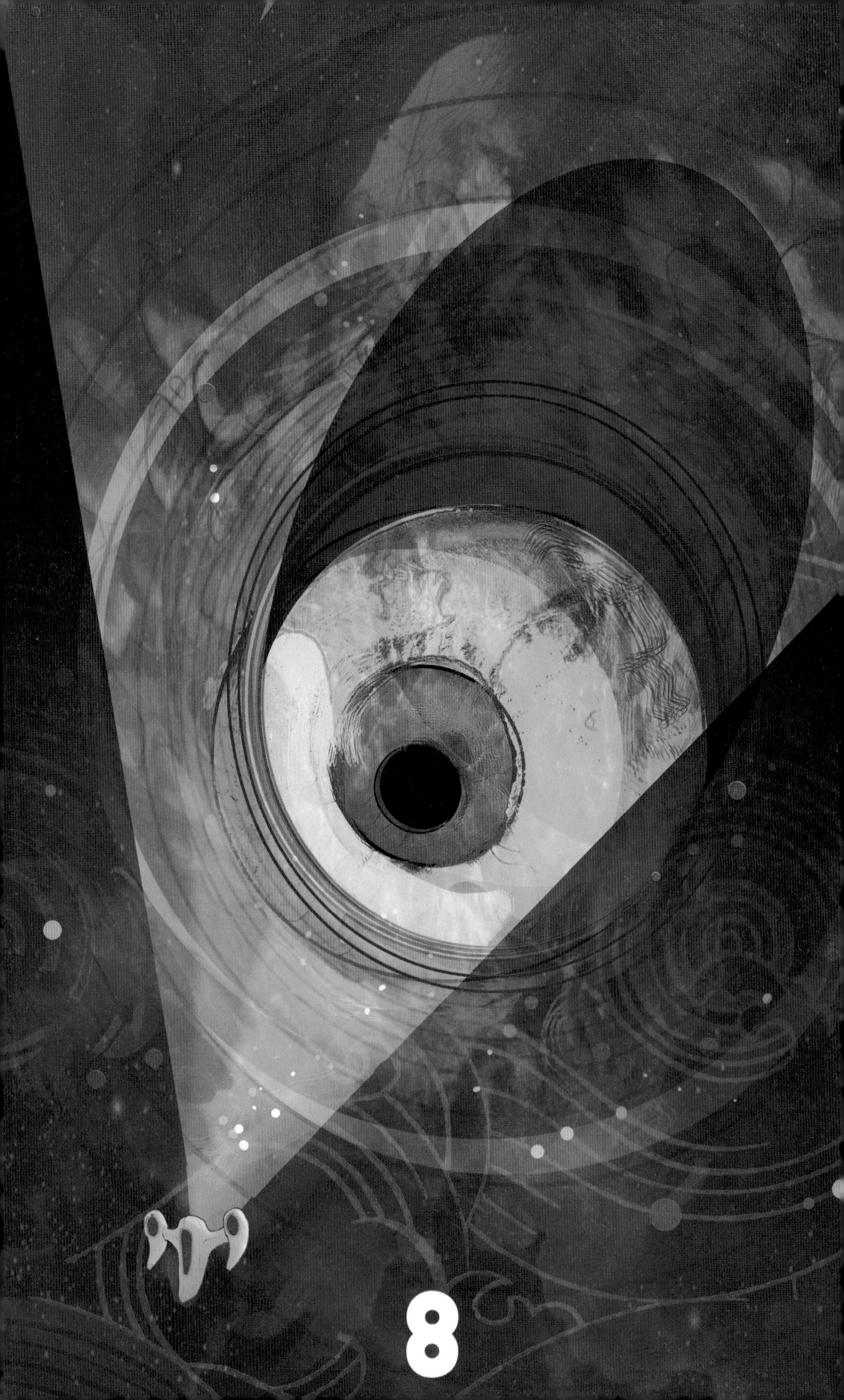
8

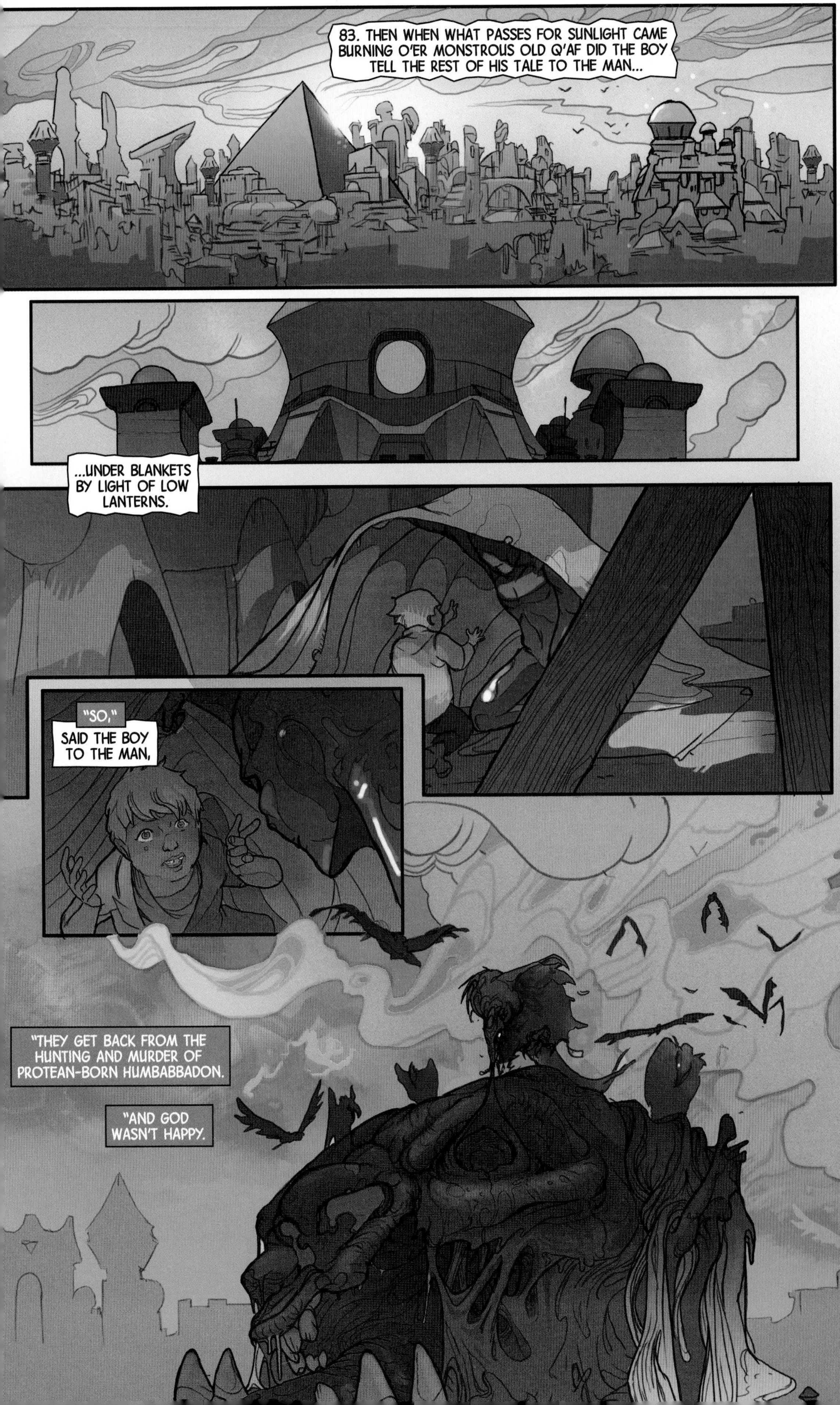
83. THEN WHEN WHAT PASSES FOR SUNLIGHT CAME BURNING O'ER MONSTROUS OLD Q'AF DID THE BOY TELL THE REST OF HIS TALE TO THE MAN...
...UNDER BLANKETS BY LIGHT OF LOW LANTERNS.
"SO,"
SAID THE BOY TO THE MAN,
"THEY GET BACK FROM THE HUNTING AND MURDER OF PROTEAN-BORN HUMBABBADON.
"AND GOD WASN'T HAPPY.

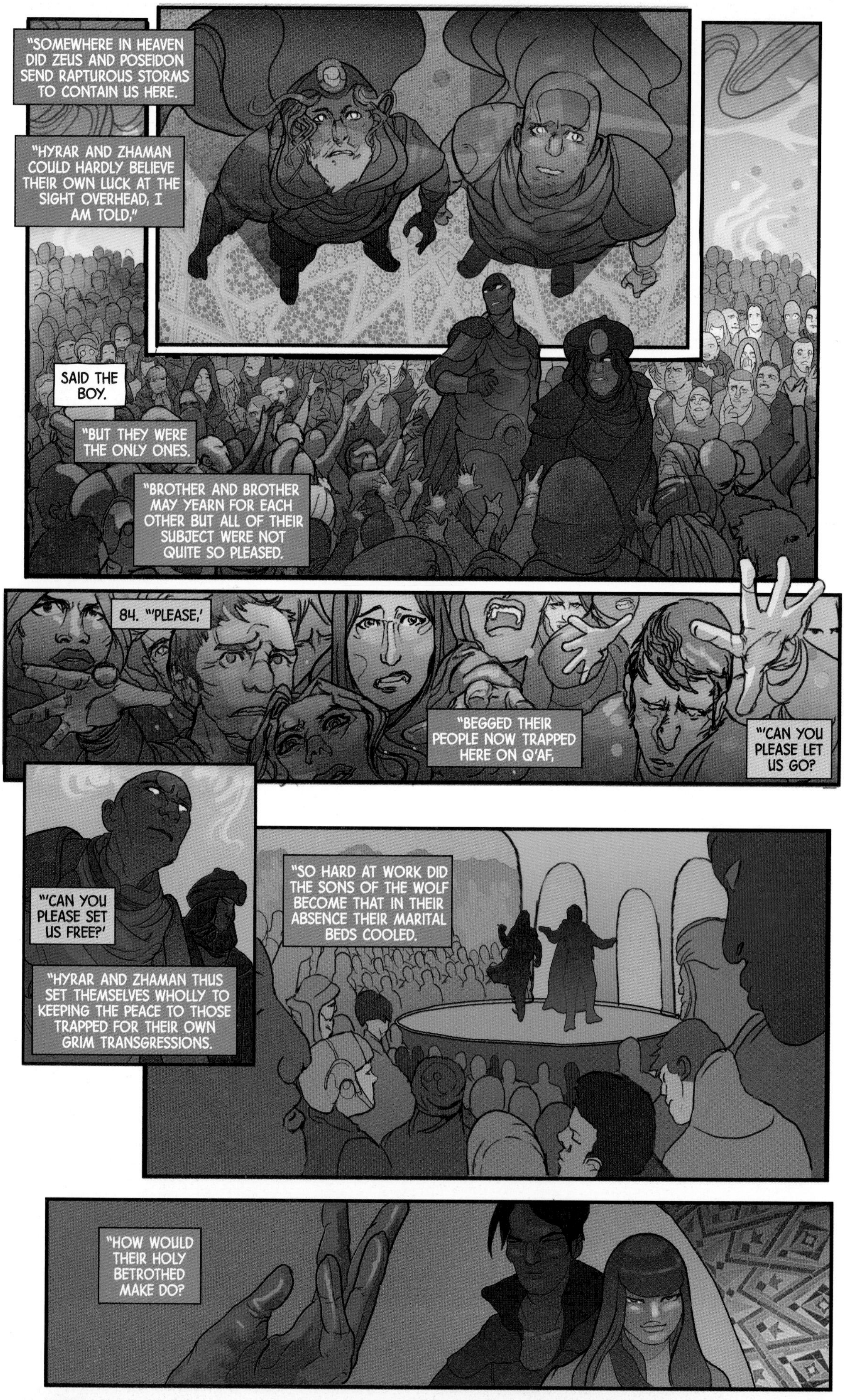
"SOMEWHERE IN HEAVEN DID ZEUS AND POSEIDON SEND RAPTUROUS STORMS TO CONTAIN US HERE.
"HYRAR AND ZHAMAN COULD HARDLY BELIEVE THEIR OWN LUCK AT THE SIGHT OVERHEAD, I AM TOLD,"
SAID THE BOY.
"BUT THEY WERE THE ONLY ONES.
"BROTHER AND BROTHER MAY YEARN FOR EACH OTHER BUT ALL OF THEIR SUBJECT WERE NOT QUITE SO PLEASED.
84. "'PLEASE,'
"BEGGED THEIR PEOPLE NOW TRAPPED HERE ON Q'AF,
"'CAN YOU PLEASE LET US GO?
"'CAN YOU PLEASE SET US FREE?'
"HYRAR AND ZHAMAN THUS SET THEMSELVES WHOLLY TO KEEPING THE PEACE TO THOSE TRAPPED FOR THEIR OWN GRIM TRANSGRESSIONS.
"SO HARD AT WORK DID THE SONS OF THE WOLF BECOME THAT IN THEIR ABSENCE THEIR MARITAL BEDS COOLED.
"HOW WOULD THEIR HOLY BETROTHED MAKE DO?

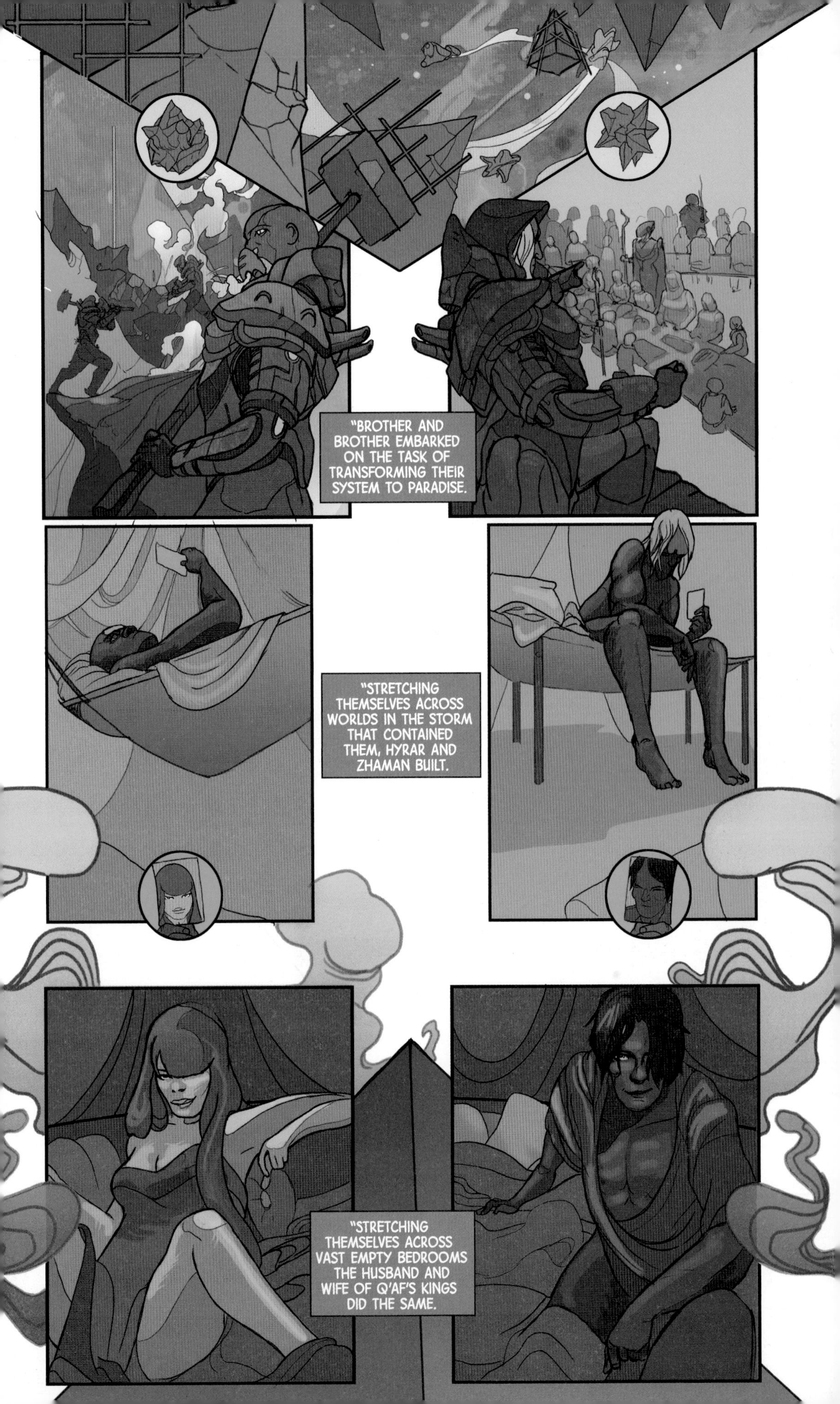
"BROTHER AND BROTHER EMBARKED ON THE TASK OF TRANSFORMING THEIR SYSTEM TO PARADISE.
"STRETCHING THEMSELVES ACROSS WORLDS IN THE STORM THAT CONTAINED THEM, HYRAR AND ZHAMAN BUILT.
"STRETCHING THEMSELVES ACROSS VAST EMPTY BEDROOMS THE HUSBAND AND WIFE OF Q'AF'S KINGS DID THE SAME.

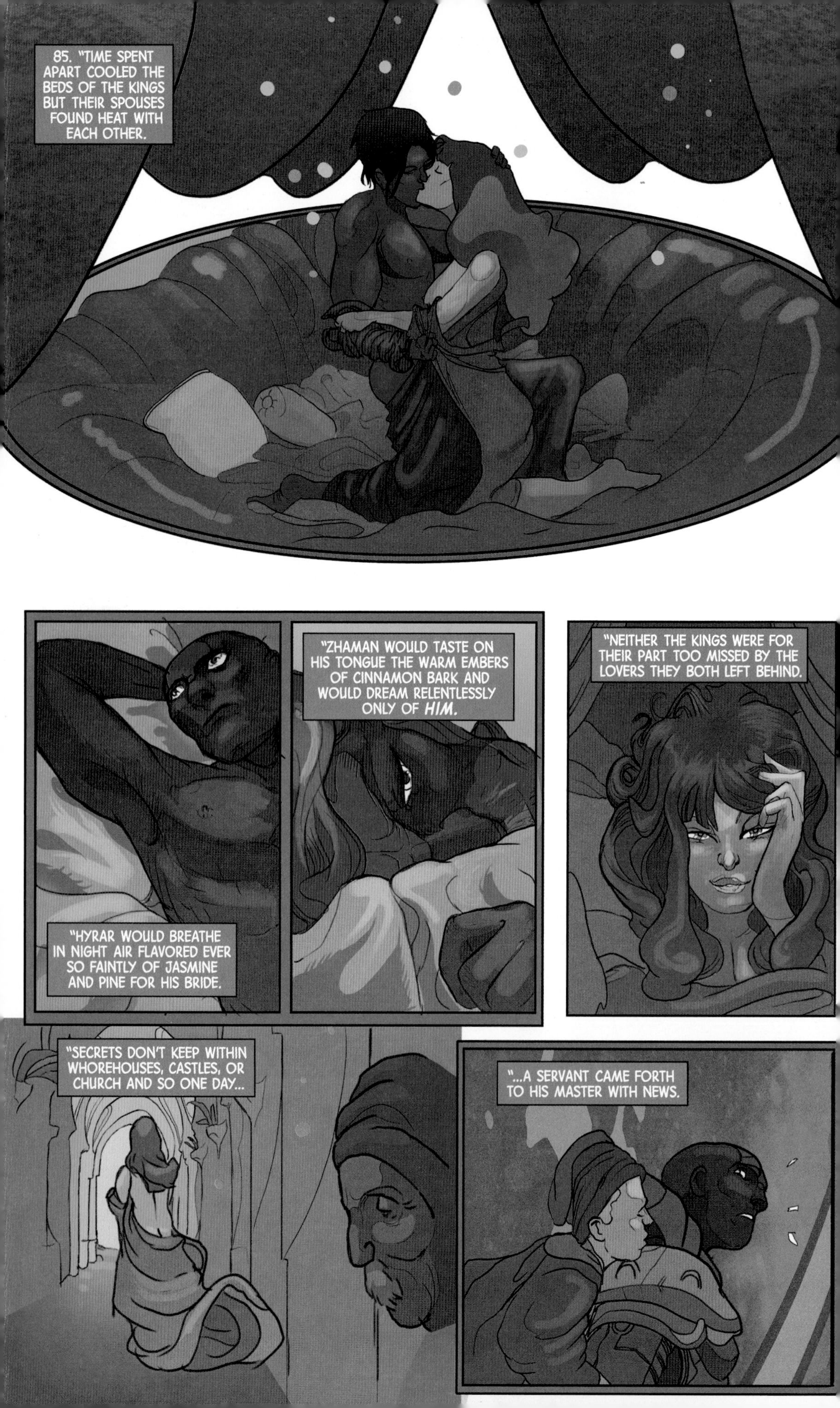
85. "TIME SPENT APART COOLED THE BEDS OF THE KINGS BUT THEIR SPOUSES FOUND HEAT WITH EACH OTHER.
"HYRAR WOULD BREATHE IN NIGHT AIR FLAVORED EVER SO FAINTLY OF JASMINE AND PINE FOR HIS BRIDE.
"ZHAMAN WOULD TASTE ON HIS TONGUE THE WARM EMBERS OF CINNAMON BARK AND WOULD DREAM RELENTLESSLY ONLY OF *HIM*.
"NEITHER THE KINGS WERE FOR THEIR PART TOO MISSED BY THE LOVERS THEY BOTH LEFT BEHIND.
"SECRETS DON'T KEEP WITHIN WHOREHOUSES, CASTLES, OR CHURCH AND SO ONE DAY...
"...A SERVANT CAME FORTH TO HIS MASTER WITH NEWS.

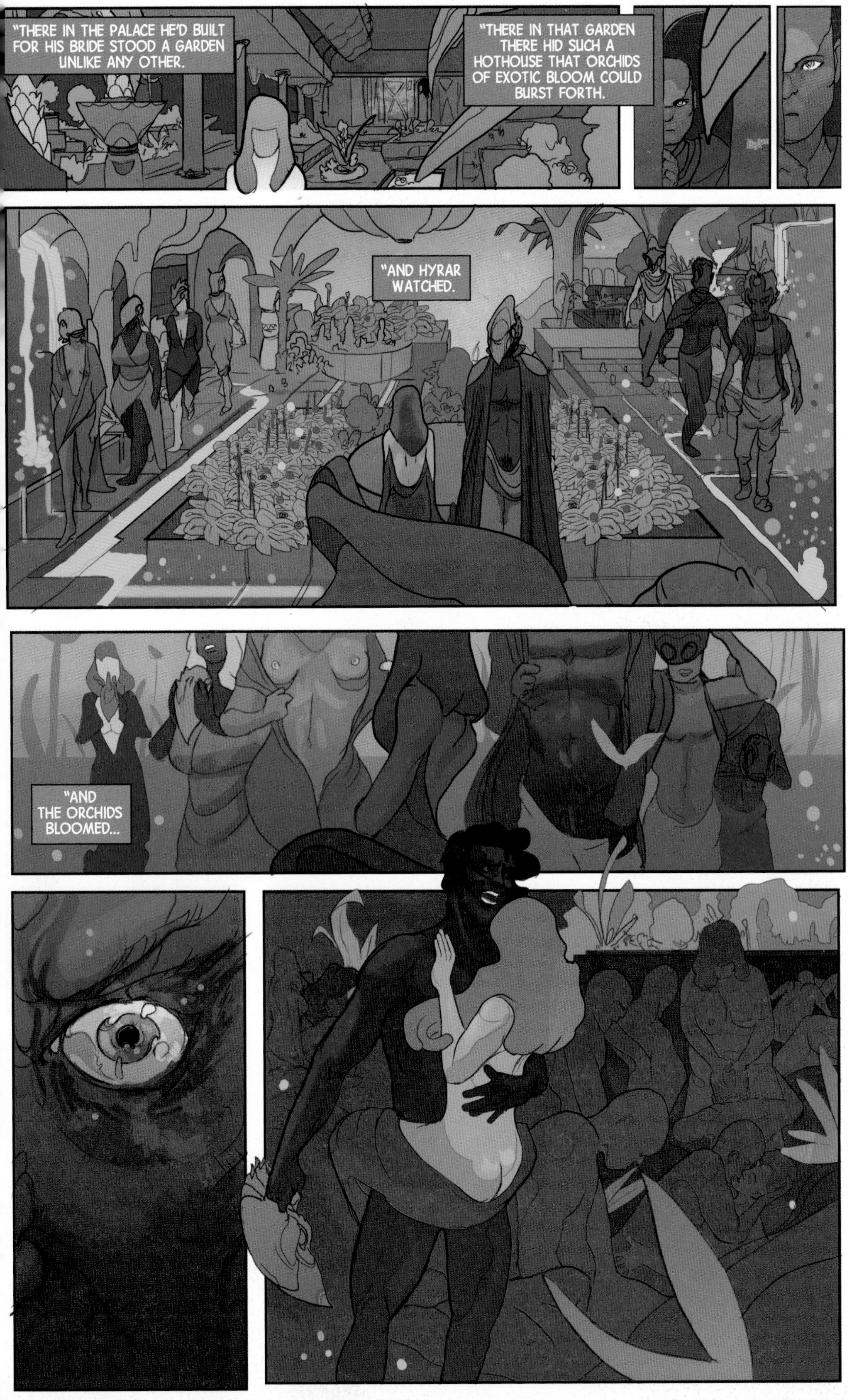
"THERE IN THE PALACE HE'D BUILT FOR HIS BRIDE STOOD A GARDEN UNLIKE ANY OTHER.
"THERE IN THAT GARDEN THERE HID SUCH A HOTHOUSE THAT ORCHIDS OF EXOTIC BLOOM COULD BURST FORTH.
"AND HYRAR WATCHED.
"AND THE ORCHIDS BLOOMED...

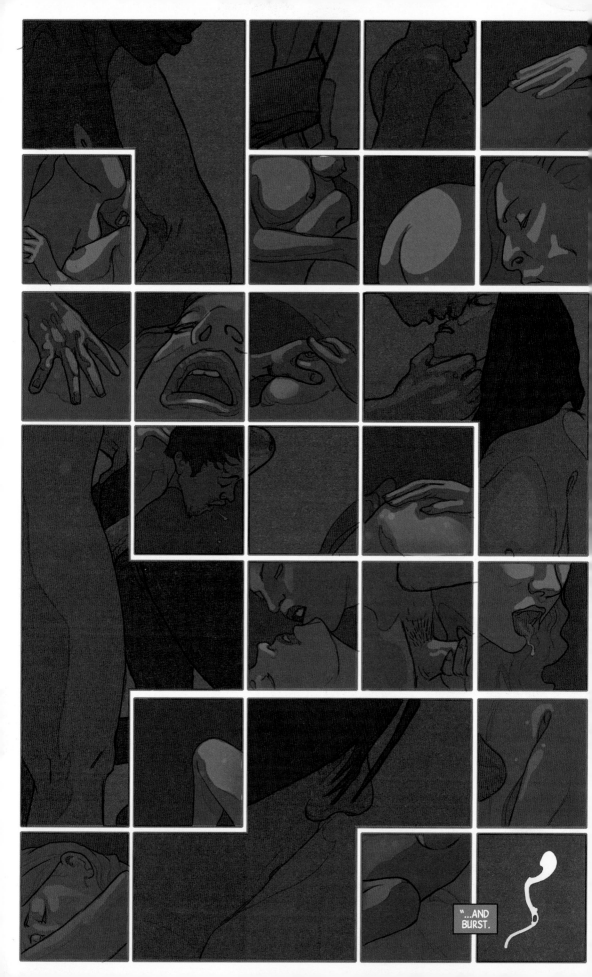

"...AND BURST.

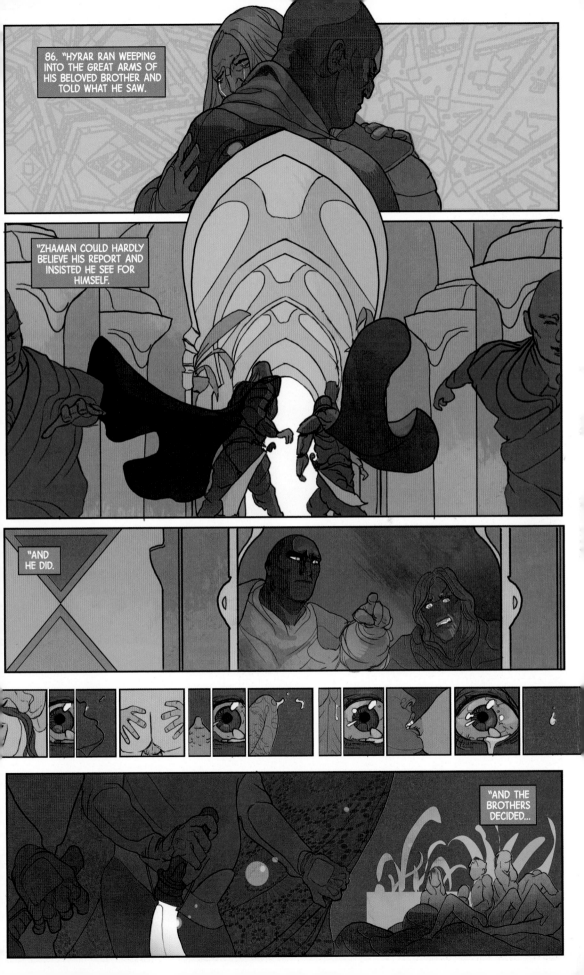

86. "HYRAR RAN WEEPING INTO THE GREAT ARMS OF HIS BELOVED BROTHER AND TOLD WHAT HE SAW.

"ZHAMAN COULD HARDLY BELIEVE HIS REPORT AND INSISTED HE SEE FOR HIMSELF.

"AND HE DID.

"AND THE BROTHERS DECIDED...

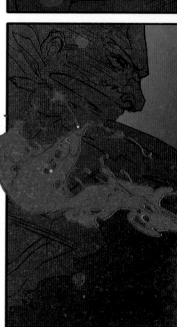
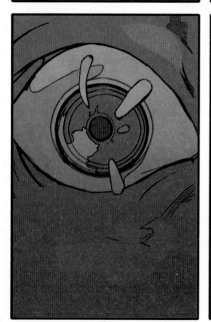
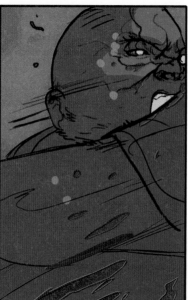
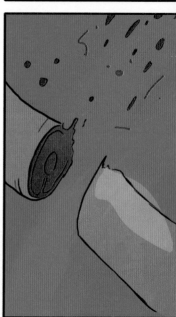

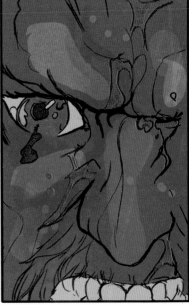

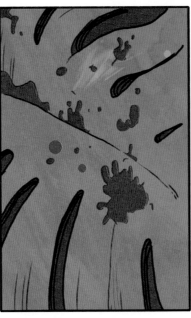

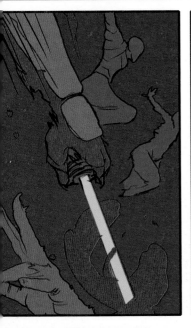
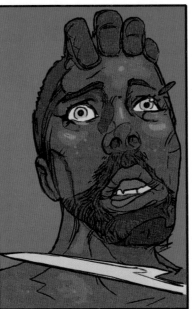
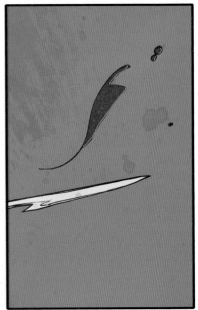

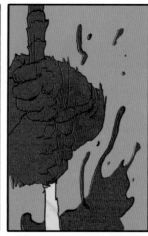
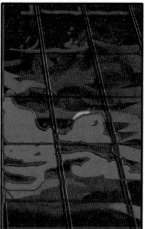
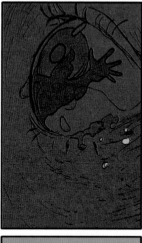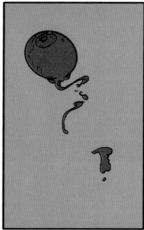
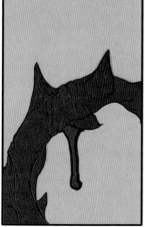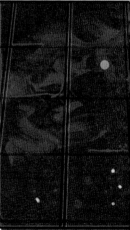

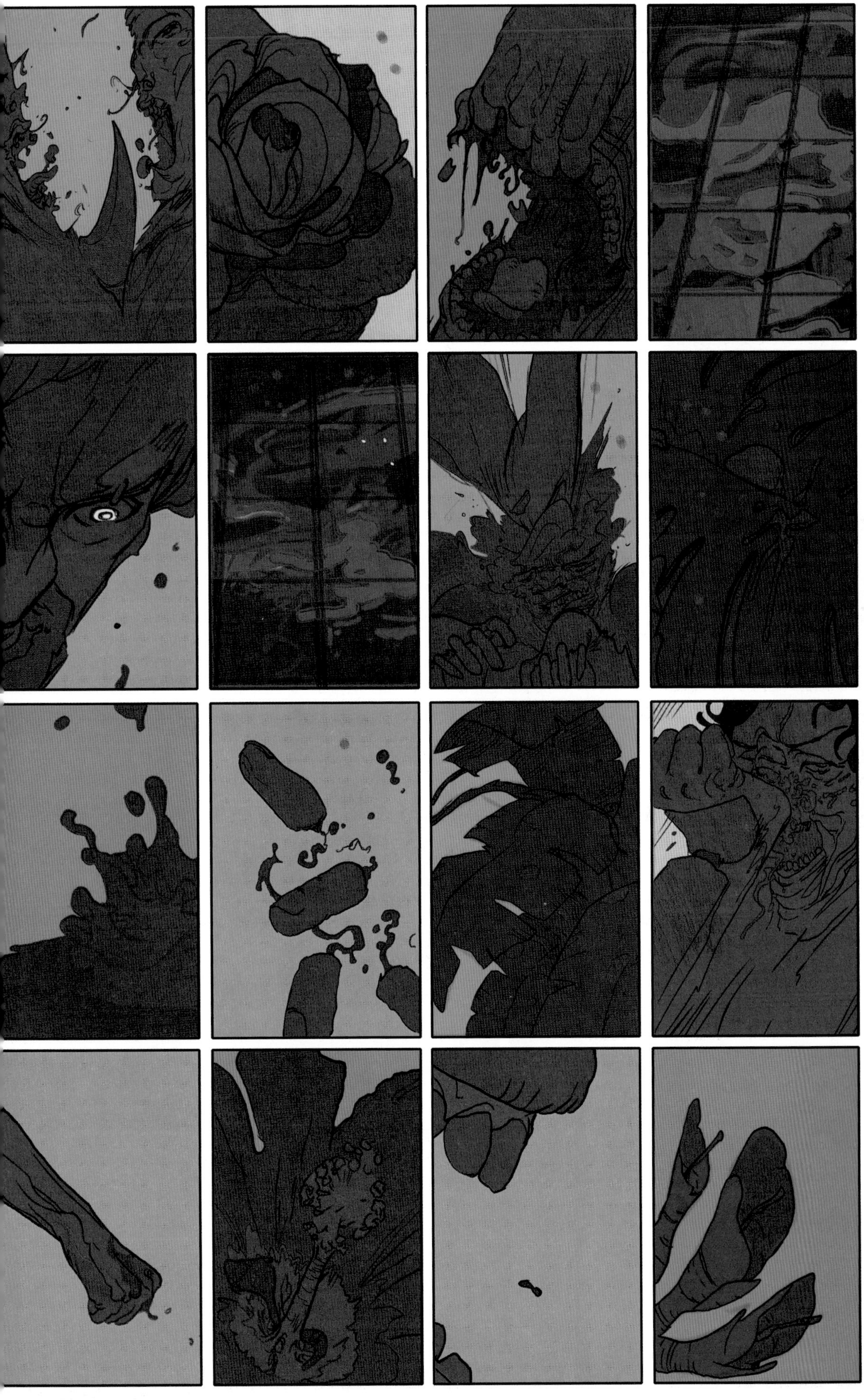

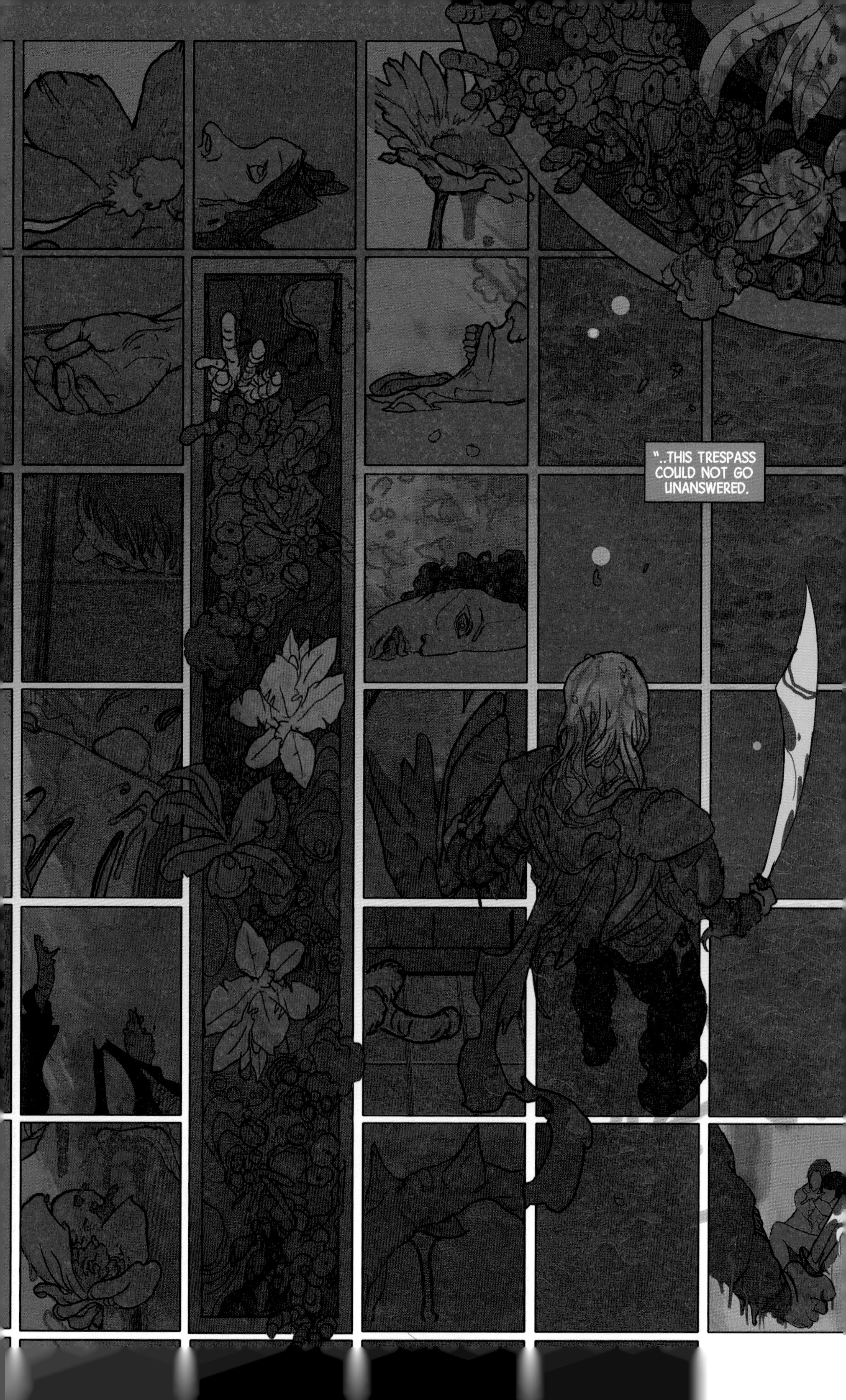
"..THIS TRESPASS COULD NOT GO UNANSWERED.

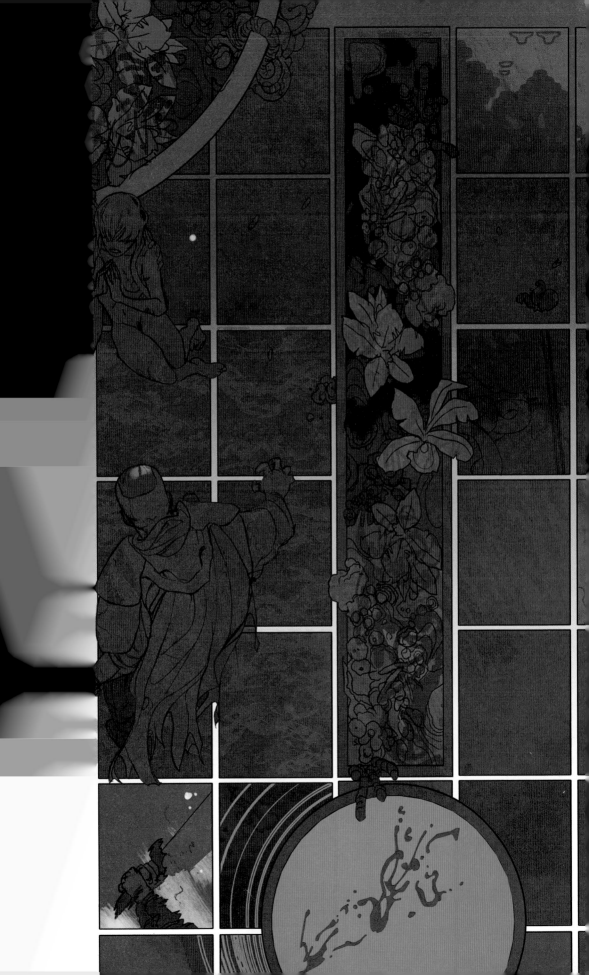

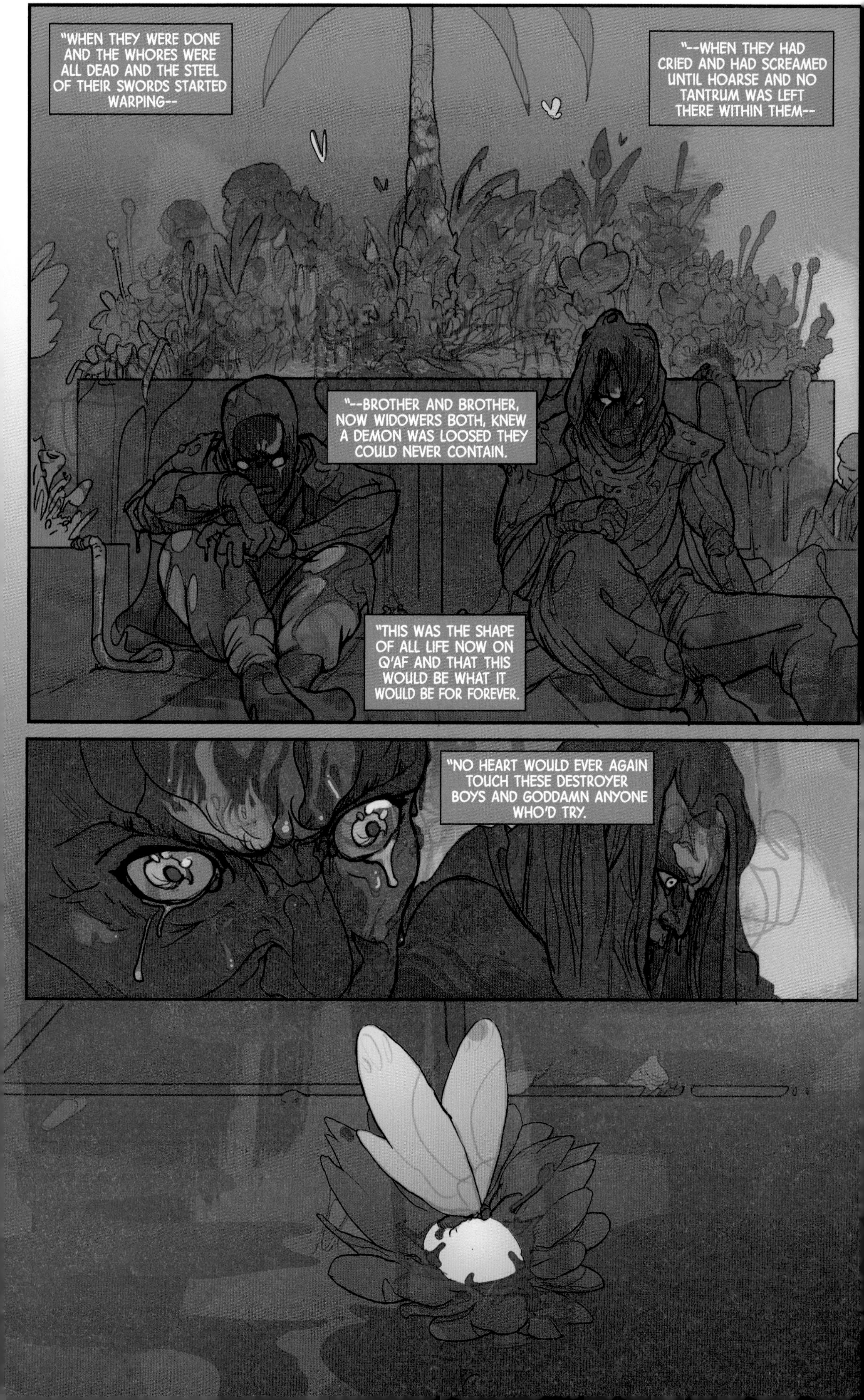
"WHEN THEY WERE DONE AND THE WHORES WERE ALL DEAD AND THE STEEL OF THEIR SWORDS STARTED WARPING--
"--WHEN THEY HAD CRIED AND HAD SCREAMED UNTIL HOARSE AND NO TANTRUM WAS LEFT THERE WITHIN THEM--
"--BROTHER AND BROTHER, NOW WIDOWERS BOTH, KNEW A DEMON WAS LOOSED THEY COULD NEVER CONTAIN.
"THIS WAS THE SHAPE OF ALL LIFE NOW ON Q'AF AND THAT THIS WOULD BE WHAT IT WOULD BE FOR FOREVER.
"NO HEART WOULD EVER AGAIN TOUCH THESE DESTROYER BOYS AND GODDAMN ANYONE WHO'D TRY.

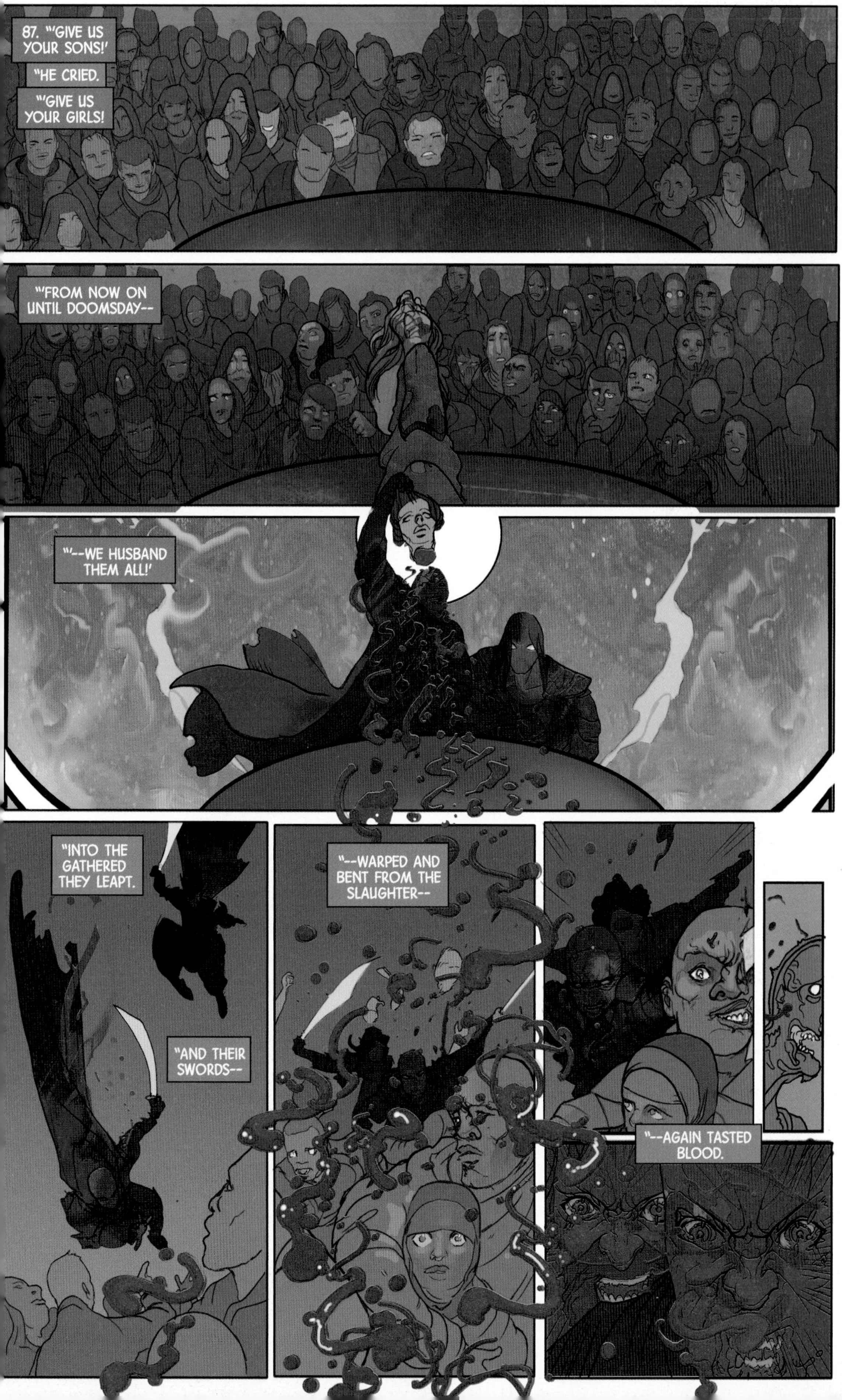
87. "'GIVE US YOUR SONS!'
"HE CRIED.
"'GIVE US YOUR GIRLS!
"FROM NOW ON UNTIL DOOMSDAY--
"'--WE HUSBAND THEM ALL!'
"INTO THE GATHERED THEY LEAPT.
"AND THEIR SWORDS--
"--WARPED AND BENT FROM THE SLAUGHTER--
"--AGAIN TASTED BLOOD.

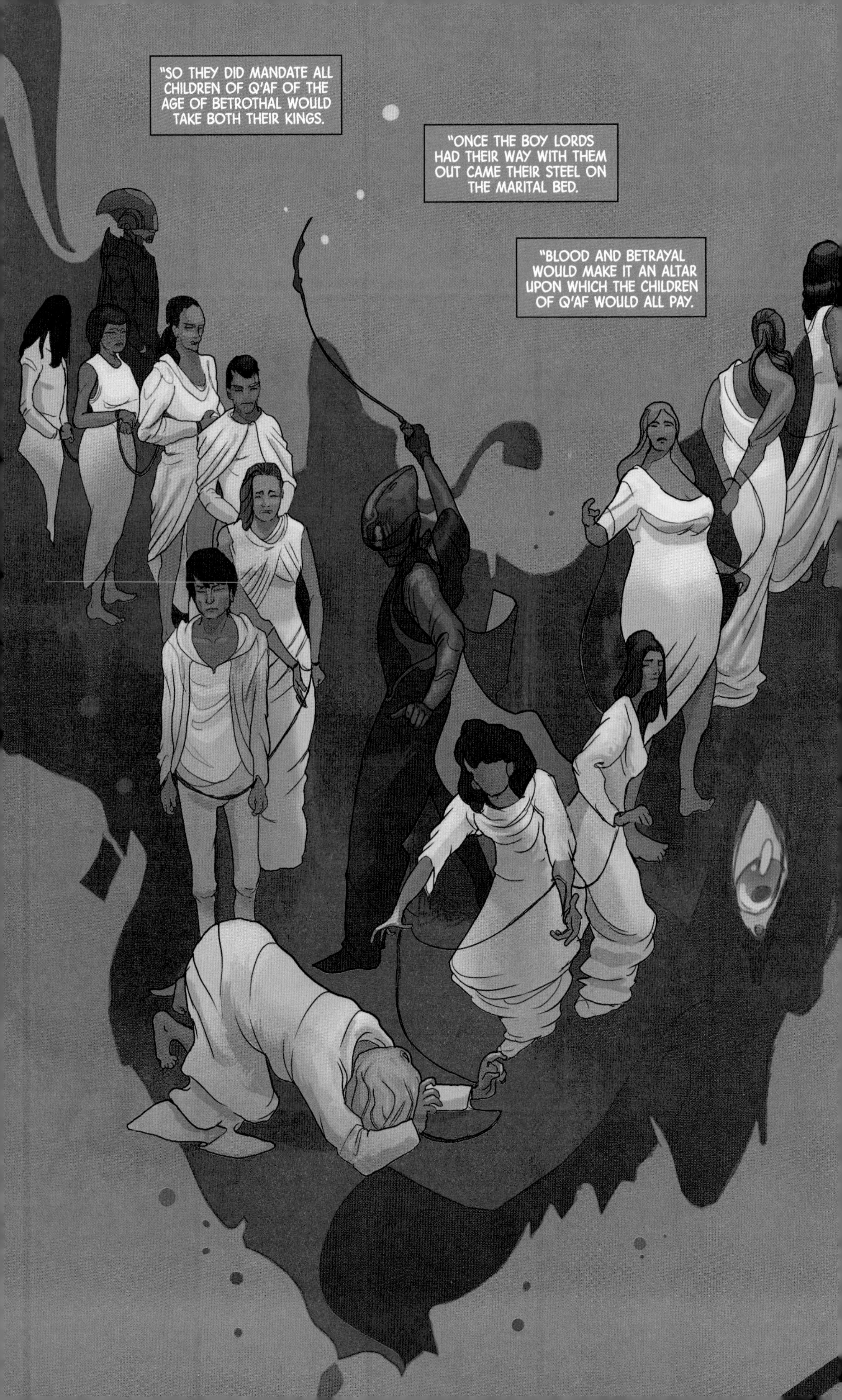
"SO THEY DID MANDATE ALL CHILDREN OF Q'AF OF THE AGE OF BETROTHAL WOULD TAKE BOTH THEIR KINGS.
"ONCE THE BOY LORDS HAD THEIR WAY WITH THEM OUT CAME THEIR STEEL ON THE MARITAL BED.
"BLOOD AND BETRAYAL WOULD MAKE IT AN ALTAR UPON WHICH THE CHILDREN OF Q'AF WOULD ALL PAY.

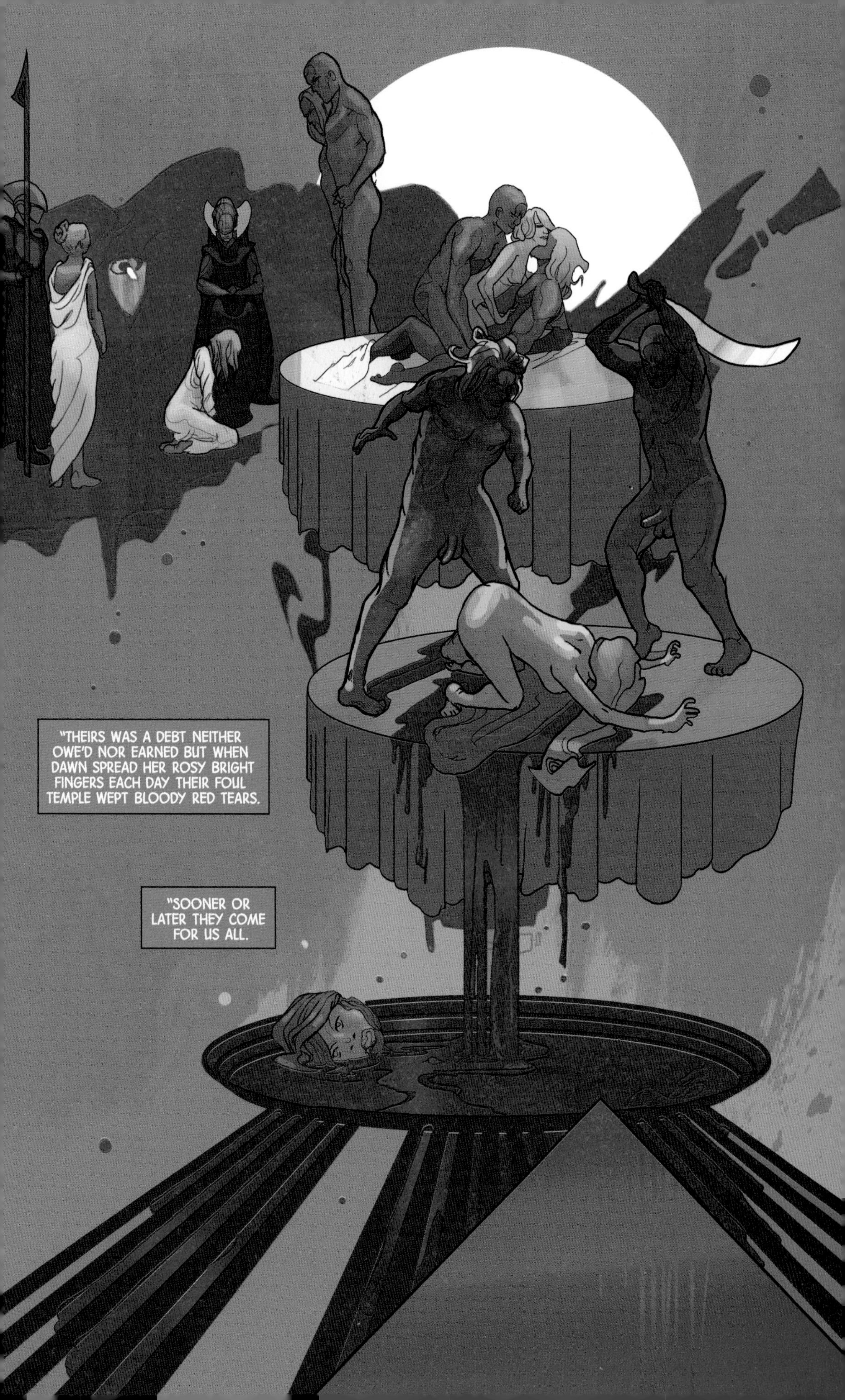
"THEIRS WAS A DEBT NEITHER OWE'D NOR EARNED BUT WHEN DAWN SPREAD HER ROSY BRIGHT FINGERS EACH DAY THEIR FOUL TEMPLE WEPT BLOODY RED TEARS.
"SOONER OR LATER THEY COME FOR US ALL.

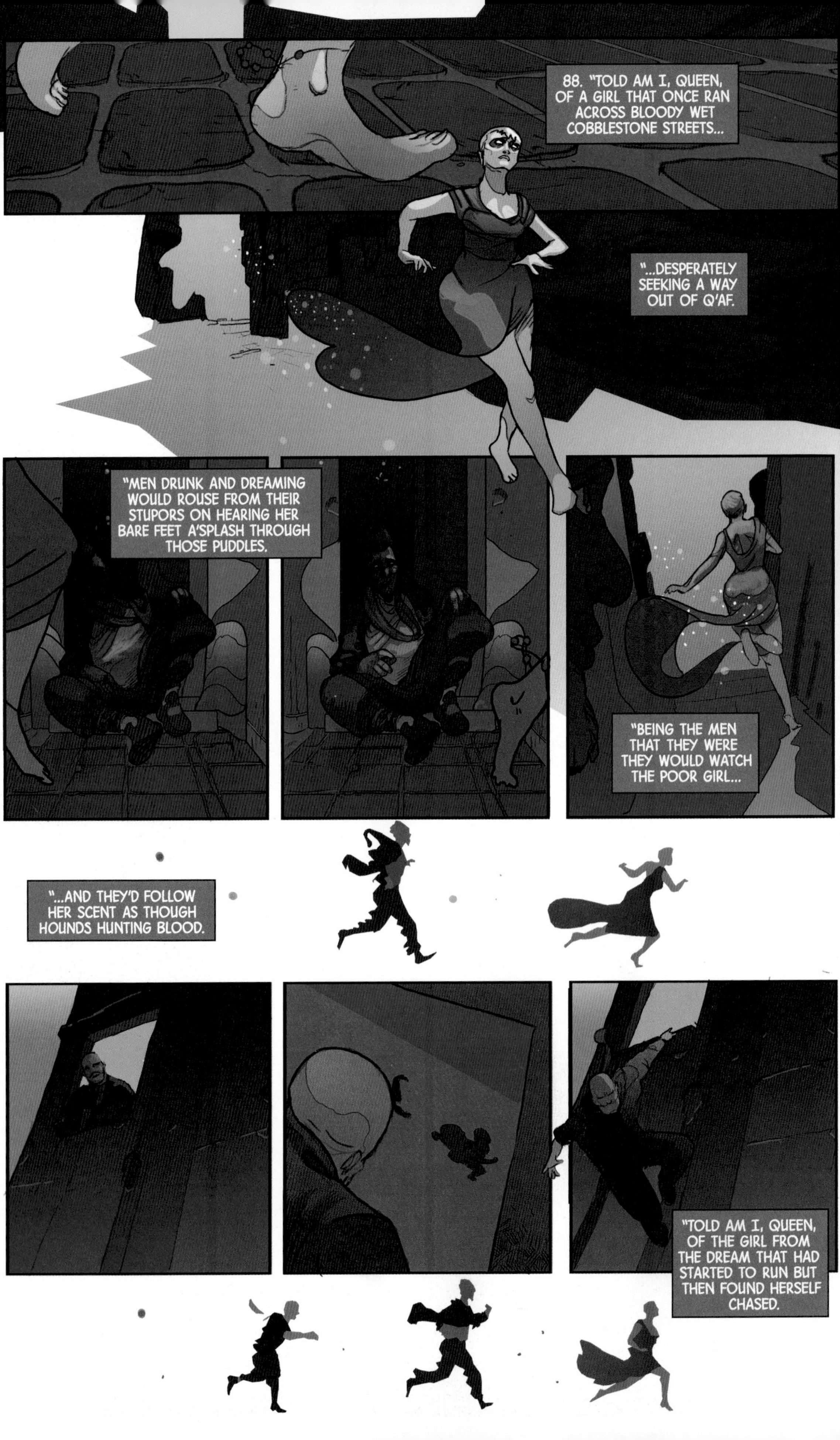
88. "TOLD AM I, QUEEN, OF A GIRL THAT ONCE RAN ACROSS BLOODY WET COBBLESTONE STREETS...
"...DESPERATELY SEEKING A WAY OUT OF Q'AF.
"MEN DRUNK AND DREAMING WOULD ROUSE FROM THEIR STUPORS ON HEARING HER BARE FEET A'SPLASH THROUGH THOSE PUDDLES.
"BEING THE MEN THAT THEY WERE THEY WOULD WATCH THE POOR GIRL...
"...AND THEY'D FOLLOW HER SCENT AS THOUGH HOUNDS HUNTING BLOOD.
"TOLD AM I, QUEEN, OF THE GIRL FROM THE DREAM THAT HAD STARTED TO RUN BUT THEN FOUND HERSELF CHASED.

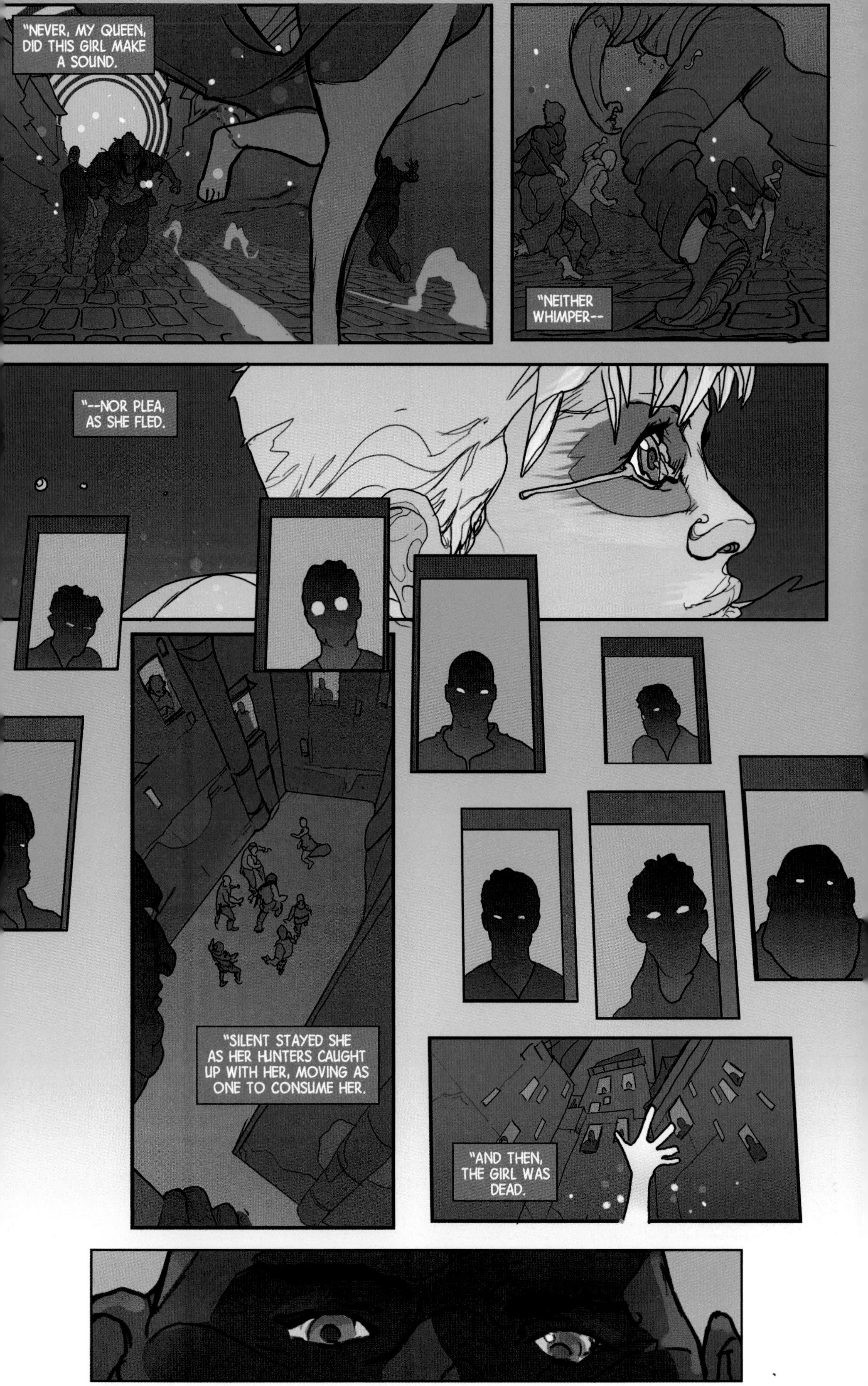
"NEVER, MY QUEEN, DID THIS GIRL MAKE A SOUND.
"NEITHER WHIMPER--
"--NOR PLEA, AS SHE FLED.
"SILENT STAYED SHE AS HER HUNTERS CAUGHT UP WITH HER, MOVING AS ONE TO CONSUME HER.
"AND THEN, THE GIRL WAS DEAD.

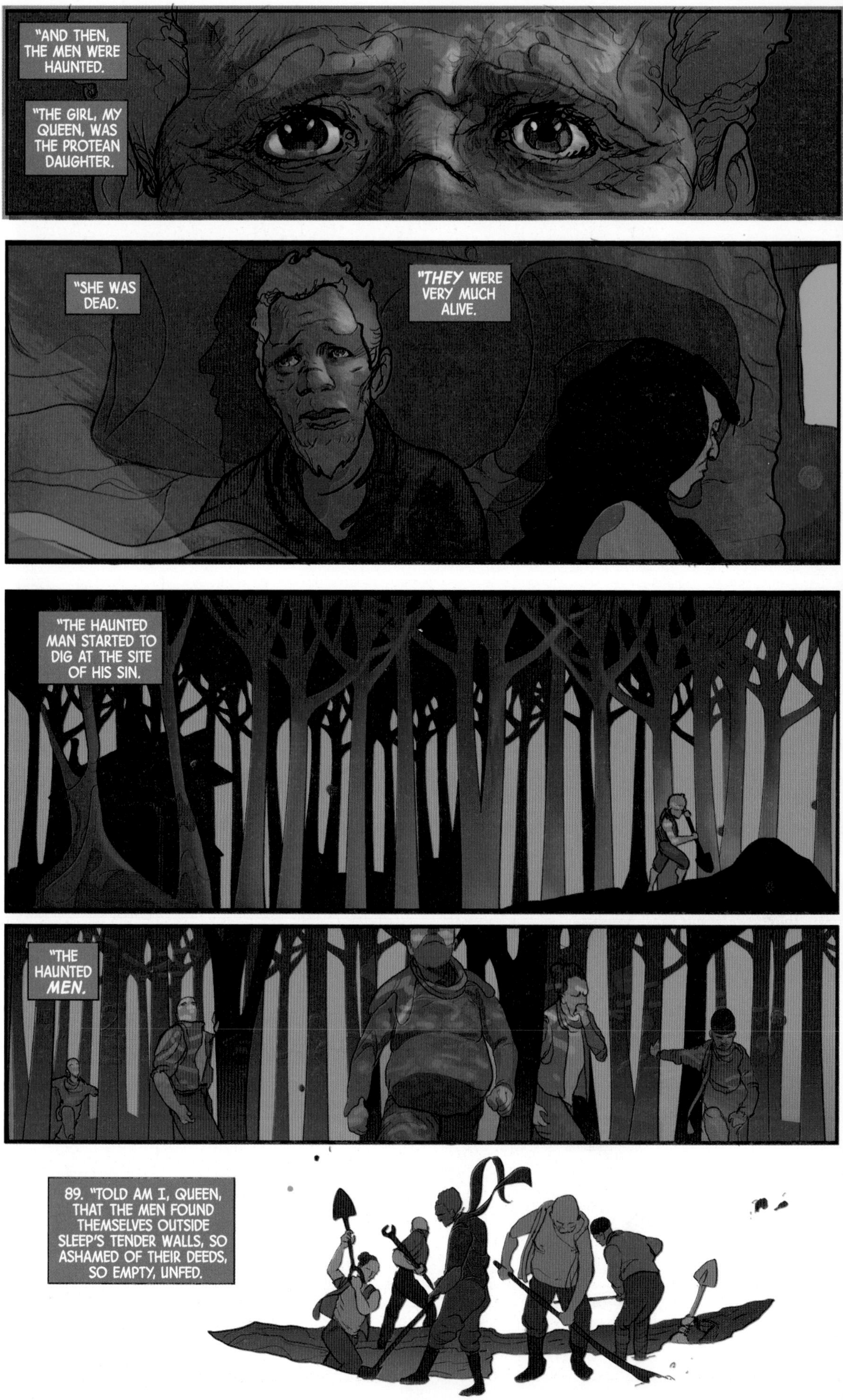
"AND THEN, THE MEN WERE HAUNTED.
"THE GIRL, MY QUEEN, WAS THE PROTEAN DAUGHTER.
"SHE WAS DEAD.
"*THEY* WERE VERY MUCH ALIVE.
"THE HAUNTED MAN STARTED TO DIG AT THE SITE OF HIS SIN.
"THE HAUNTED *MEN.*
89. "TOLD AM I, QUEEN, THAT THE MEN FOUND THEMSELVES OUTSIDE SLEEP'S TENDER WALLS, SO ASHAMED OF THEIR DEEDS, SO EMPTY, UNFED.

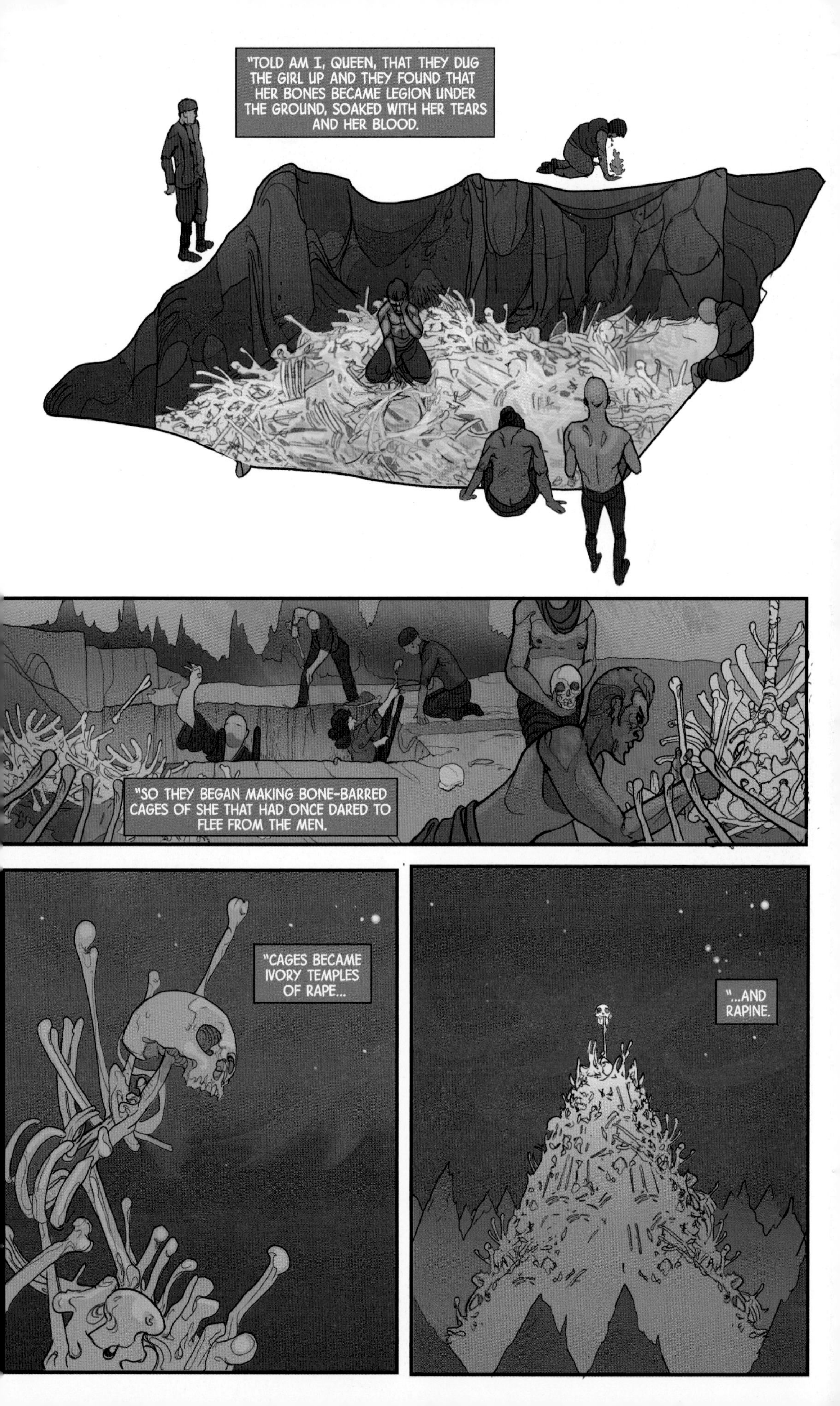
"TOLD AM I, QUEEN, THAT THEY DUG THE GIRL UP AND THEY FOUND THAT HER BONES BECAME LEGION UNDER THE GROUND, SOAKED WITH HER TEARS AND HER BLOOD.
"SO THEY BEGAN MAKING BONE-BARRED CAGES OF SHE THAT HAD ONCE DARED TO FLEE FROM THE MEN.
"CAGES BECAME IVORY TEMPLES OF RAPE...
"...AND RAPINE.

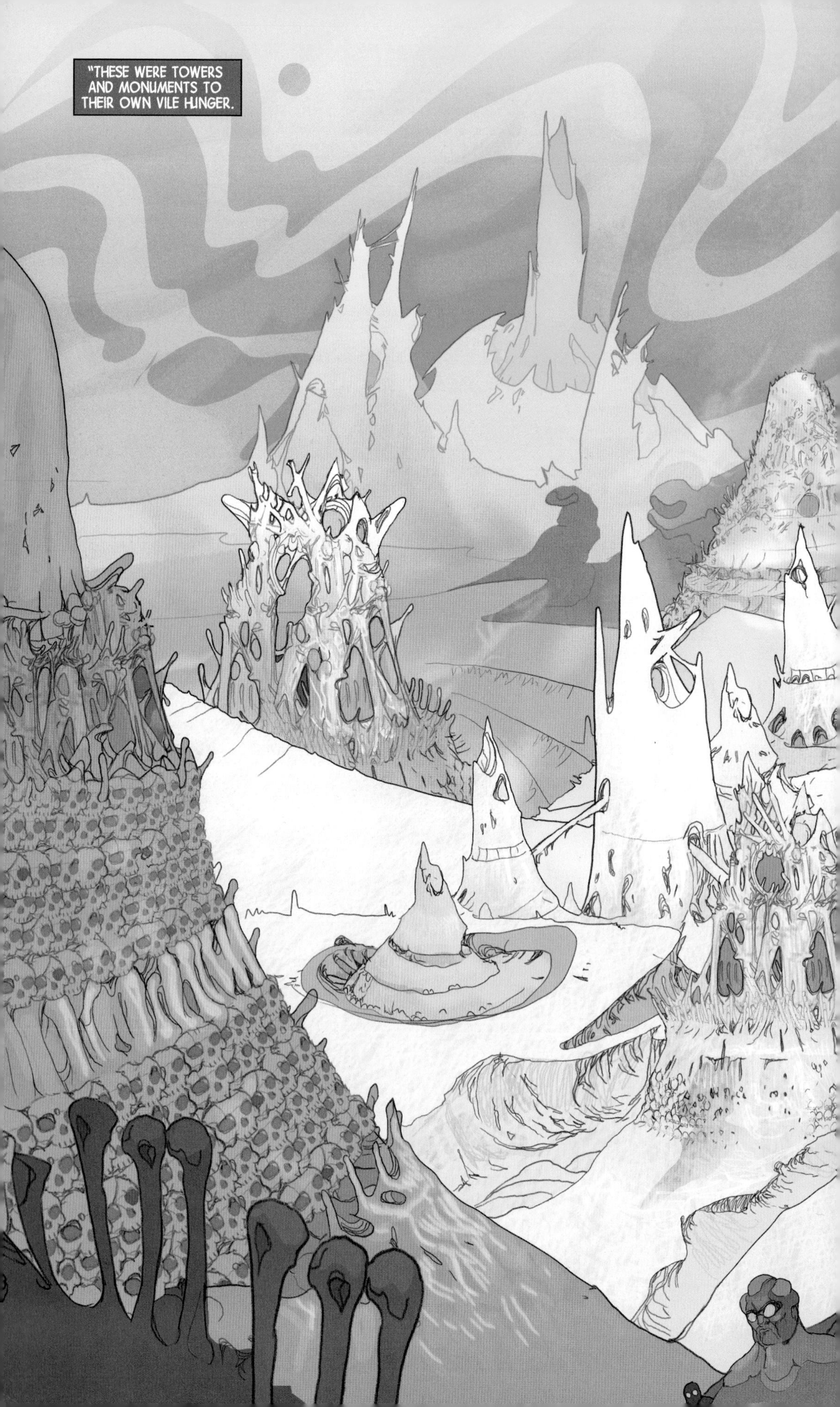
"THESE WERE TOWERS AND MONUMENTS TO THEIR OWN VILE HUNGER.

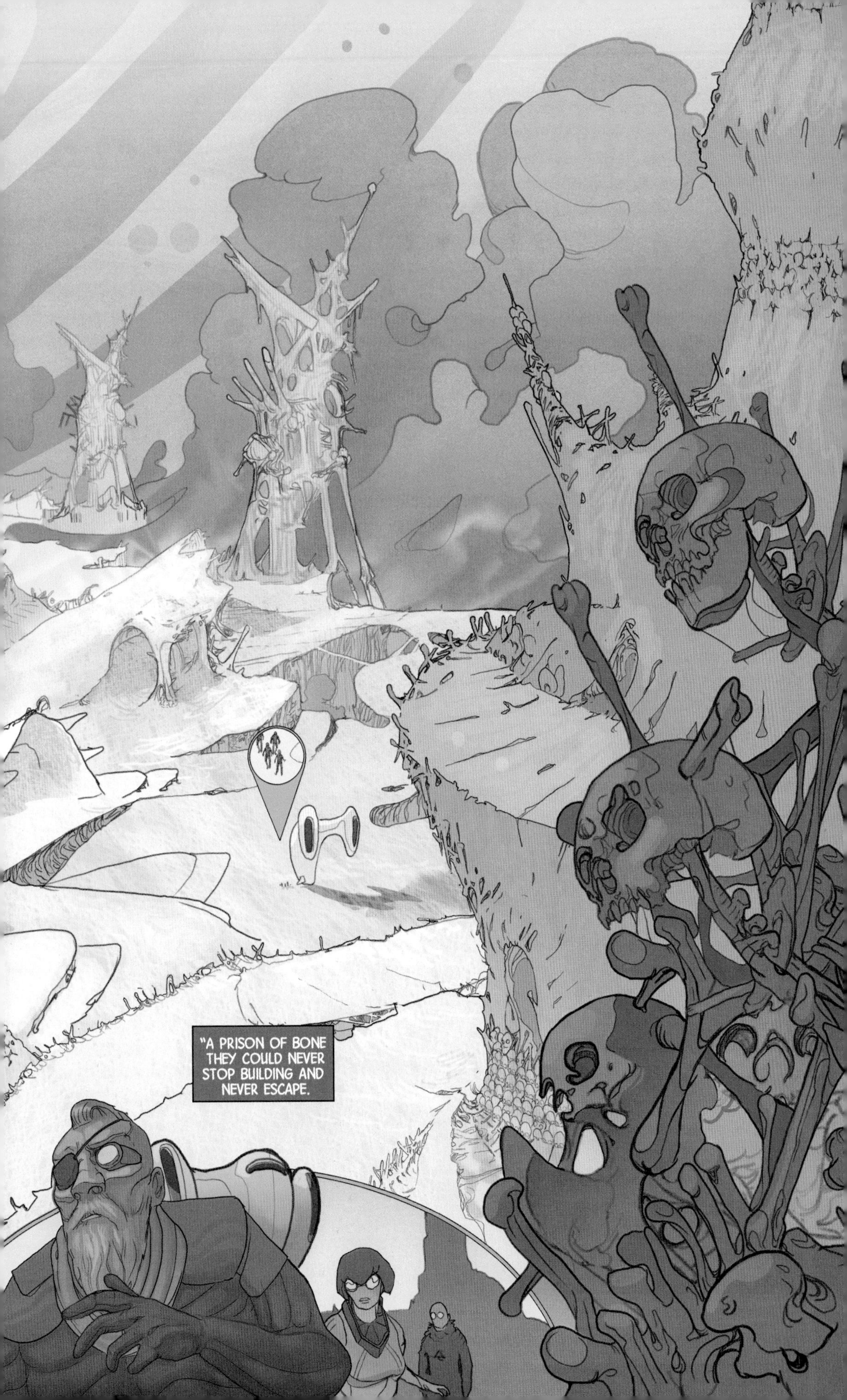
"A PRISON OF BONE THEY COULD NEVER STOP BUILDING AND NEVER ESCAPE.

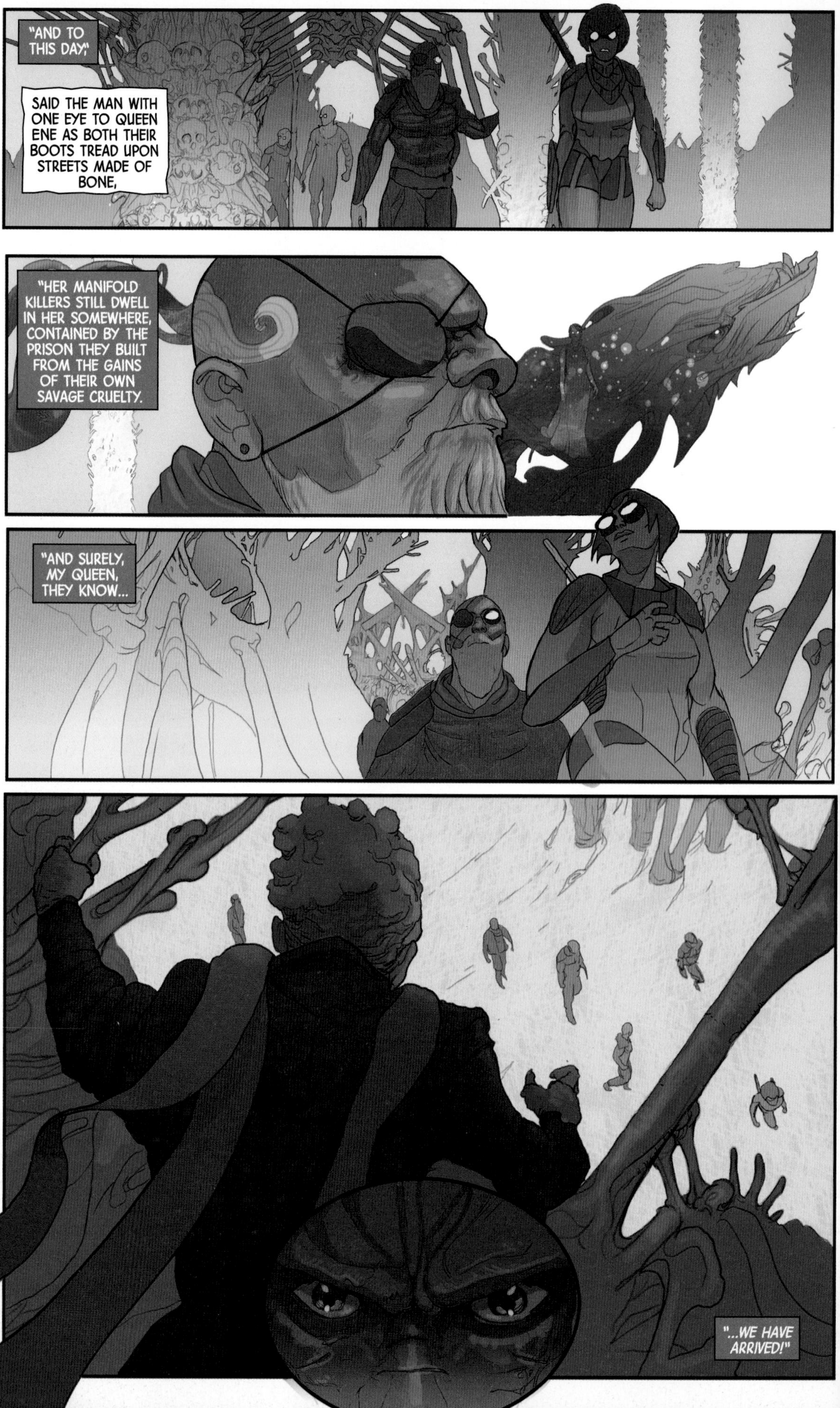
"AND TO THIS DAY,"
SAID THE MAN WITH ONE EYE TO QUEEN ENE AS BOTH THEIR BOOTS TREAD UPON STREETS MADE OF BONE,
"HER MANIFOLD KILLERS STILL DWELL IN HER SOMEWHERE, CONTAINED BY THE PRISON THEY BUILT FROM THE GAINS OF THEIR OWN SAVAGE CRUELTY.
"AND SURELY, MY QUEEN, THEY KNOW...
"...WE HAVE ARRIVED!"

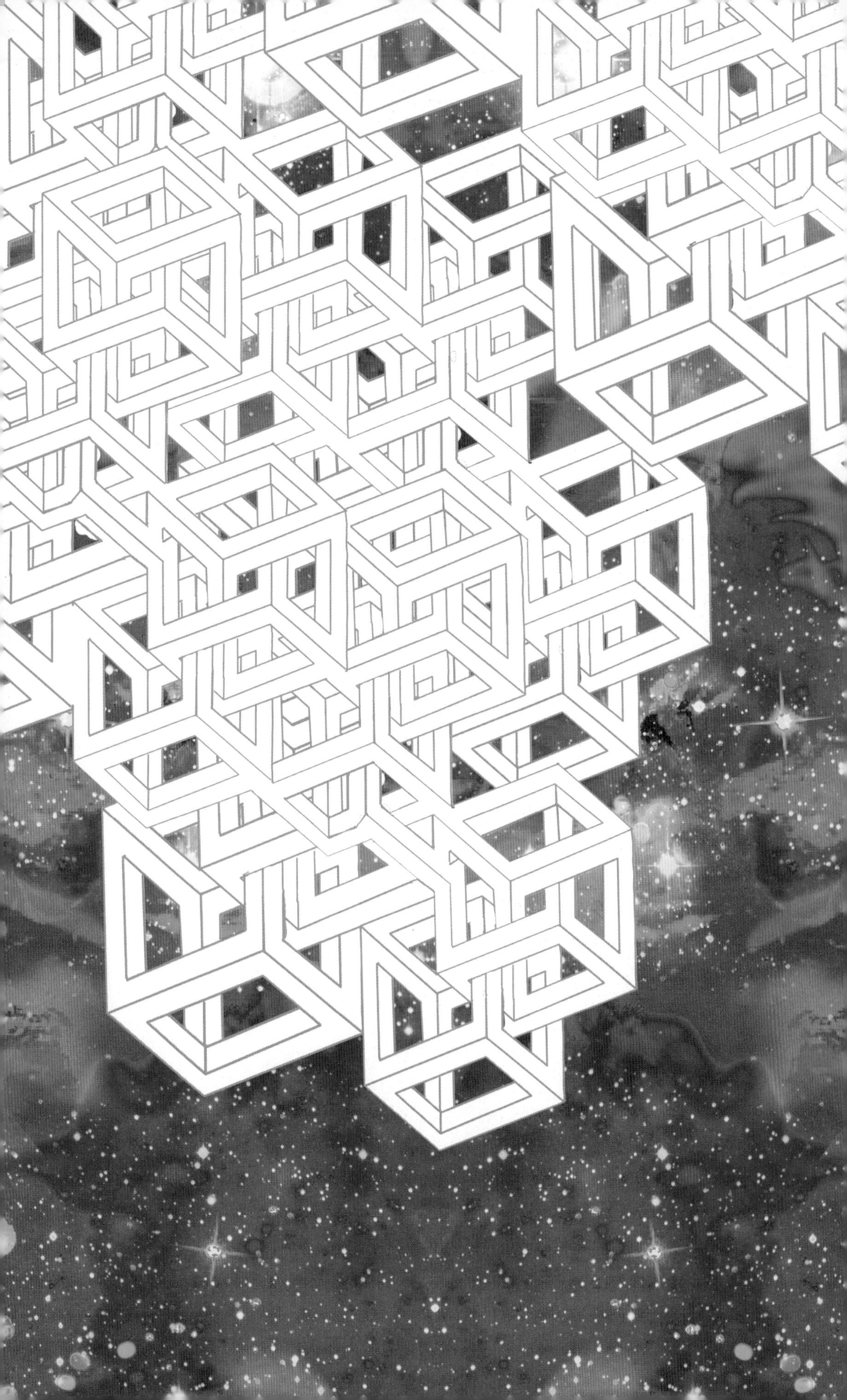

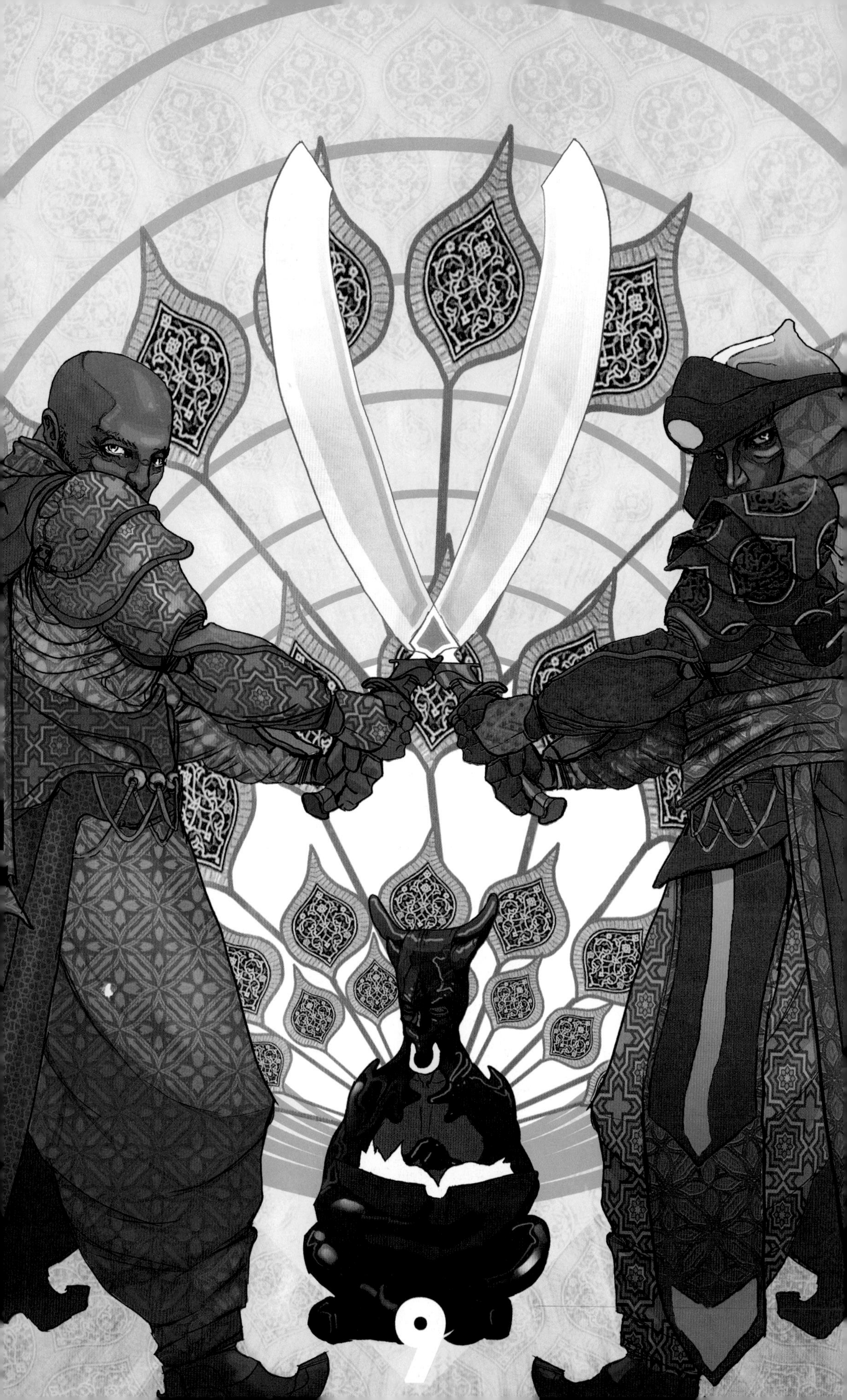

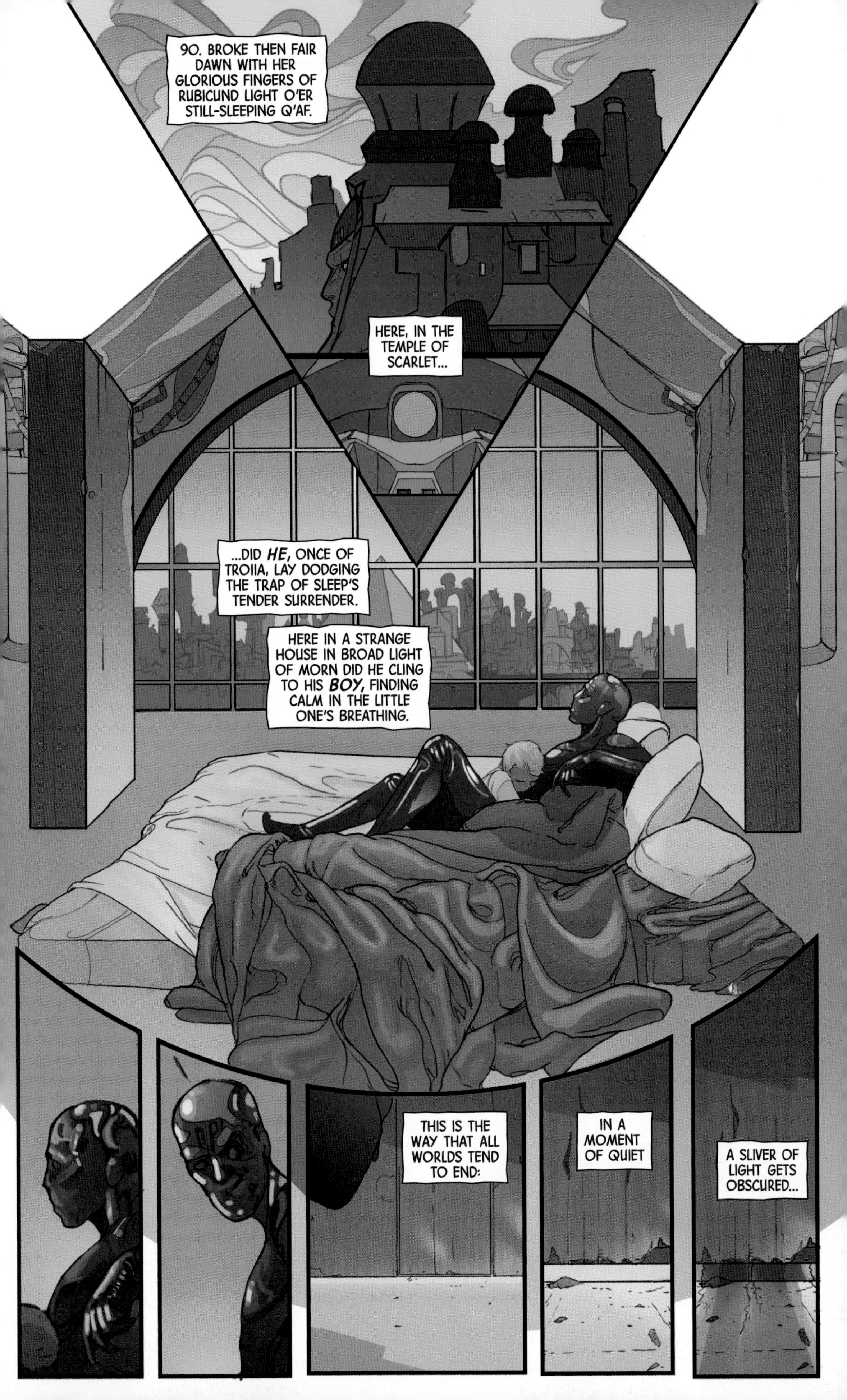
90. BROKE THEN FAIR DAWN WITH HER GLORIOUS FINGERS OF RUBICUND LIGHT O'ER STILL-SLEEPING Q'AF.
HERE, IN THE TEMPLE OF SCARLET...
...DID HE, ONCE OF TROIIA, LAY DODGING THE TRAP OF SLEEP'S TENDER SURRENDER.
HERE IN A STRANGE HOUSE IN BROAD LIGHT OF MORN DID HE CLING TO HIS BOY, FINDING CALM IN THE LITTLE ONE'S BREATHING.
THIS IS THE WAY THAT ALL WORLDS TEND TO END:
IN A MOMENT OF QUIET
A SLIVER OF LIGHT GETS OBSCURED...

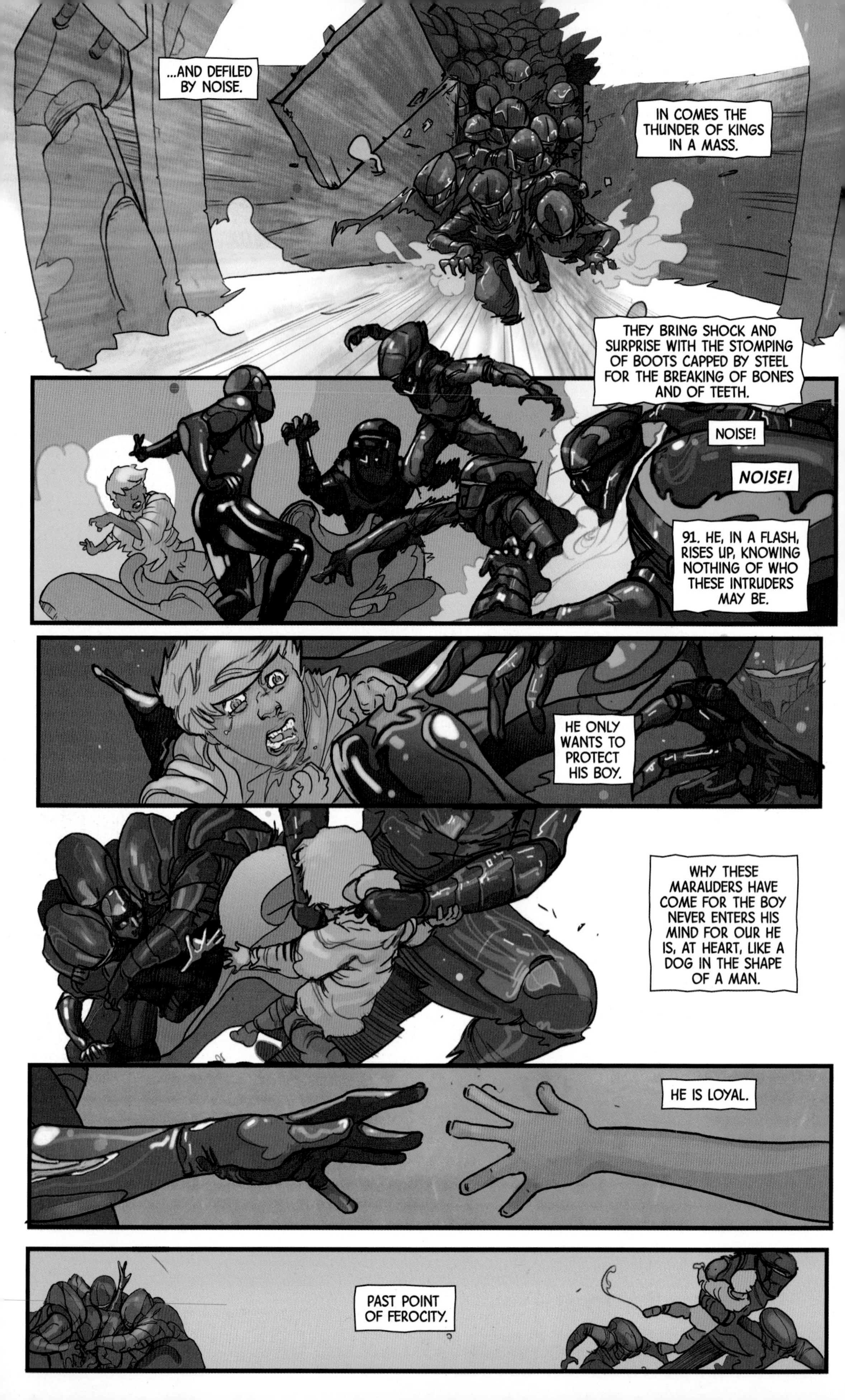
...AND DEFILED BY NOISE.
IN COMES THE THUNDER OF KINGS IN A MASS.
THEY BRING SHOCK AND SURPRISE WITH THE STOMPING OF BOOTS CAPPED BY STEEL FOR THE BREAKING OF BONES AND OF TEETH.
NOISE!
NOISE!
91. HE, IN A FLASH, RISES UP, KNOWING NOTHING OF WHO THESE INTRUDERS MAY BE.
HE ONLY WANTS TO PROTECT HIS BOY.
WHY THESE MARAUDERS HAVE COME FOR THE BOY NEVER ENTERS HIS MIND FOR OUR HE IS, AT HEART, LIKE A DOG IN THE SHAPE OF A MAN.
HE IS LOYAL.
PAST POINT OF FEROCITY.

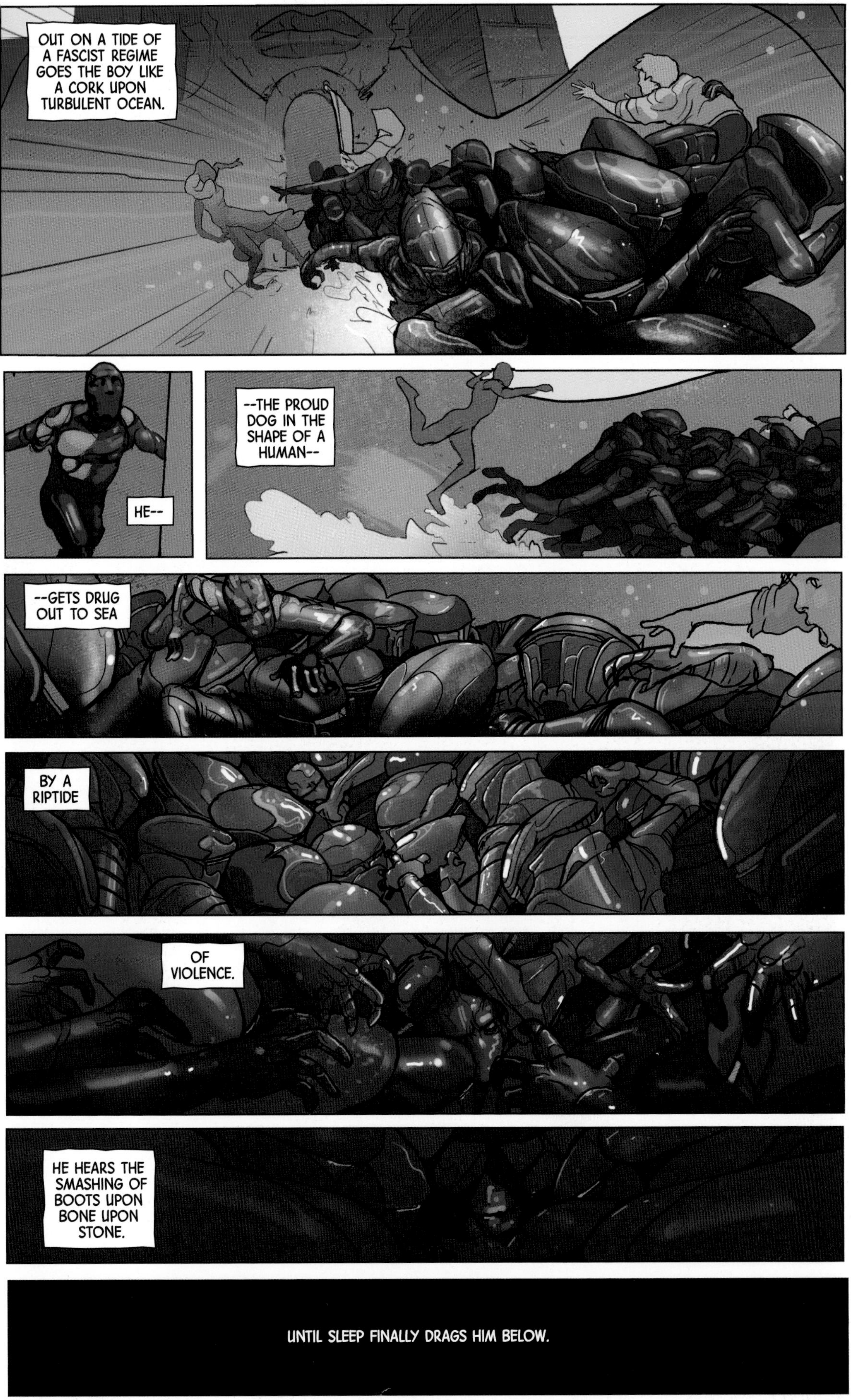
OUT ON A TIDE OF A FASCIST REGIME GOES THE BOY LIKE A CORK UPON TURBULENT OCEAN.
HE--
--THE PROUD DOG IN THE SHAPE OF A HUMAN--
--GETS DRUG OUT TO SEA
BY A RIPTIDE
OF VIOLENCE.
HE HEARS THE SMASHING OF BOOTS UPON BONE UPON STONE.
UNTIL SLEEP FINALLY DRAGS HIM BELOW.

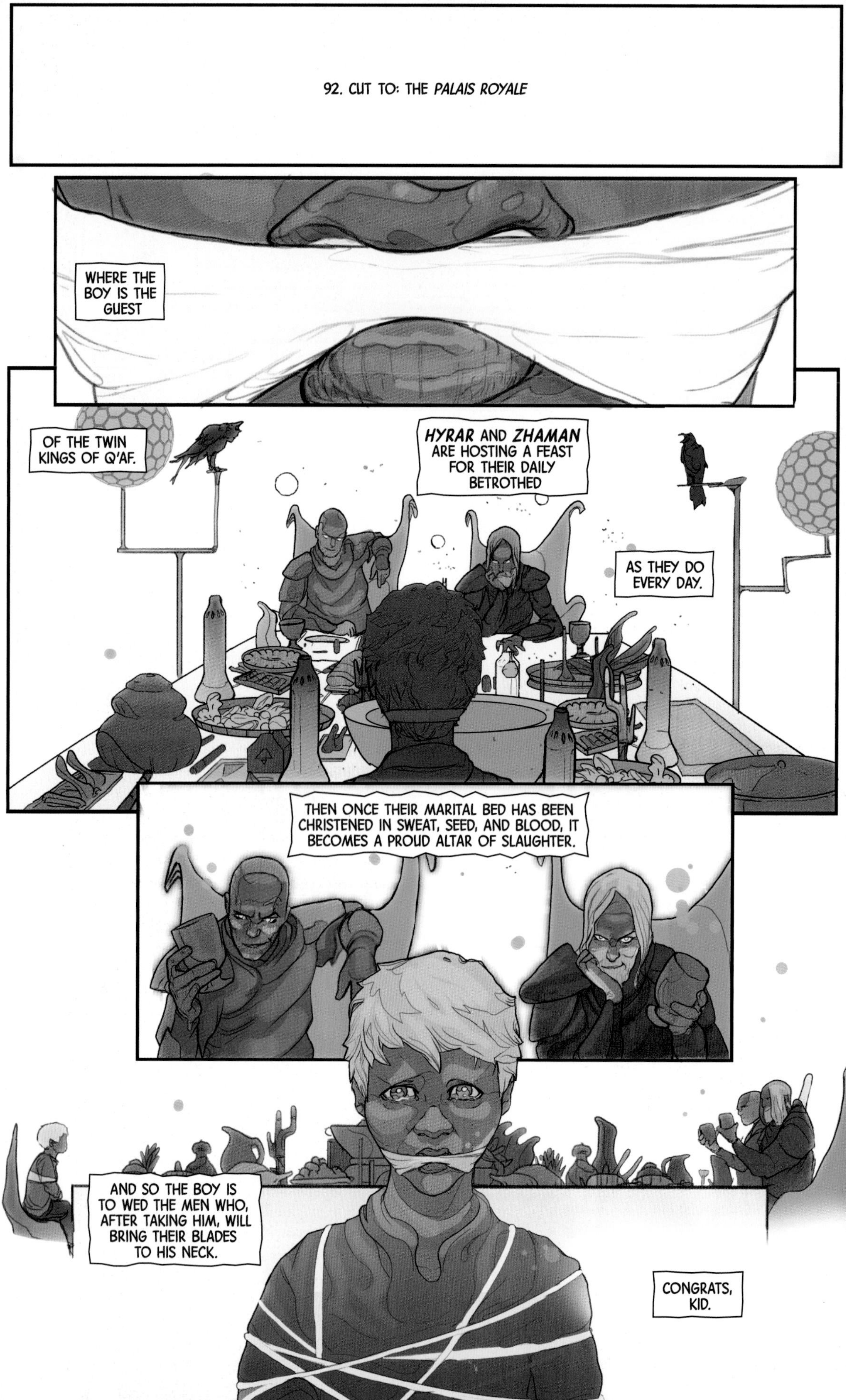
92. CUT TO: THE *PALAIS ROYALE*
WHERE THE BOY IS THE GUEST
OF THE TWIN KINGS OF Q'AF.
HYRAR AND *ZHAMAN* ARE HOSTING A FEAST FOR THEIR DAILY BETROTHED
AS THEY DO EVERY DAY.
THEN ONCE THEIR MARITAL BED HAS BEEN CHRISTENED IN SWEAT, SEED, AND BLOOD, IT BECOMES A PROUD ALTAR OF SLAUGHTER.
AND SO THE BOY IS TO WED THE MEN WHO, AFTER TAKING HIM, WILL BRING THEIR BLADES TO HIS NECK.
CONGRATS, KID.

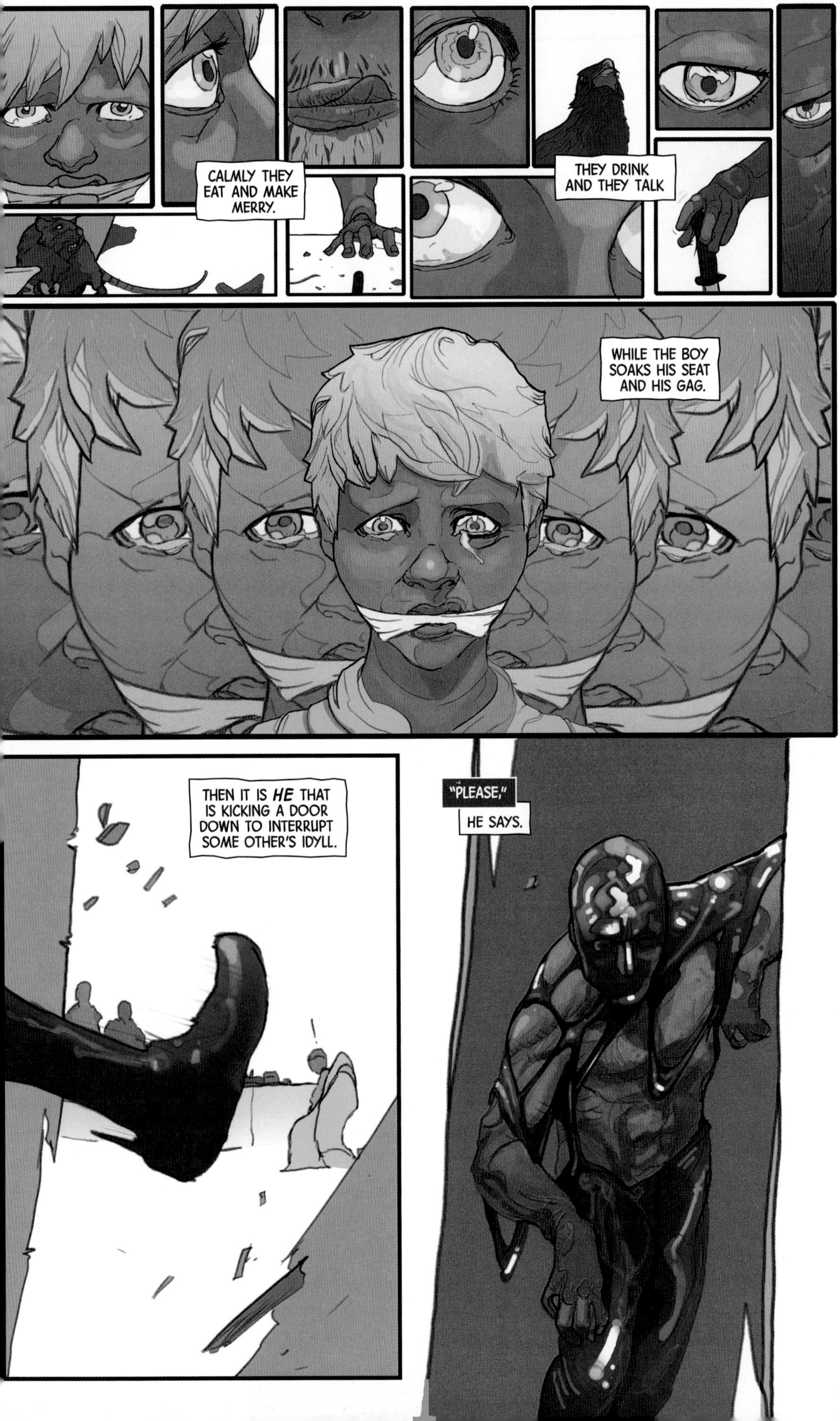
CALMLY THEY EAT AND MAKE MERRY.
THEY DRINK AND THEY TALK
WHILE THE BOY SOAKS HIS SEAT AND HIS GAG.
THEN IT IS HE THAT IS KICKING A DOOR DOWN TO INTERRUPT SOME OTHER'S IDYLL.
"PLEASE,"
HE SAYS.

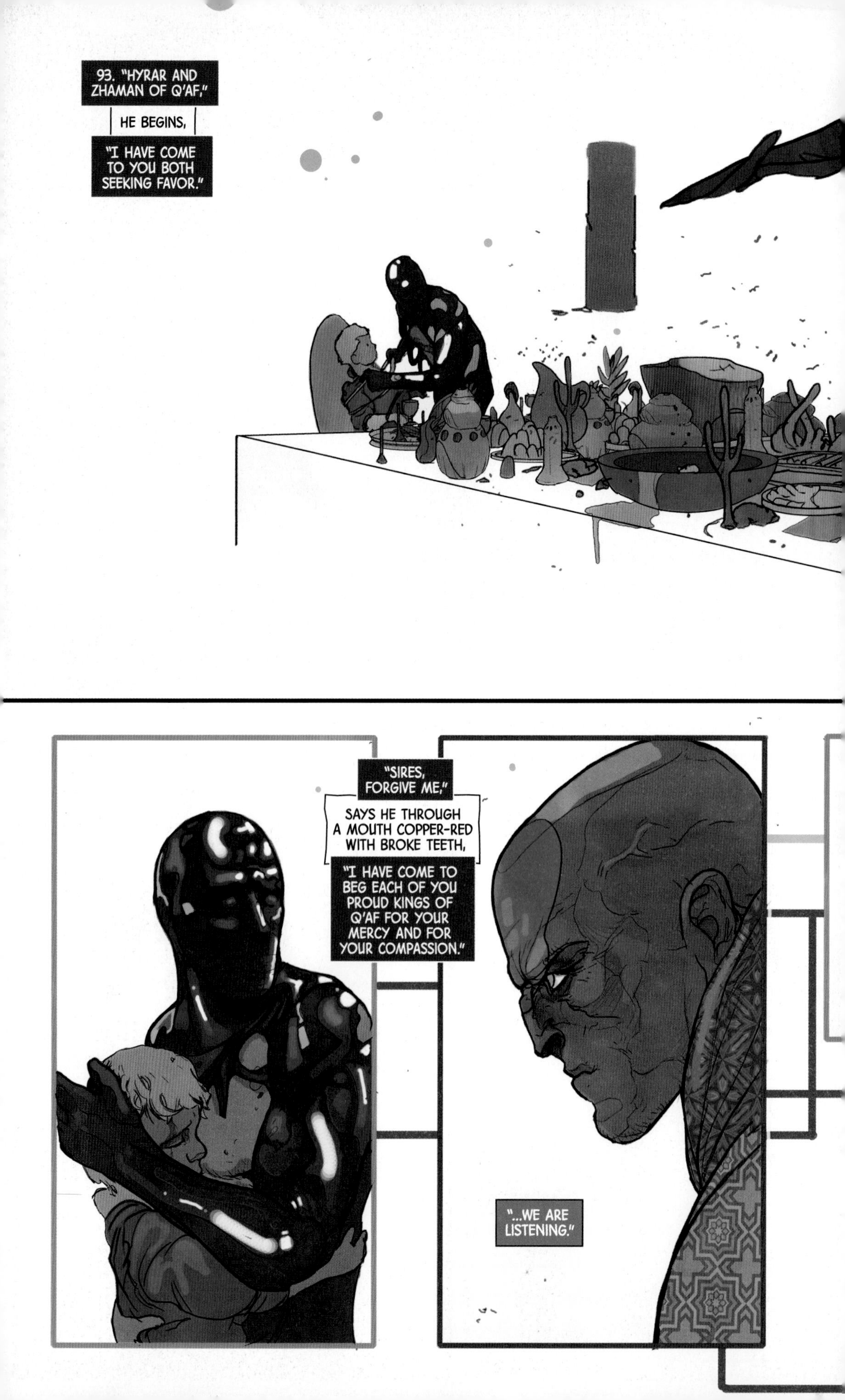
93. "HYRAR AND ZHAMAN OF Q'AF,"
HE BEGINS,
"I HAVE COME TO YOU BOTH SEEKING FAVOR."
"SIRES, FORGIVE ME,"
SAYS HE THROUGH A MOUTH COPPER-RED WITH BROKE TEETH,
"I HAVE COME TO BEG EACH OF YOU PROUD KINGS OF Q'AF FOR YOUR MERCY AND FOR YOUR COMPASSION."
"...WE ARE LISTENING."

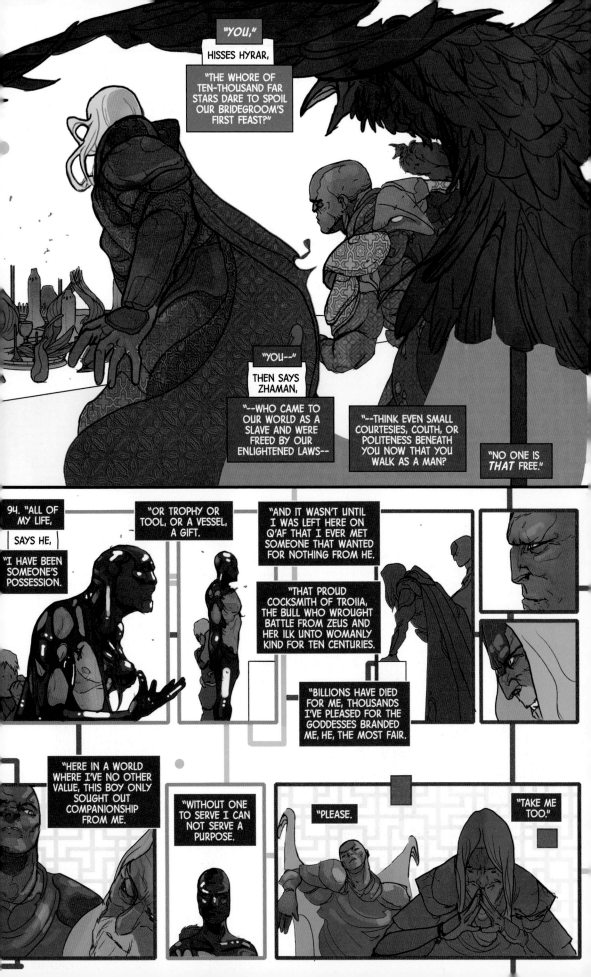

"YOU,"

HISSES HYRAR,

"THE WHORE OF TEN-THOUSAND FAR STARS DARE TO SPOIL OUR BRIDEGROOM'S FIRST FEAST?"

"YOU--"

THEN SAYS ZHAMAN,

"--WHO CAME TO OUR WORLD AS A SLAVE AND WERE FREED BY OUR ENLIGHTENED LAWS--

"--THINK EVEN SMALL COURTESIES, COUTH, OR POLITENESS BENEATH YOU NOW THAT YOU WALK AS A MAN?"

"NO ONE IS *THAT* FREE."

94. "ALL OF MY LIFE,

SAYS HE,

"I HAVE BEEN SOMEONE'S POSSESSION.

"OR TROPHY OR TOOL, OR A VESSEL, A GIFT.

"AND IT WASN'T UNTIL I WAS LEFT HERE ON Q'AF THAT I EVER MET SOMEONE THAT WANTED FOR NOTHING FROM HE.

"THAT PROUD COCKSMITH OF TROIIA, THE BULL WHO WROUGHT BATTLE FROM ZEUS AND HER ILK UNTO WOMANLY KIND FOR TEN CENTURIES.

"BILLIONS HAVE DIED FOR ME, THOUSANDS I'VE PLEASED FOR THE GODDESSES BRANDED ME, HE, THE MOST FAIR.

"HERE IN A WORLD WHERE I'VE NO OTHER VALUE, THIS BOY ONLY SOUGHT OUT COMPANIONSHIP FROM ME.

"WITHOUT ONE TO SERVE I CAN NOT SERVE A PURPOSE.

"PLEASE.

"TAKE ME TOO."

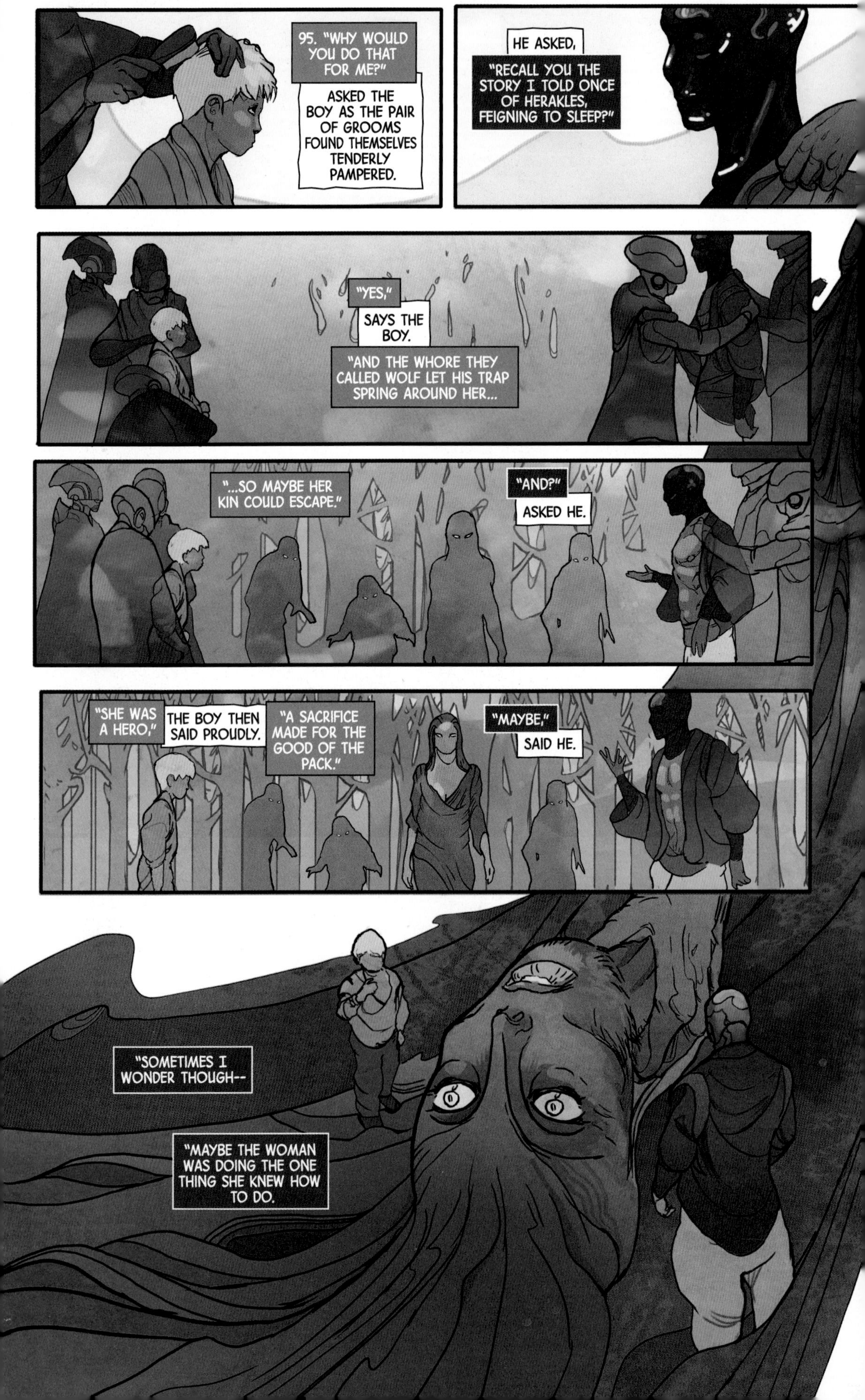
95. "WHY WOULD YOU DO THAT FOR ME?"
ASKED THE BOY AS THE PAIR OF GROOMS FOUND THEMSELVES TENDERLY PAMPERED.
HE ASKED,
"RECALL YOU THE STORY I TOLD ONCE OF HERAKLES, FEIGNING TO SLEEP?"
"YES,"
SAYS THE BOY.
"AND THE WHORE THEY CALLED WOLF LET HIS TRAP SPRING AROUND HER...
"...SO MAYBE HER KIN COULD ESCAPE."
"AND?"
ASKED HE.
"SHE WAS A HERO,"
THE BOY THEN SAID PROUDLY.
"A SACRIFICE MADE FOR THE GOOD OF THE PACK."
"MAYBE,"
SAID HE.
"SOMETIMES I WONDER THOUGH--
"MAYBE THE WOMAN WAS DOING THE ONE THING SHE KNEW HOW TO DO.

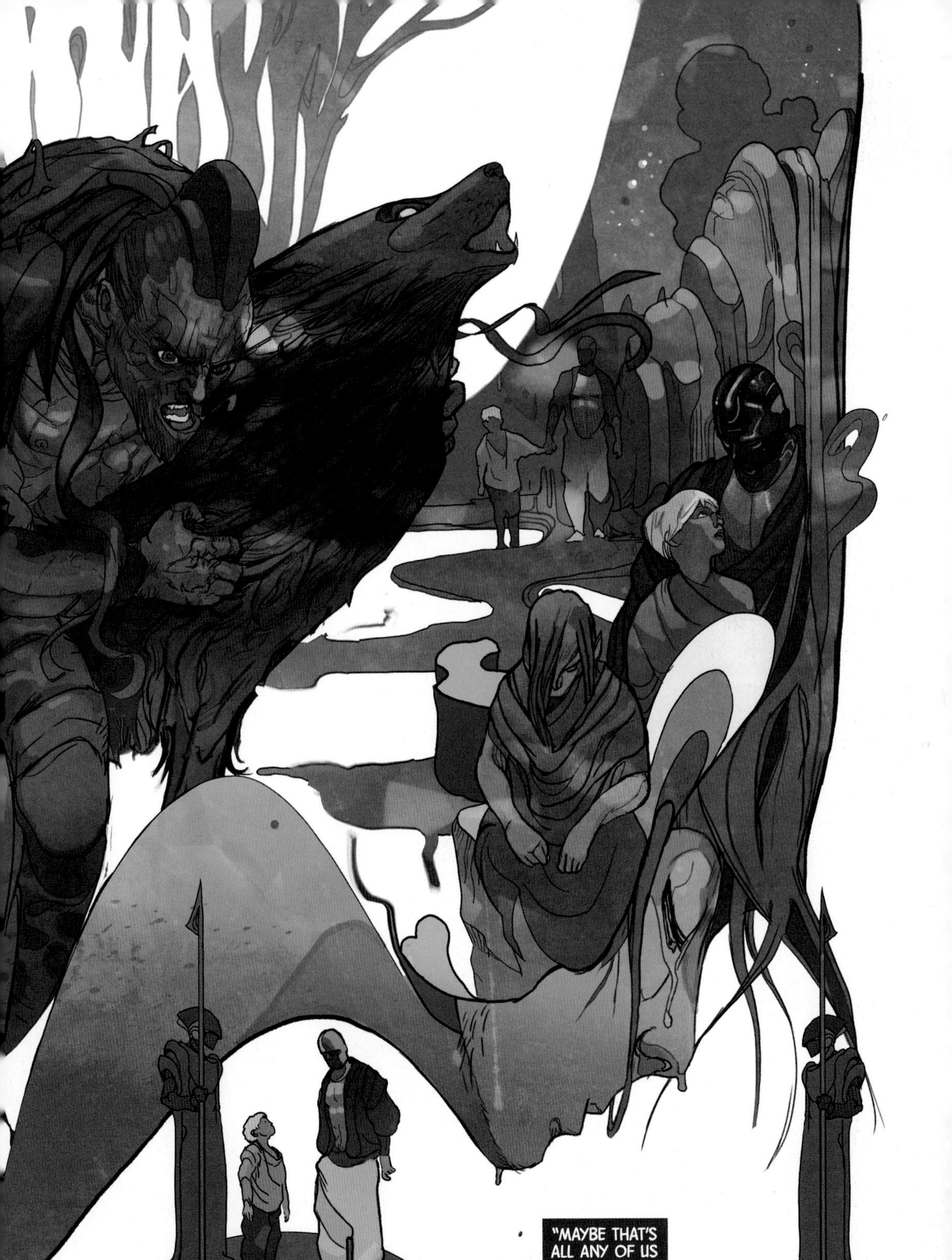
"MAYBE THAT'S ALL ANY OF US CAN DO.

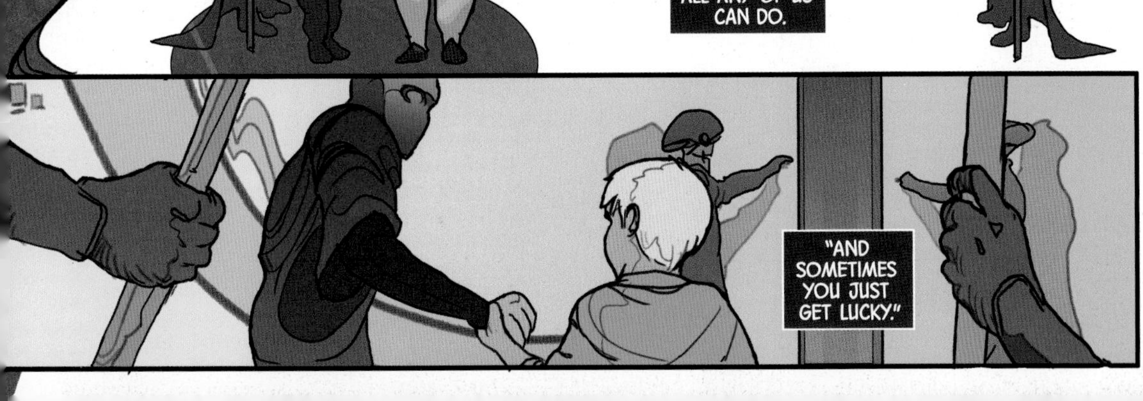
"AND SOMETIMES YOU JUST GET LUCKY."

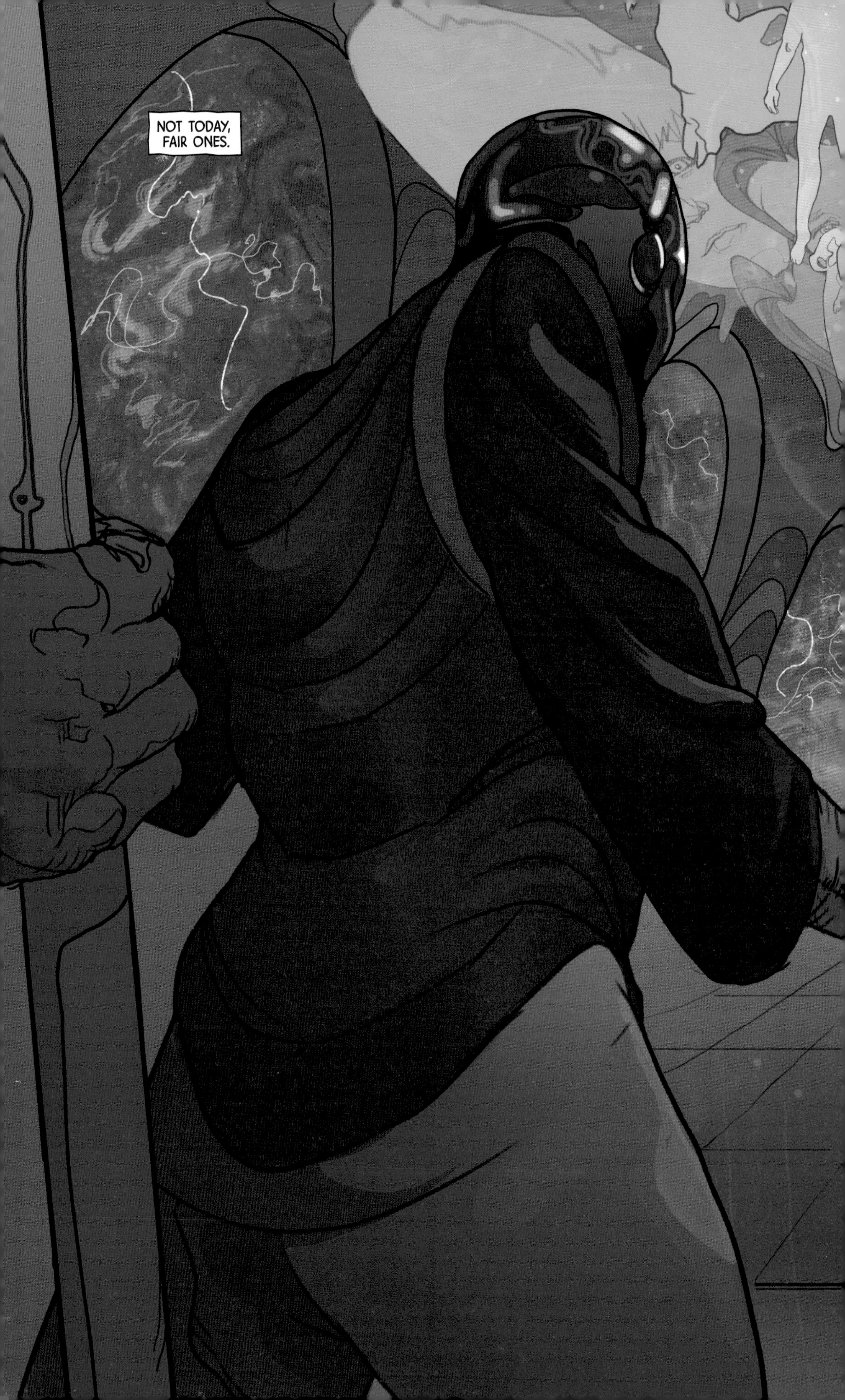
NOT TODAY, FAIR ONES.

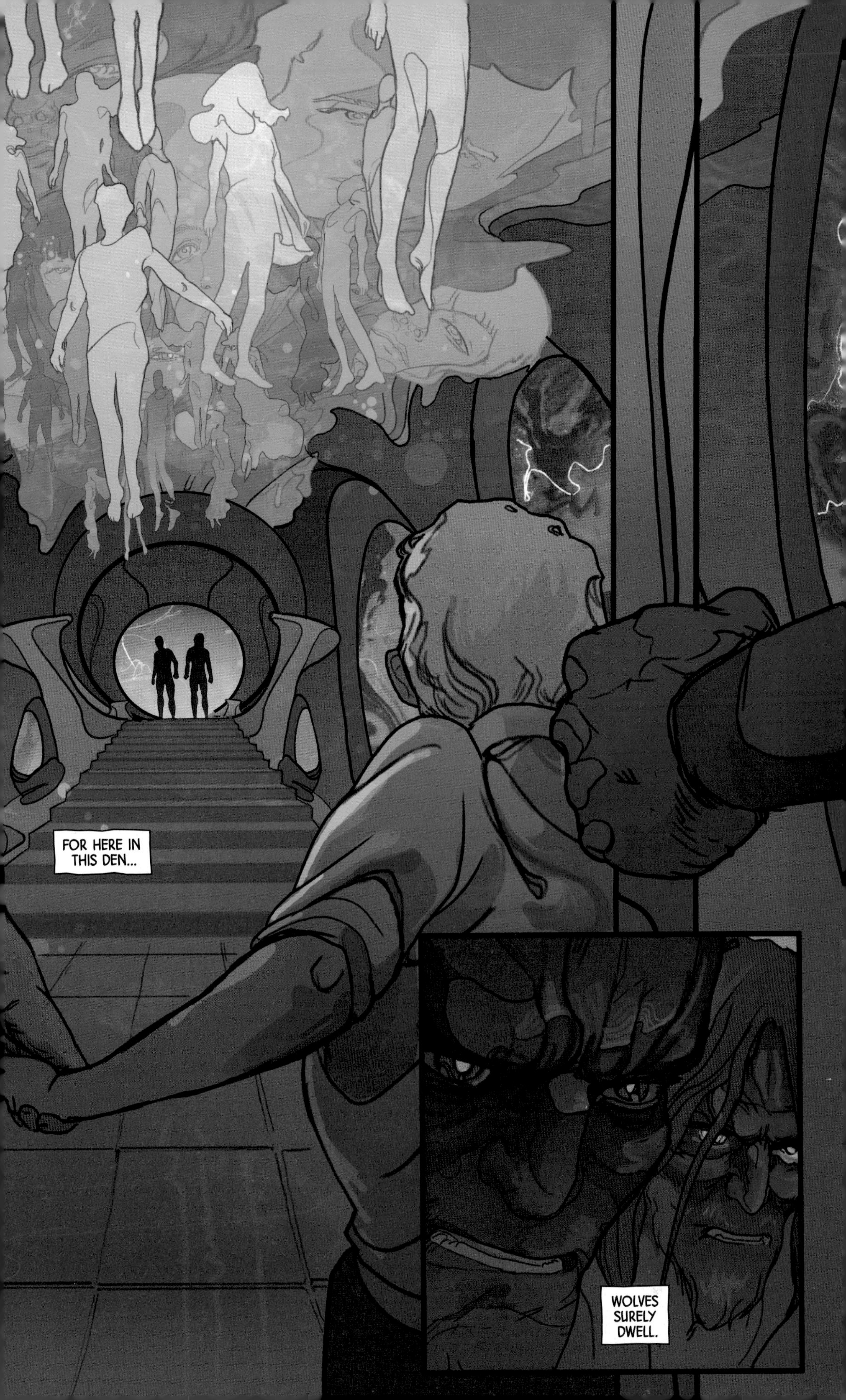
FOR HERE IN THIS DEN...
WOLVES SURELY DWELL.

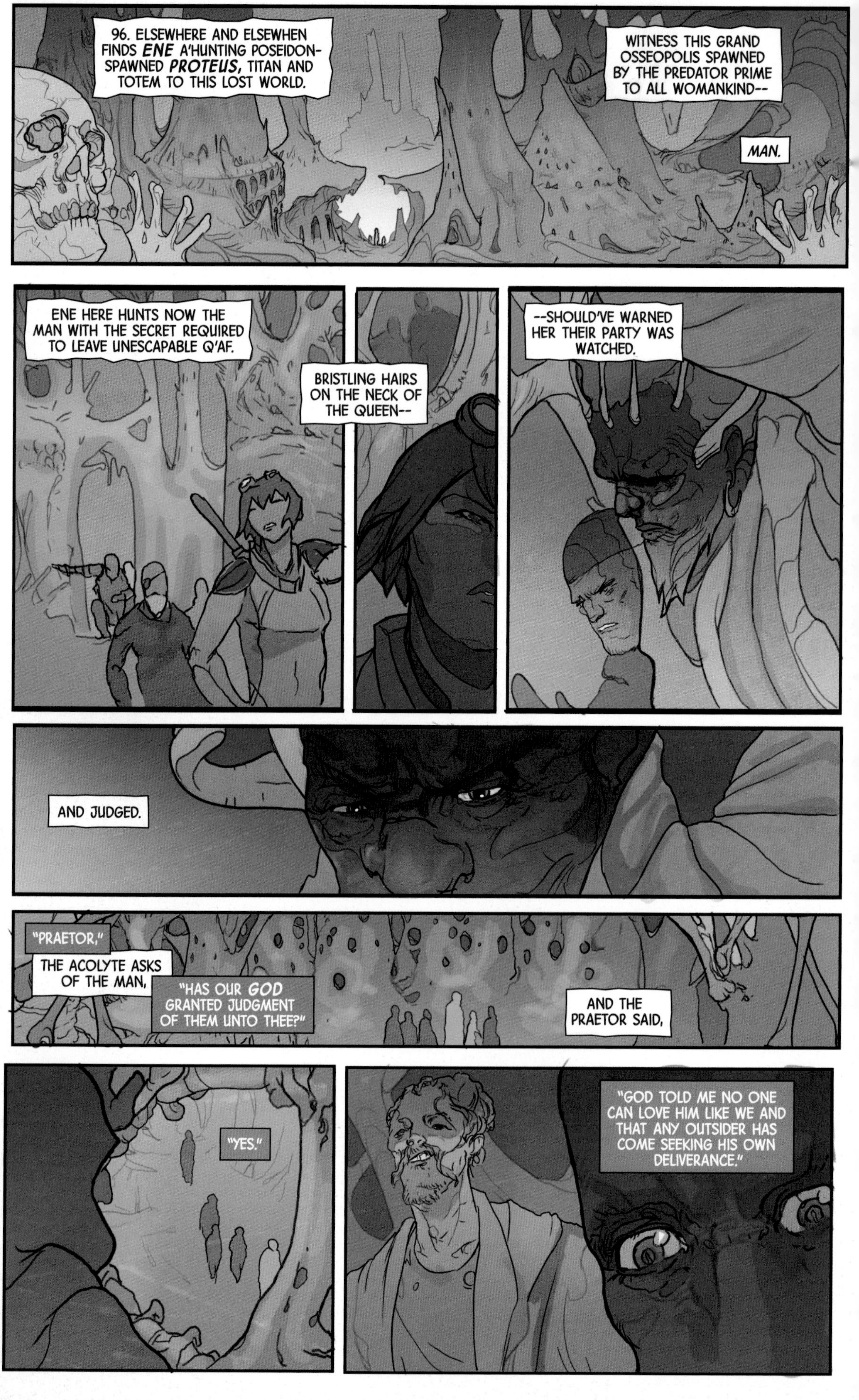
96. ELSEWHERE AND ELSEWHEN FINDS ENE A'HUNTING POSEIDON-SPAWNED PROTEUS, TITAN AND TOTEM TO THIS LOST WORLD.
WITNESS THIS GRAND OSSEOPOLIS SPAWNED BY THE PREDATOR PRIME TO ALL WOMANKIND--
MAN.
ENE HERE HUNTS NOW THE MAN WITH THE SECRET REQUIRED TO LEAVE UNESCAPABLE Q'AF.
BRISTLING HAIRS ON THE NECK OF THE QUEEN--
--SHOULD'VE WARNED HER THEIR PARTY WAS WATCHED.
AND JUDGED.
"PRAETOR,"
THE ACOLYTE ASKS OF THE MAN,
"HAS OUR GOD GRANTED JUDGMENT OF THEM UNTO THEE?"
AND THE PRAETOR SAID,
"YES."
"GOD TOLD ME NO ONE CAN LOVE HIM LIKE WE AND THAT ANY OUTSIDER HAS COME SEEKING HIS OWN DELIVERANCE."

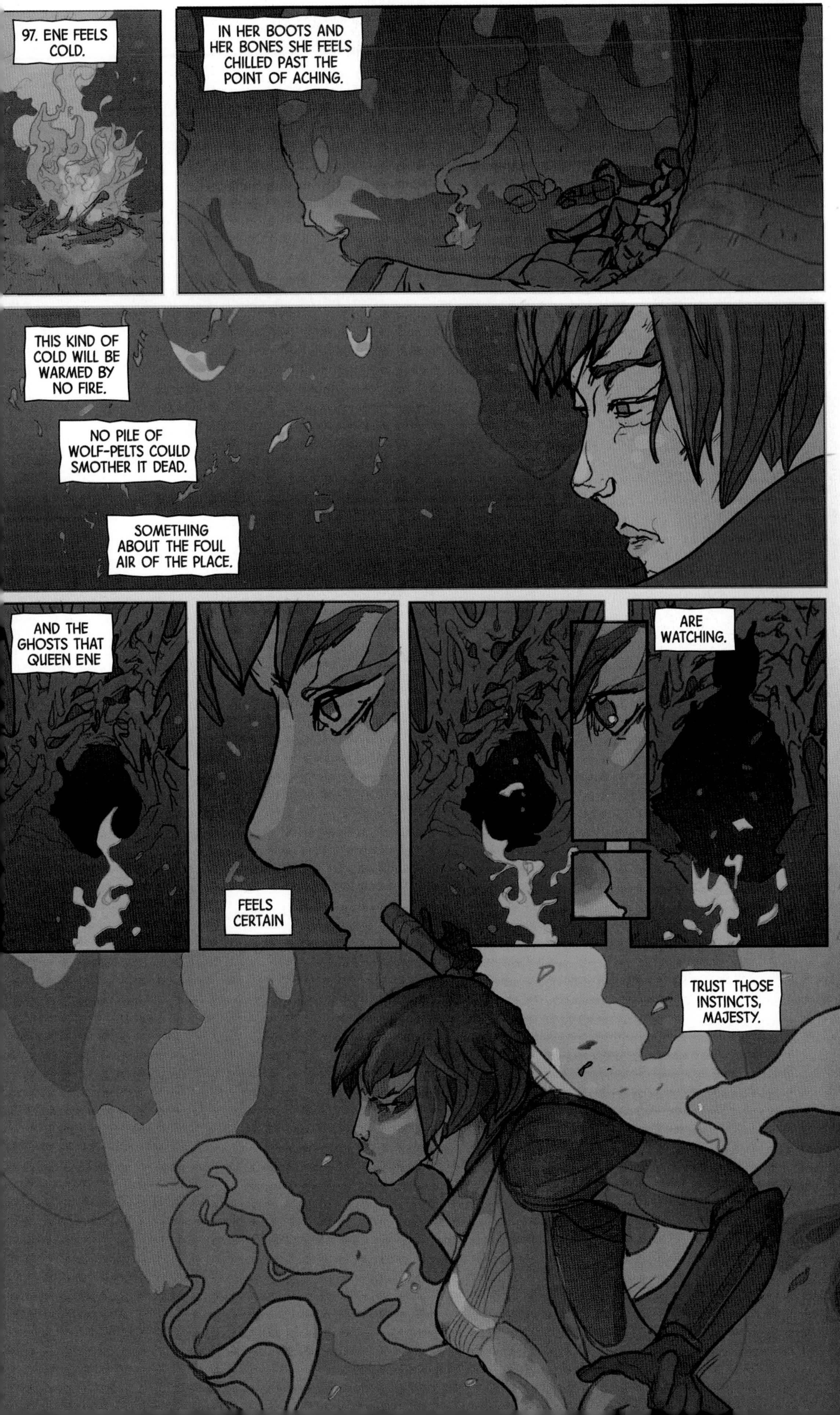
97. ENE FEELS COLD.
IN HER BOOTS AND HER BONES SHE FEELS CHILLED PAST THE POINT OF ACHING.
THIS KIND OF COLD WILL BE WARMED BY NO FIRE.
NO PILE OF WOLF-PELTS COULD SMOTHER IT DEAD.
SOMETHING ABOUT THE FOUL AIR OF THE PLACE.
AND THE GHOSTS THAT QUEEN ENE
FEELS CERTAIN
ARE WATCHING.
TRUST THOSE INSTINCTS, MAJESTY.

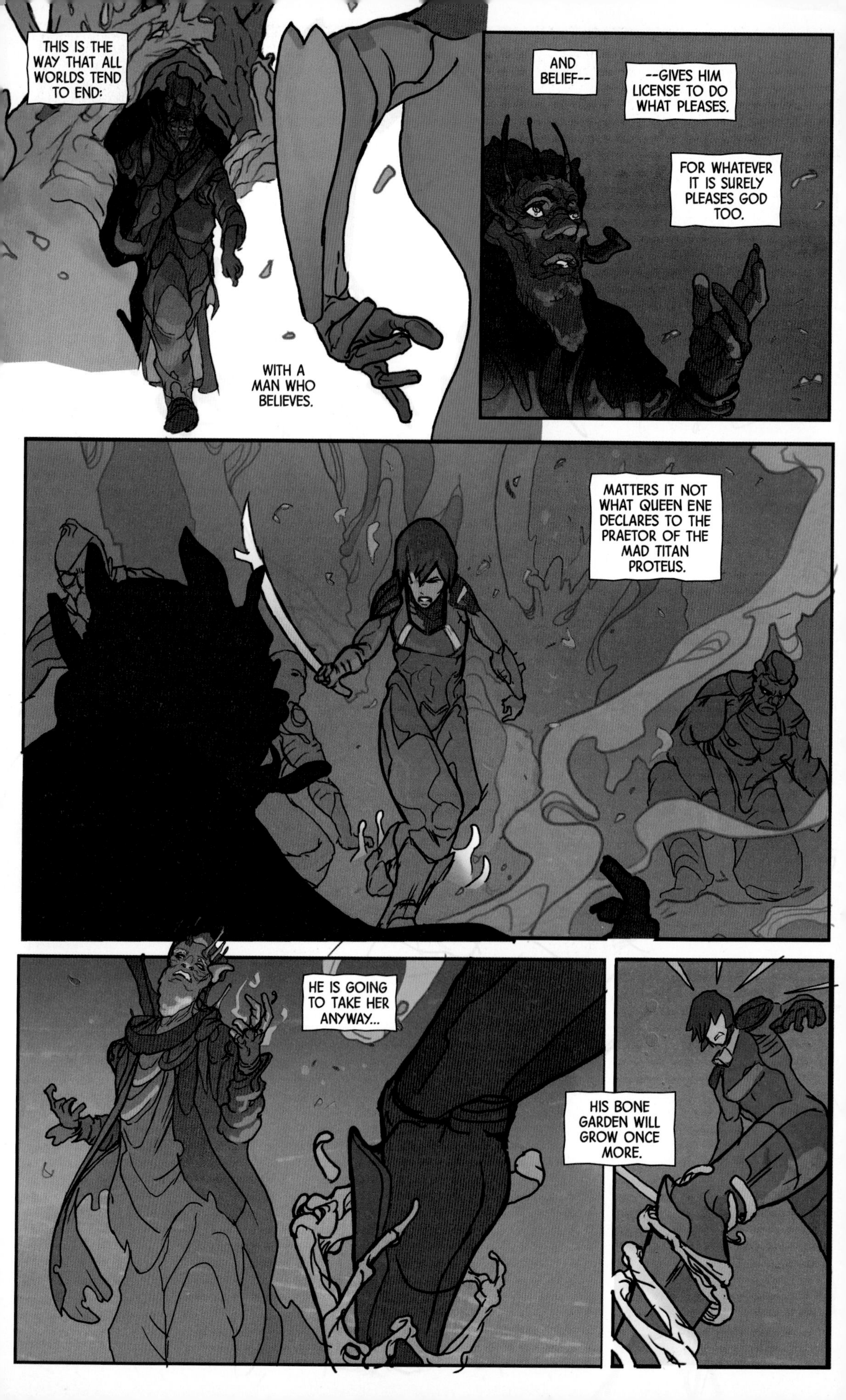
THIS IS THE WAY THAT ALL WORLDS TEND TO END:
WITH A MAN WHO BELIEVES.
AND BELIEF--
--GIVES HIM LICENSE TO DO WHAT PLEASES.
FOR WHATEVER IT IS SURELY PLEASES GOD TOO.
MATTERS IT NOT WHAT QUEEN ENE DECLARES TO THE PRAETOR OF THE MAD TITAN PROTEUS.
HE IS GOING TO TAKE HER ANYWAY...
HIS BONE GARDEN WILL GROW ONCE MORE.

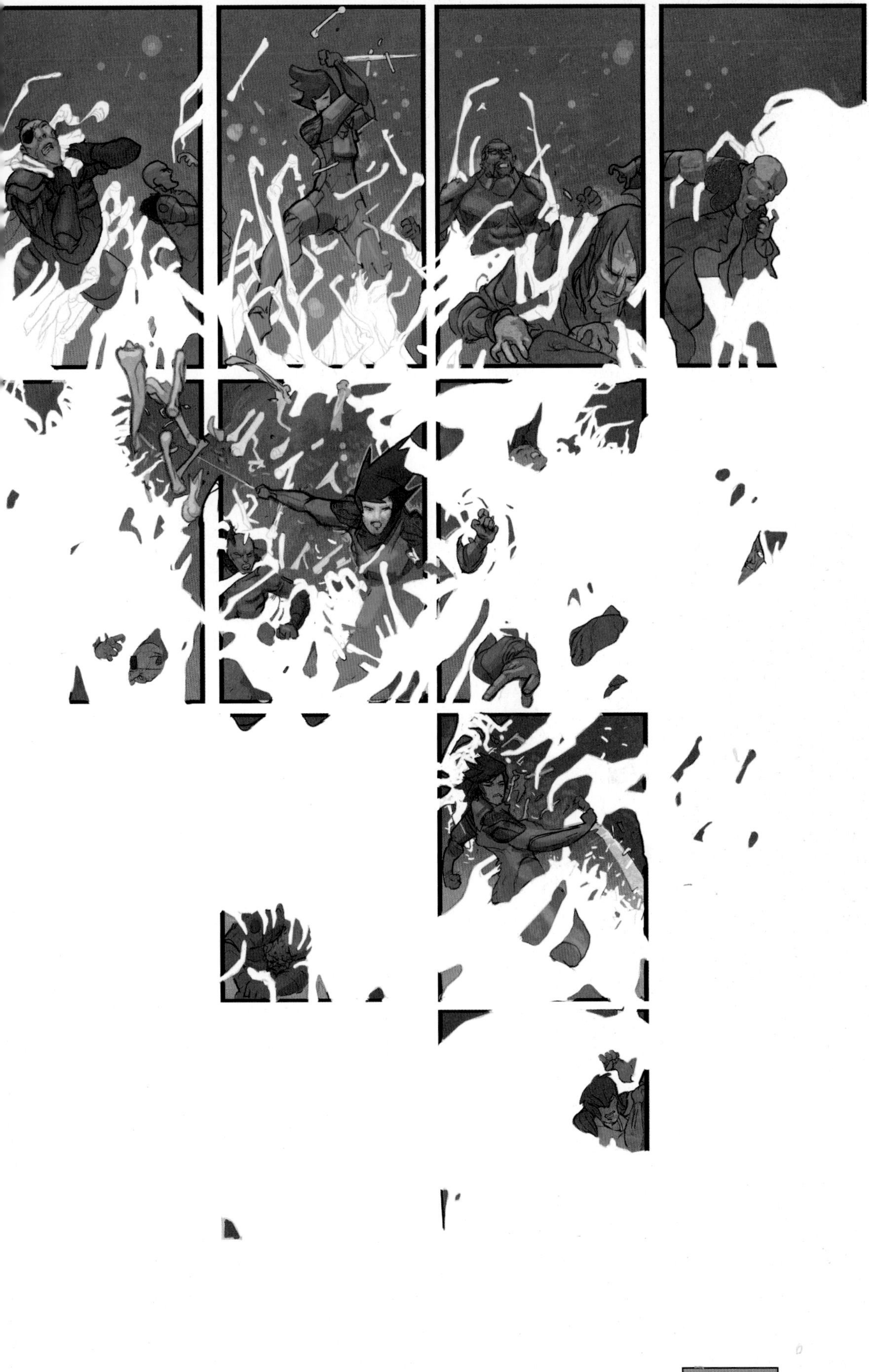
IT'S WHAT GOD WANTS.

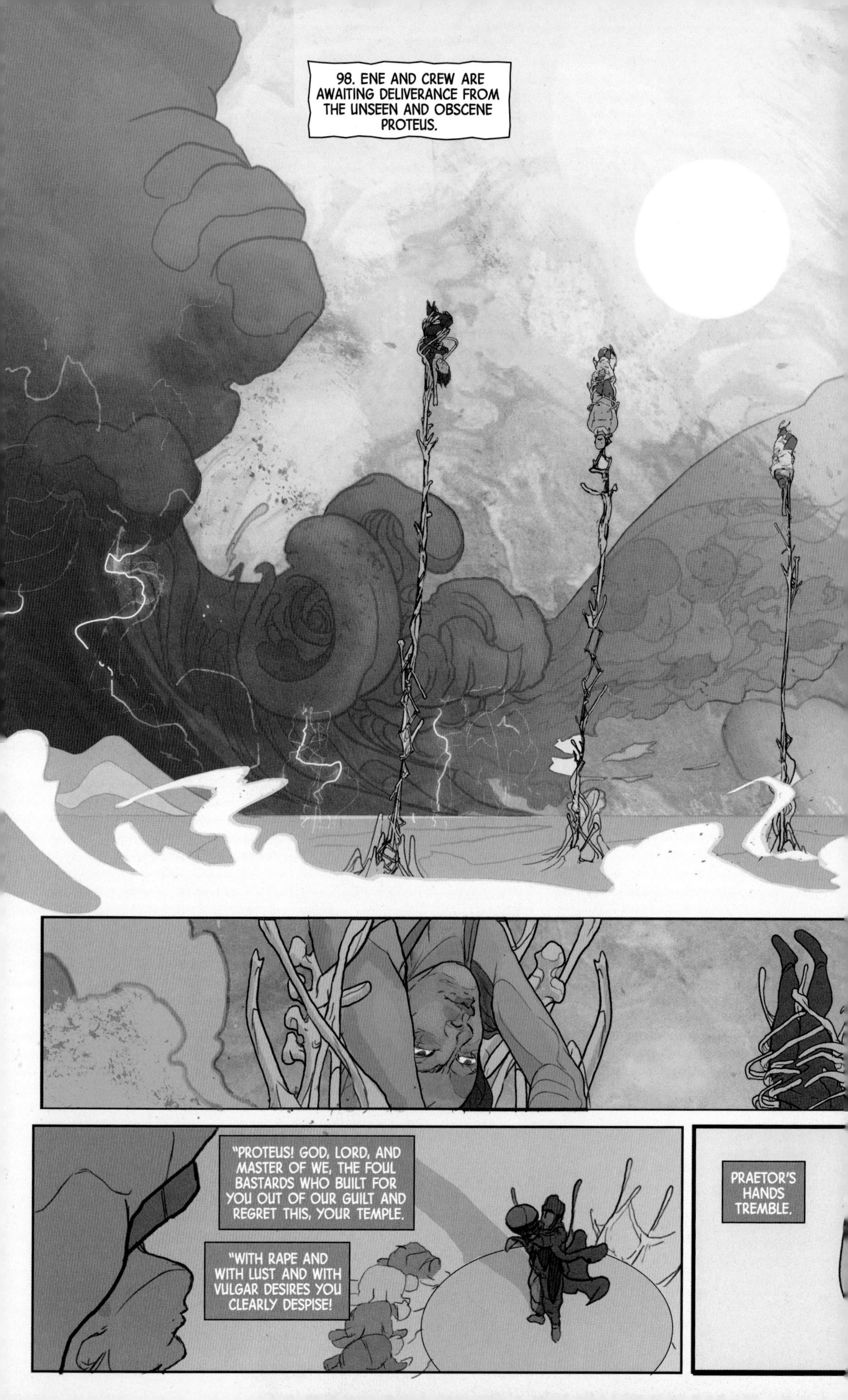
98. ENE AND CREW ARE AWAITING DELIVERANCE FROM THE UNSEEN AND OBSCENE PROTEUS.
"PROTEUS! GOD, LORD, AND MASTER OF WE, THE FOUL BASTARDS WHO BUILT FOR YOU OUT OF OUR GUILT AND REGRET THIS, YOUR TEMPLE.
"WITH RAPE AND WITH LUST AND WITH VULGAR DESIRES YOU CLEARLY DESPISE!
PRAETOR'S HANDS TREMBLE.

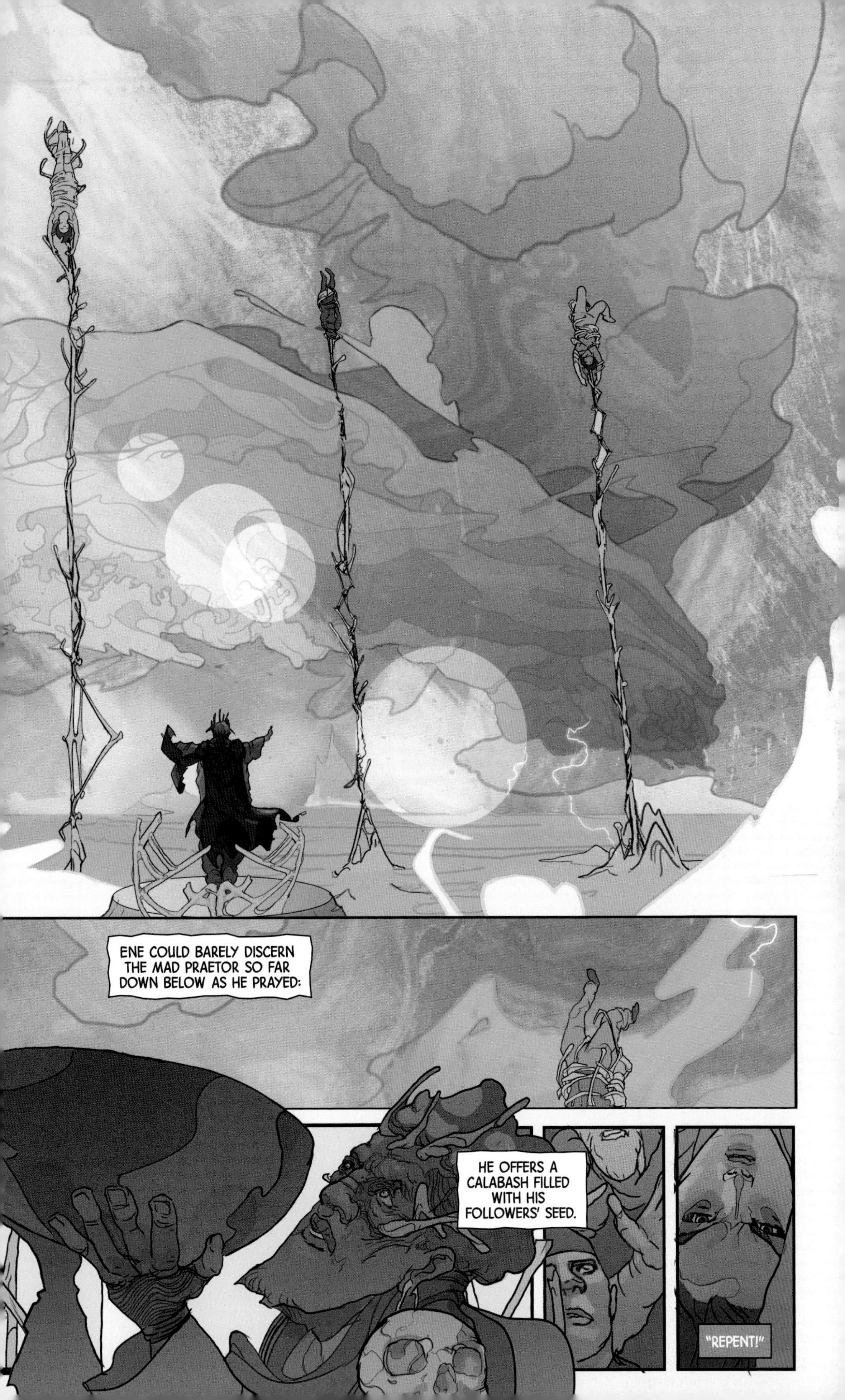
ENE COULD BARELY DISCERN THE MAD PRAETOR SO FAR DOWN BELOW AS HE PRAYED:
HE OFFERS A CALABASH FILLED WITH HIS FOLLOWERS' SEED.
"REPENT!"

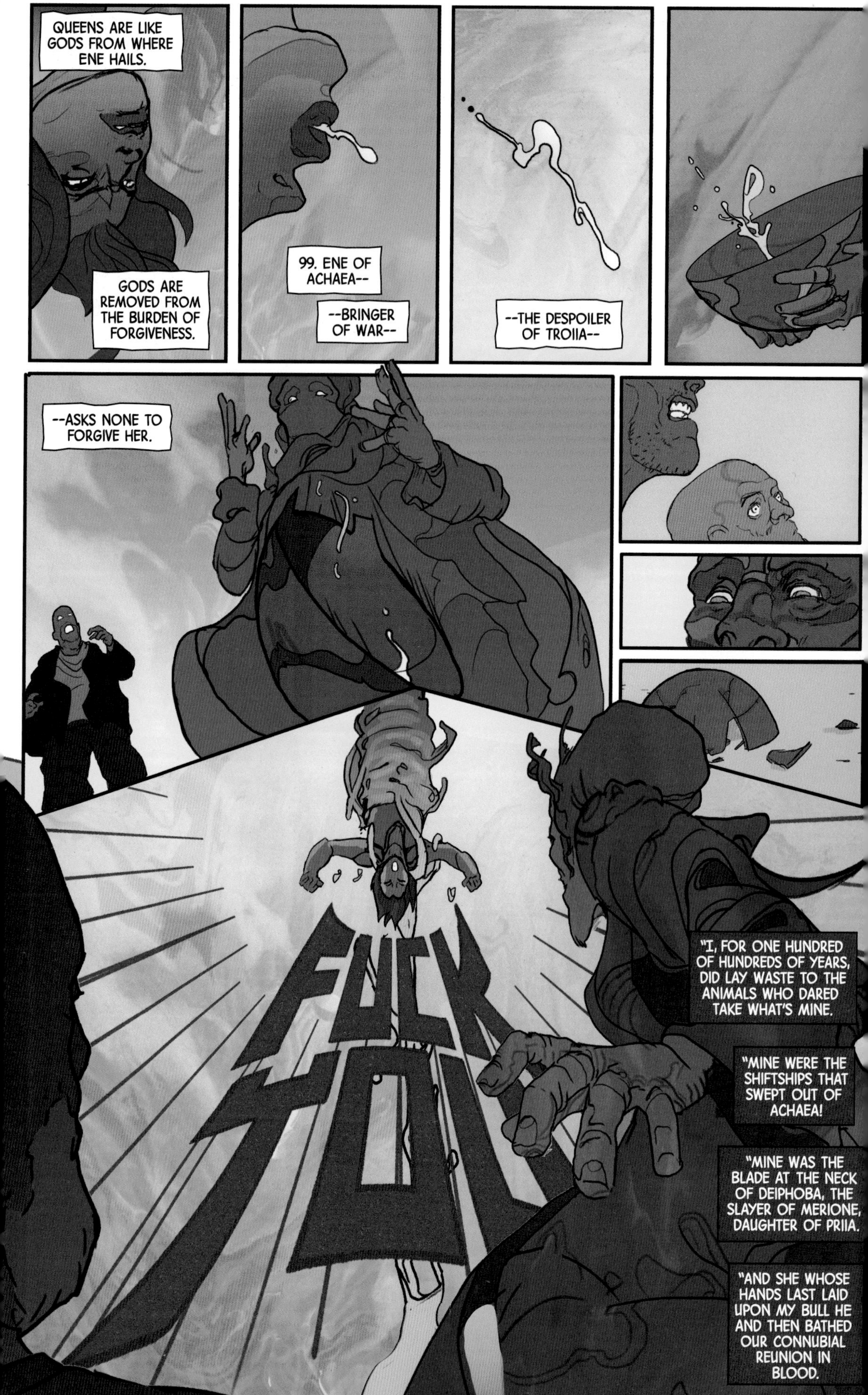
QUEENS ARE LIKE GODS FROM WHERE ENE HAILS.
GODS ARE REMOVED FROM THE BURDEN OF FORGIVENESS.
99. ENE OF ACHAEA--
--BRINGER OF WAR--
--THE DESPOILER OF TROIIA--
--ASKS NONE TO FORGIVE HER.
FUCK YOU
"I, FOR ONE HUNDRED OF HUNDREDS OF YEARS, DID LAY WASTE TO THE ANIMALS WHO DARED TAKE WHAT'S MINE.
"MINE WERE THE SHIFTSHIPS THAT SWEPT OUT OF ACHAEA!
"MINE WAS THE BLADE AT THE NECK OF DEIPHOBA, THE SLAYER OF MERIONE, DAUGHTER OF PRIIA.
"AND SHE WHOSE HANDS LAST LAID UPON MY BULL HE AND THEN BATHED OUR CONNUBIAL REUNION IN BLOOD.

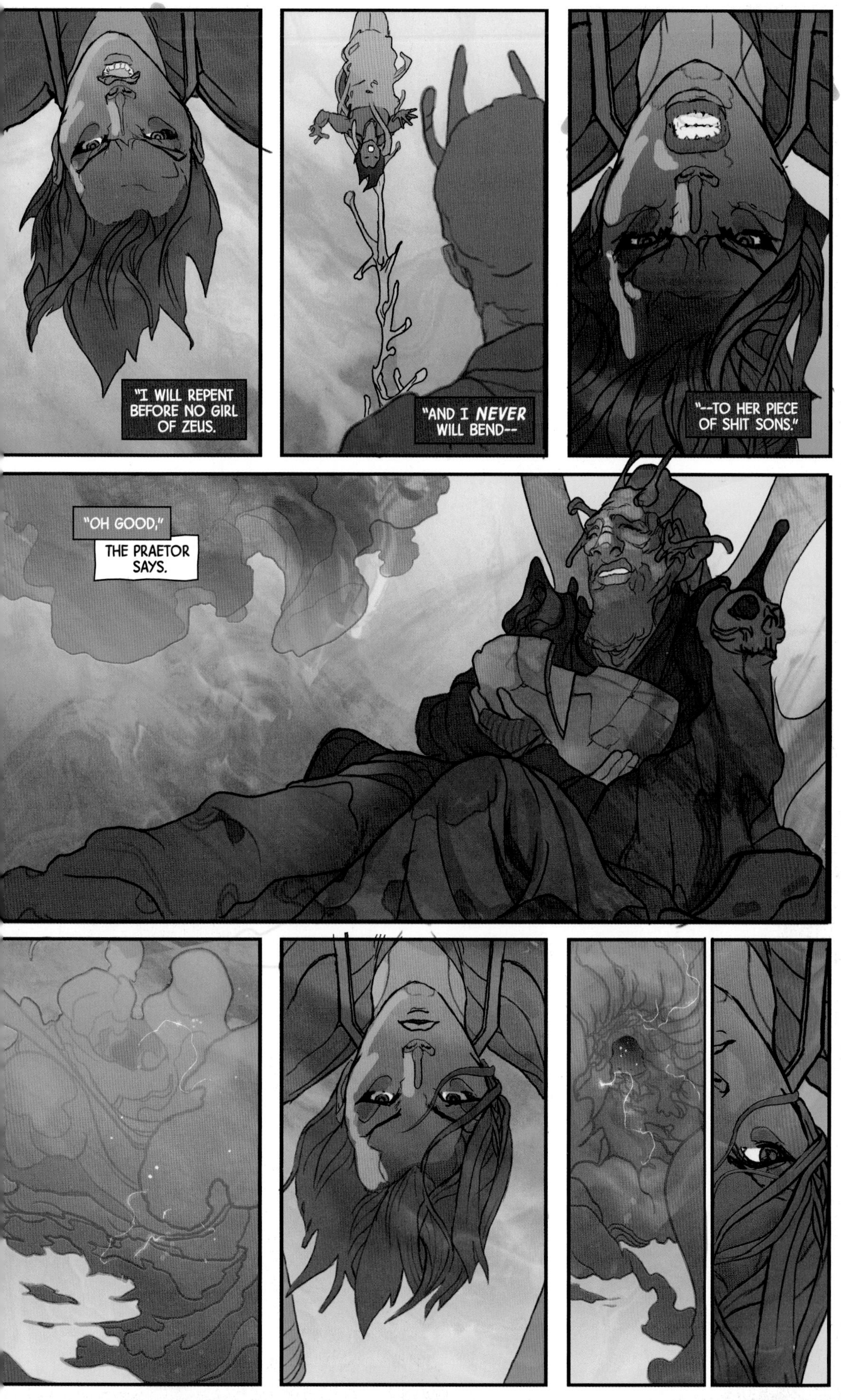
"I WILL REPENT BEFORE NO GIRL OF ZEUS.
"AND I NEVER WILL BEND--
"--TO HER PIECE OF SHIT SONS."
"OH GOOD,"
THE PRAETOR SAYS.

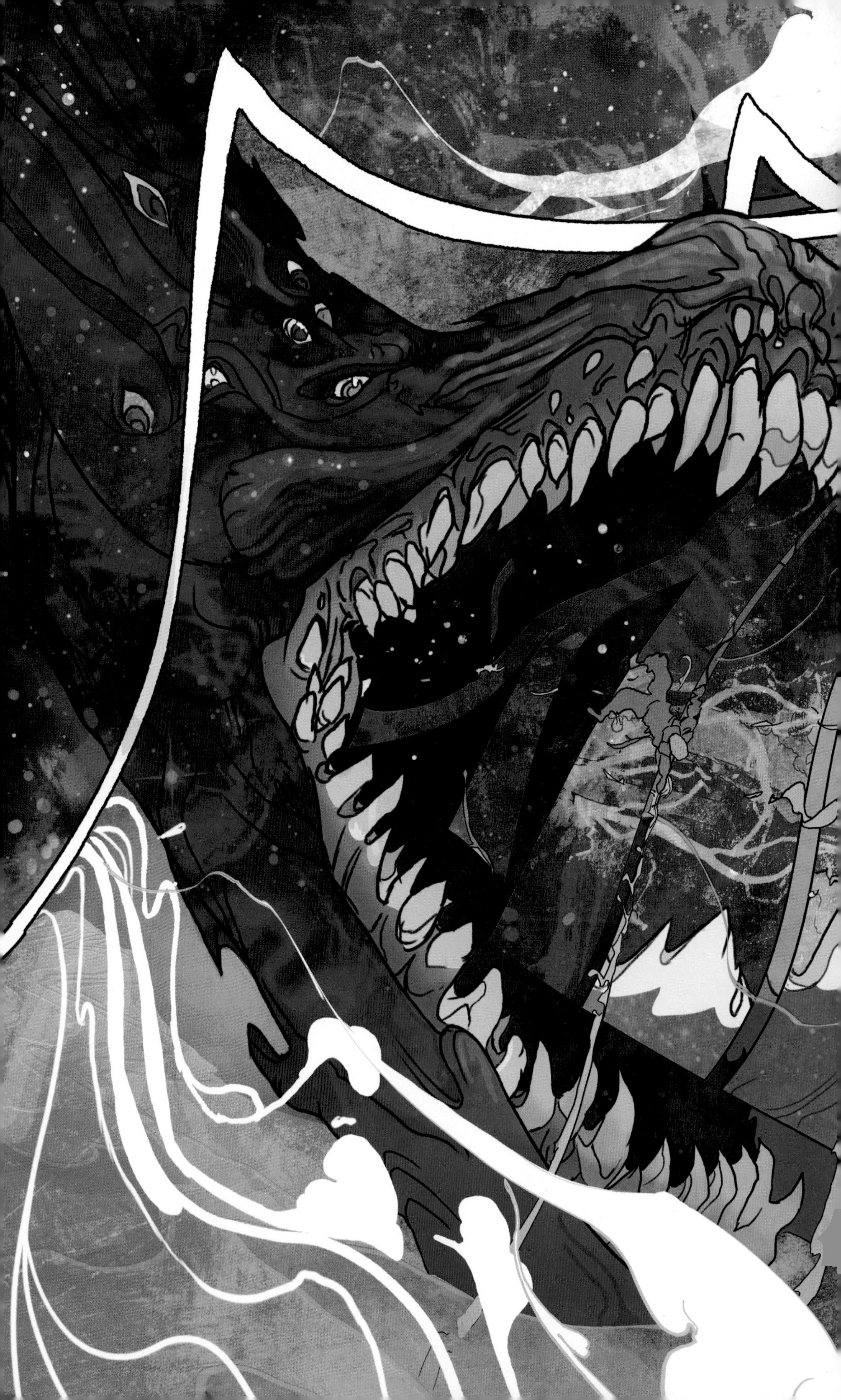

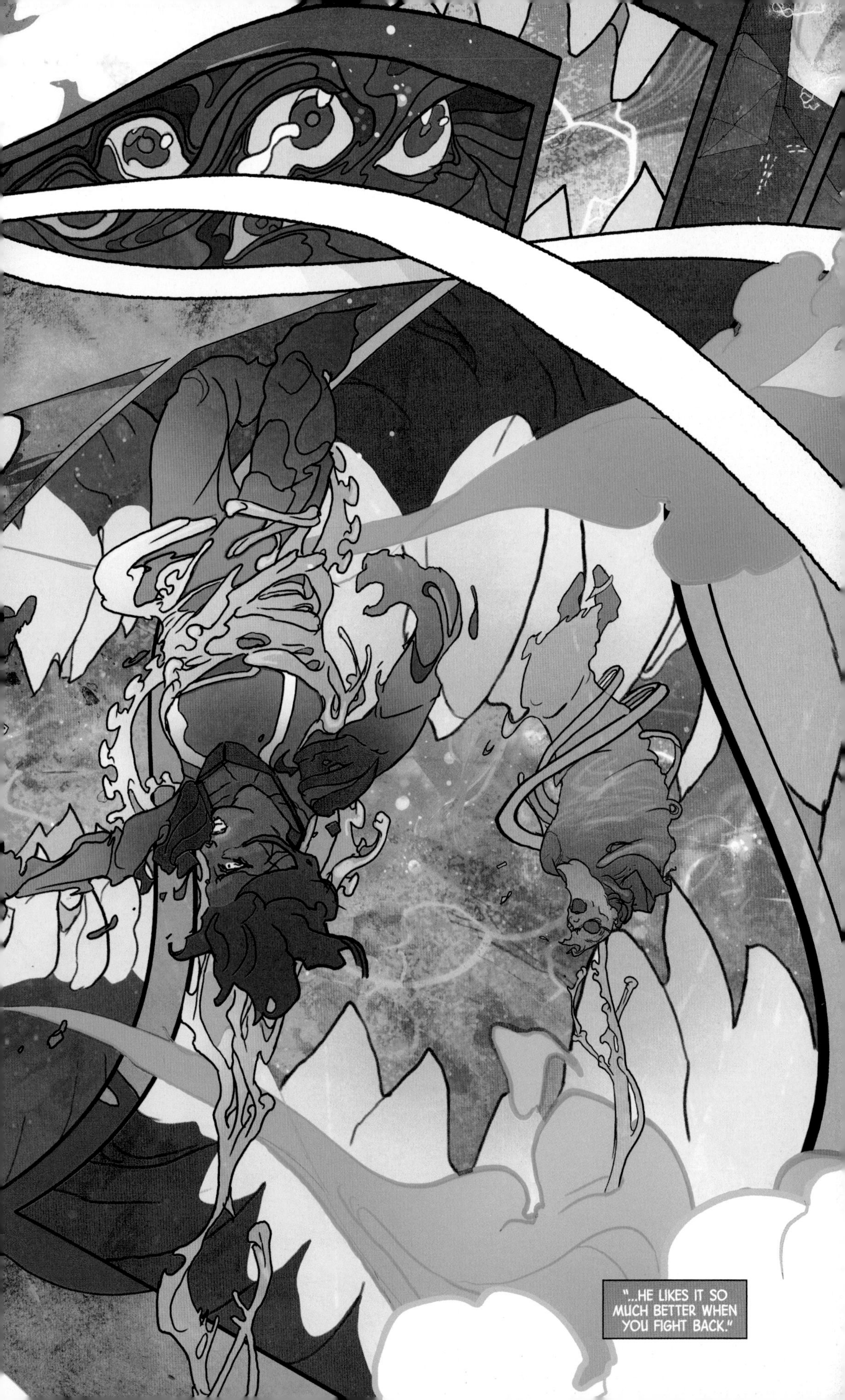
"...HE LIKES IT SO MUCH BETTER WHEN YOU FIGHT BACK."

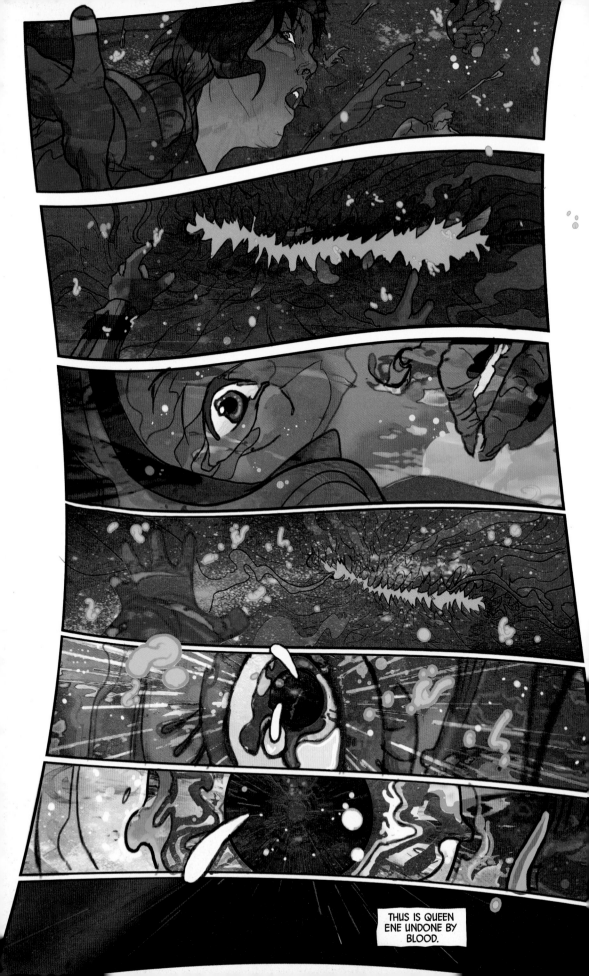

THUS IS QUEEN ENE UNDONE BY BLOOD.

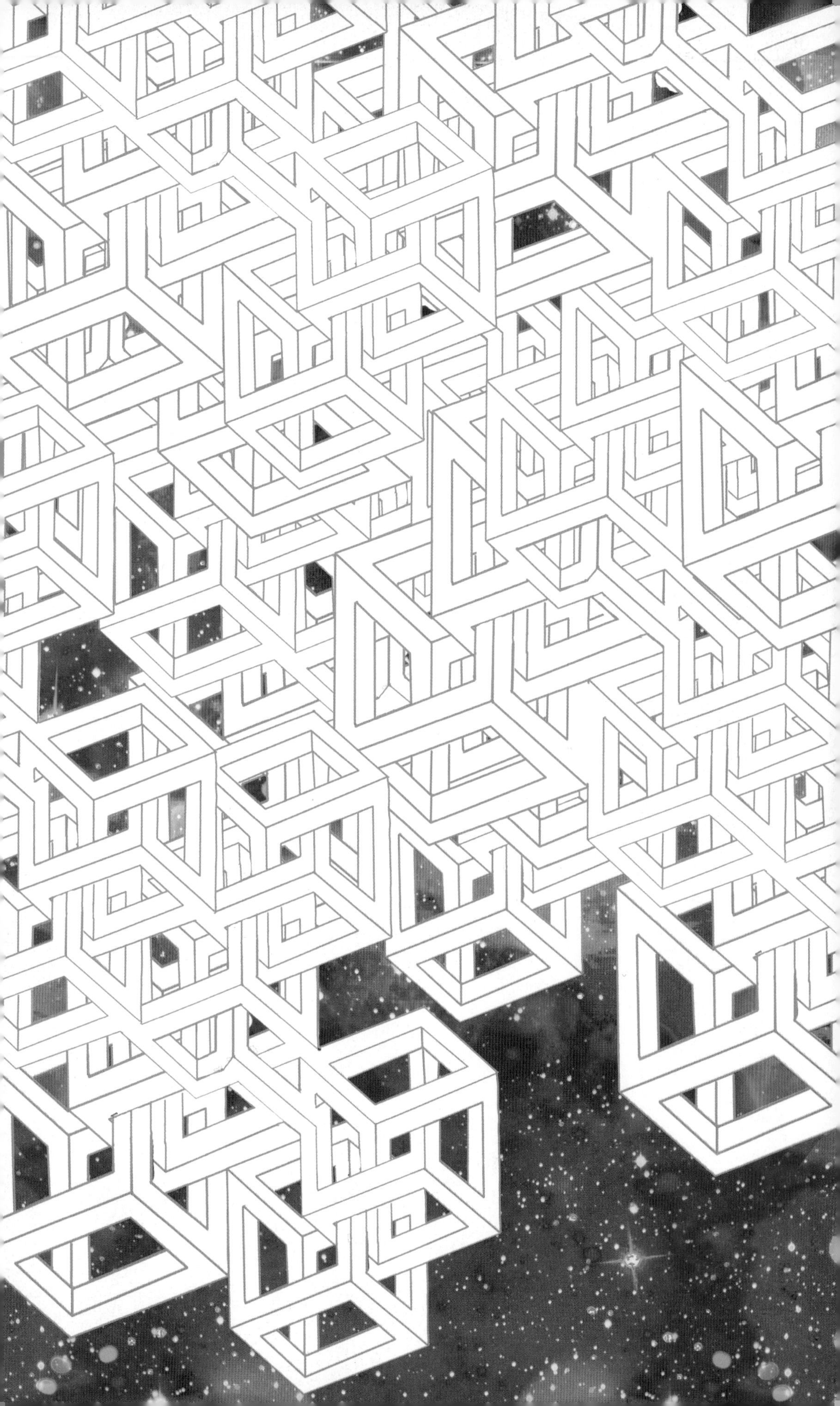

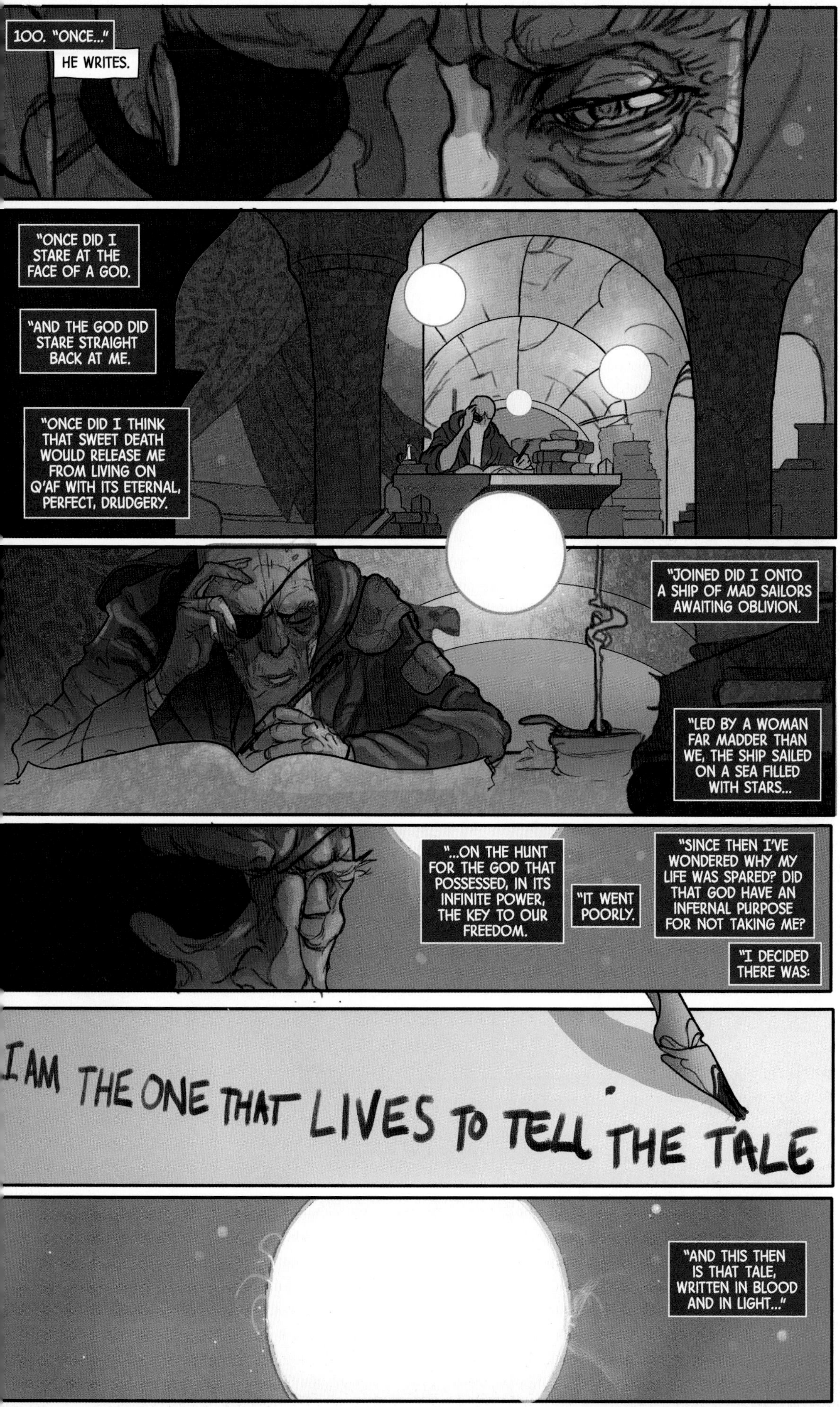
100. "ONCE..."
HE WRITES.
"ONCE DID I STARE AT THE FACE OF A GOD.
"AND THE GOD DID STARE STRAIGHT BACK AT ME.
"ONCE DID I THINK THAT SWEET DEATH WOULD RELEASE ME FROM LIVING ON Q'AF WITH ITS ETERNAL, PERFECT, DRUDGERY.
"JOINED DID I ONTO A SHIP OF MAD SAILORS AWAITING OBLIVION.
"LED BY A WOMAN FAR MADDER THAN WE, THE SHIP SAILED ON A SEA FILLED WITH STARS...
"...ON THE HUNT FOR THE GOD THAT POSSESSED, IN ITS INFINITE POWER, THE KEY TO OUR FREEDOM.
"IT WENT POORLY.
"SINCE THEN I'VE WONDERED WHY MY LIFE WAS SPARED? DID THAT GOD HAVE AN INFERNAL PURPOSE FOR NOT TAKING ME?
"I DECIDED THERE WAS:
I AM THE ONE THAT LIVES TO TELL THE TALE
"AND THIS THEN IS THAT TALE, WRITTEN IN BLOOD AND IN LIGHT..."

101. ENE, SO PROUD AND SO STRONG, WHO DID HUNT FOR THE GODSPAWN CALLED PROTEUS FOUND, TO HER HORROR UNENDING, THE TITAN OF Q'AF WAS MORE MAD THAN EVEN SHE.

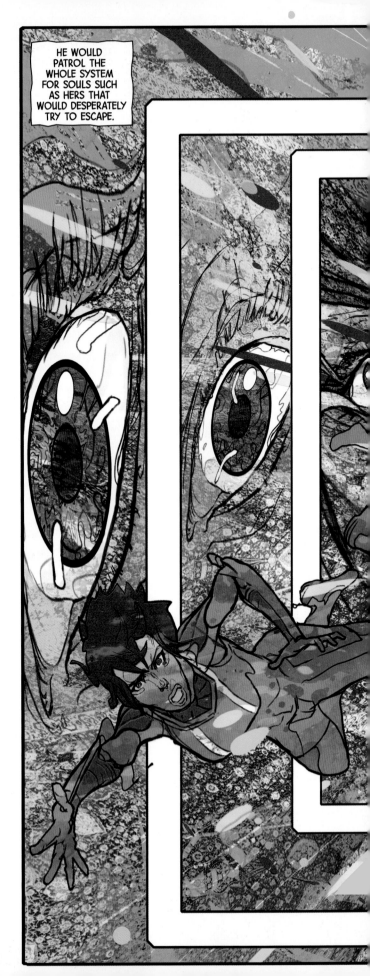

HE WOULD PATROL THE WHOLE SYSTEM FOR SOULS SUCH AS HERS THAT WOULD DESPERATELY TRY TO ESCAPE.

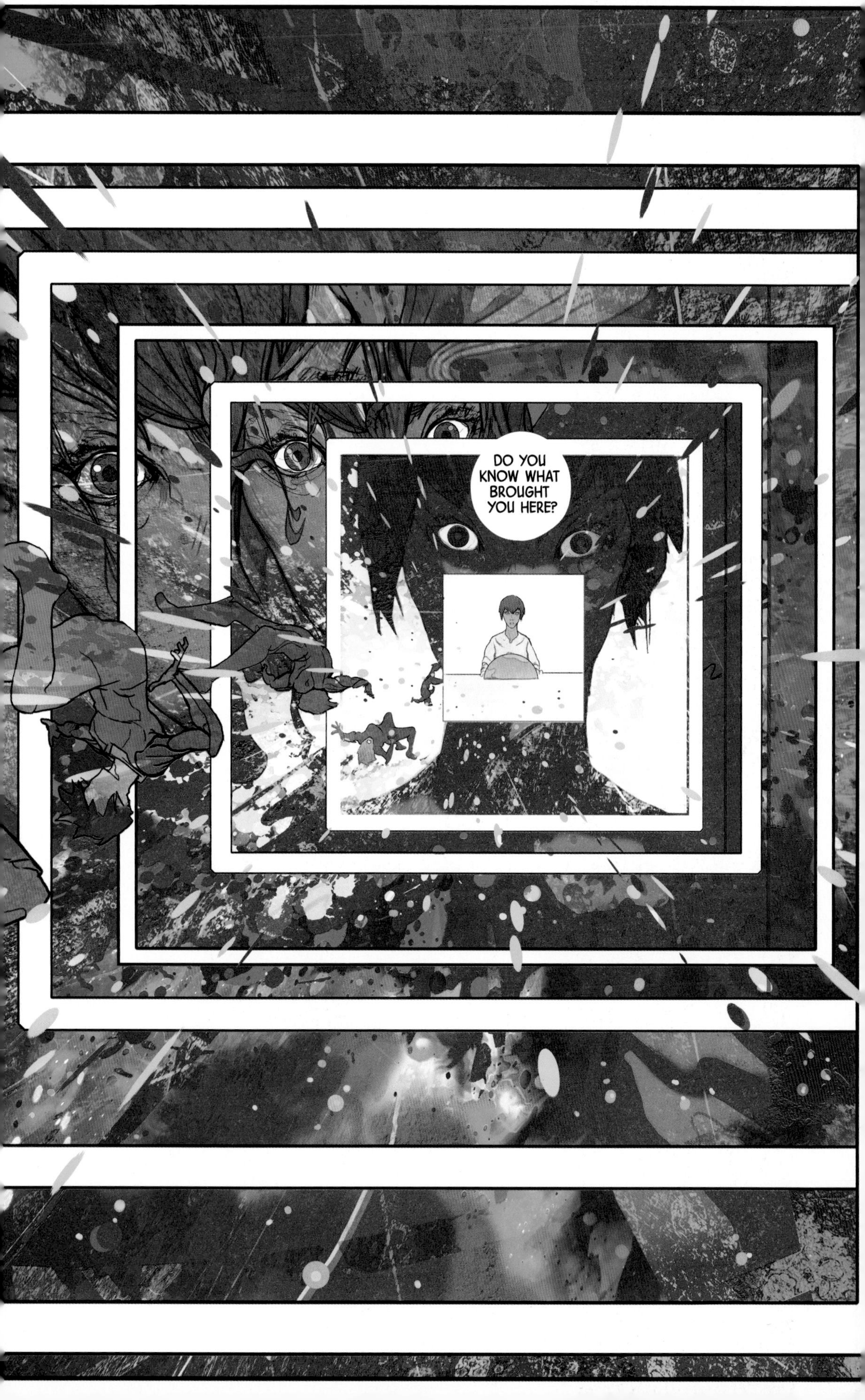
DO YOU KNOW WHAT BROUGHT YOU HERE?

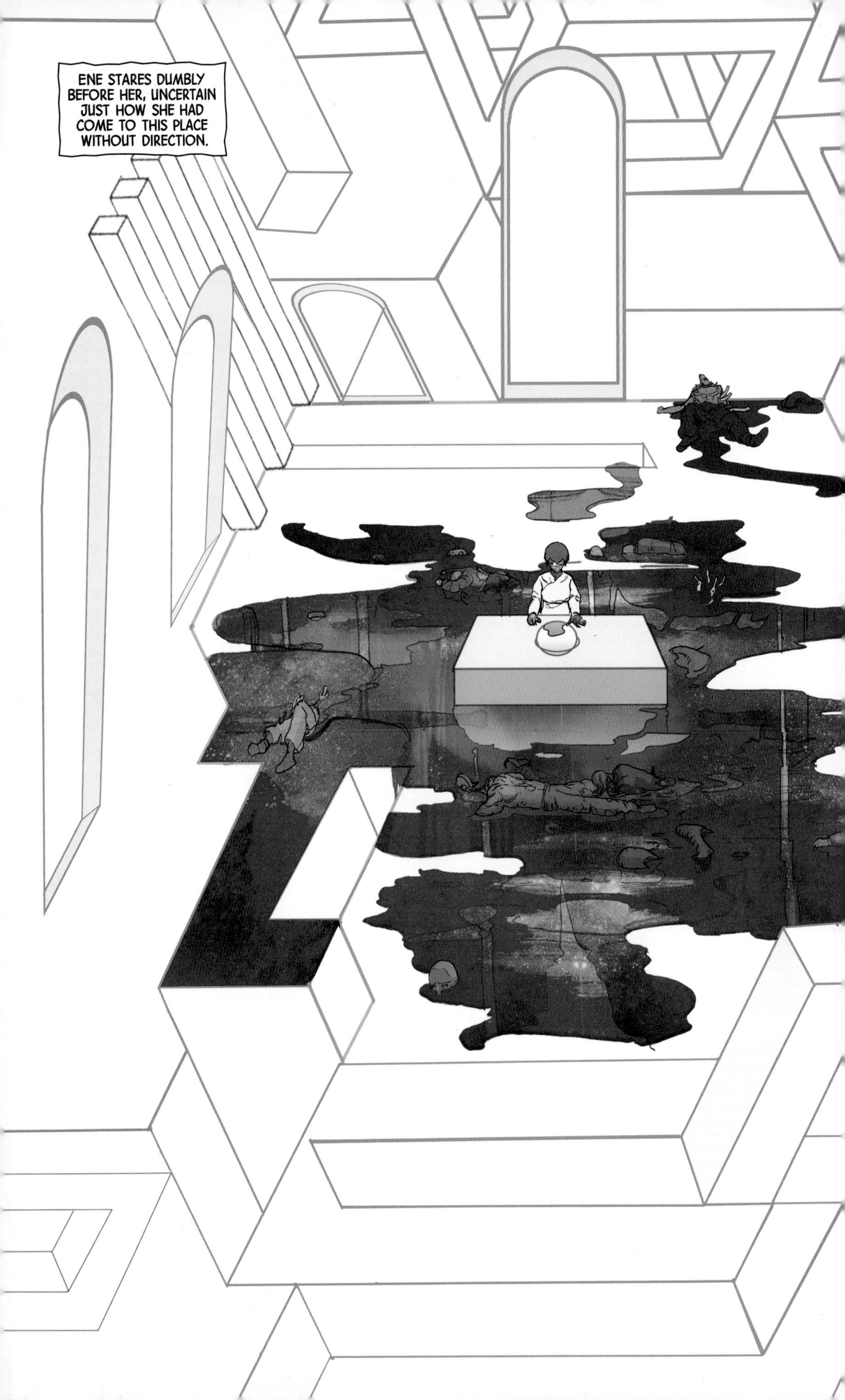
ENE STARES DUMBLY BEFORE HER, UNCERTAIN JUST HOW SHE HAD COME TO THIS PLACE WITHOUT DIRECTION.

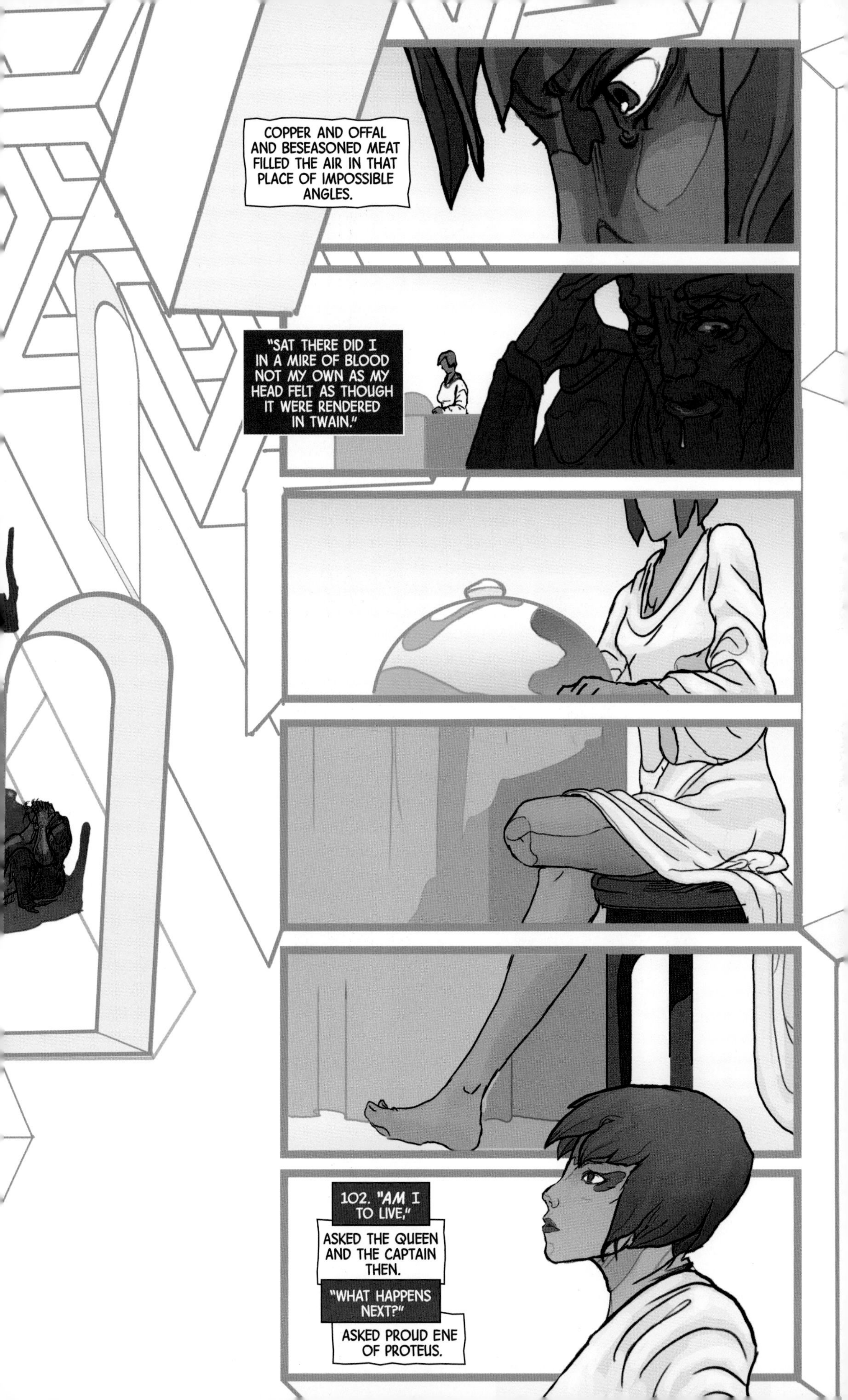
COPPER AND OFFAL AND BESEASONED MEAT FILLED THE AIR IN THAT PLACE OF IMPOSSIBLE ANGLES.
"SAT THERE DID I IN A MIRE OF BLOOD NOT MY OWN AS MY HEAD FELT AS THOUGH IT WERE RENDERED IN TWAIN."
102. "AM I TO LIVE,"
ASKED THE QUEEN AND THE CAPTAIN THEN.
"WHAT HAPPENS NEXT?"
ASKED PROUD ENE OF PROTEUS.

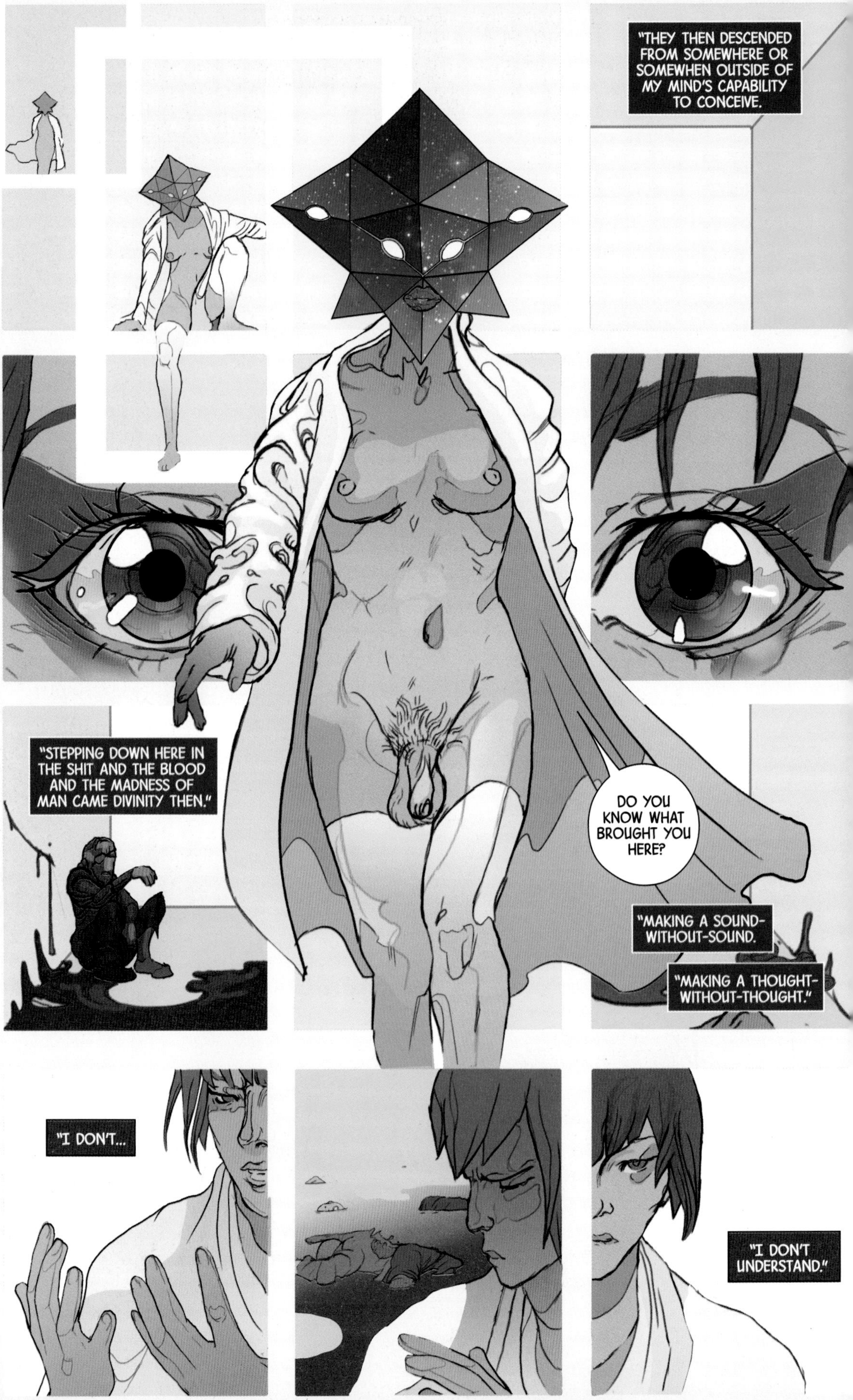
"THEY THEN DESCENDED FROM SOMEWHERE OR SOMEWHEN OUTSIDE OF MY MIND'S CAPABILITY TO CONCEIVE.
"STEPPING DOWN HERE IN THE SHIT AND THE BLOOD AND THE MADNESS OF MAN CAME DIVINITY THEN."
DO YOU KNOW WHAT BROUGHT YOU HERE?
"MAKING A SOUND-WITHOUT-SOUND.
"MAKING A THOUGHT-WITHOUT-THOUGHT."
"I DON'T...
"I DON'T UNDERSTAND."

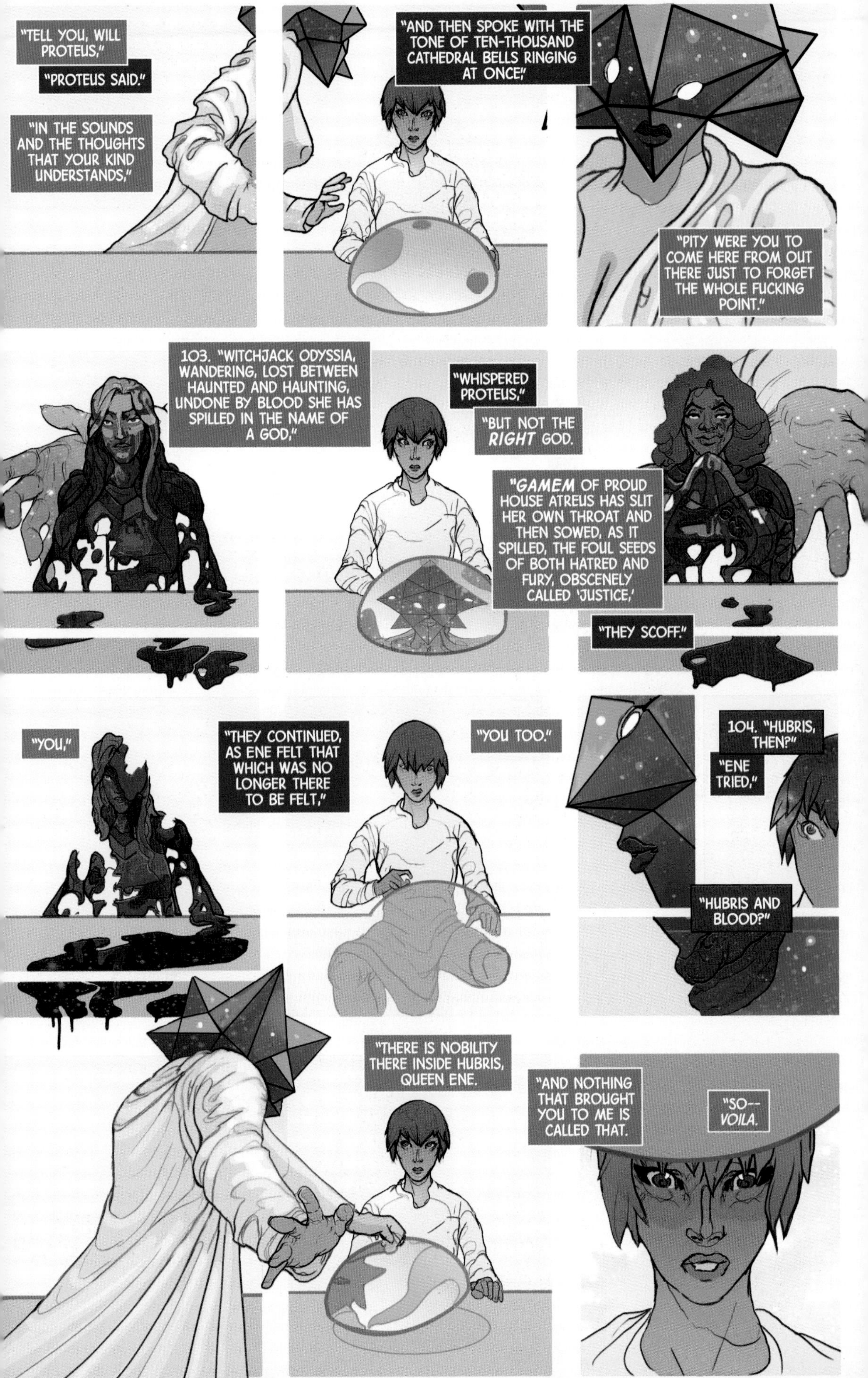
"TELL YOU, WILL PROTEUS,"
"PROTEUS SAID."
"IN THE SOUNDS AND THE THOUGHTS THAT YOUR KIND UNDERSTANDS,"
"AND THEN SPOKE WITH THE TONE OF TEN-THOUSAND CATHEDRAL BELLS RINGING AT ONCE."
"PITY WERE YOU TO COME HERE FROM OUT THERE JUST TO FORGET THE WHOLE FUCKING POINT."
103. "WITCHJACK ODYSSIA, WANDERING, LOST BETWEEN HAUNTED AND HAUNTING, UNDONE BY BLOOD SHE HAS SPILLED IN THE NAME OF A GOD,"
"WHISPERED PROTEUS,"
"BUT NOT THE *RIGHT* GOD.
"*GAMEM* OF PROUD HOUSE ATREUS HAS SLIT HER OWN THROAT AND THEN SOWED, AS IT SPILLED, THE FOUL SEEDS OF BOTH HATRED AND FURY, OBSCENELY CALLED 'JUSTICE,'
"THEY SCOFF."
"YOU,"
"THEY CONTINUED, AS ENE FELT THAT WHICH WAS NO LONGER THERE TO BE FELT,"
"YOU TOO."
104. "HUBRIS, THEN?"
"ENE TRIED,"
"HUBRIS AND BLOOD?"
"THERE IS NOBILITY THERE INSIDE HUBRIS, QUEEN ENE.
"AND NOTHING THAT BROUGHT YOU TO ME IS CALLED THAT.
"SO-- *VOILA.*

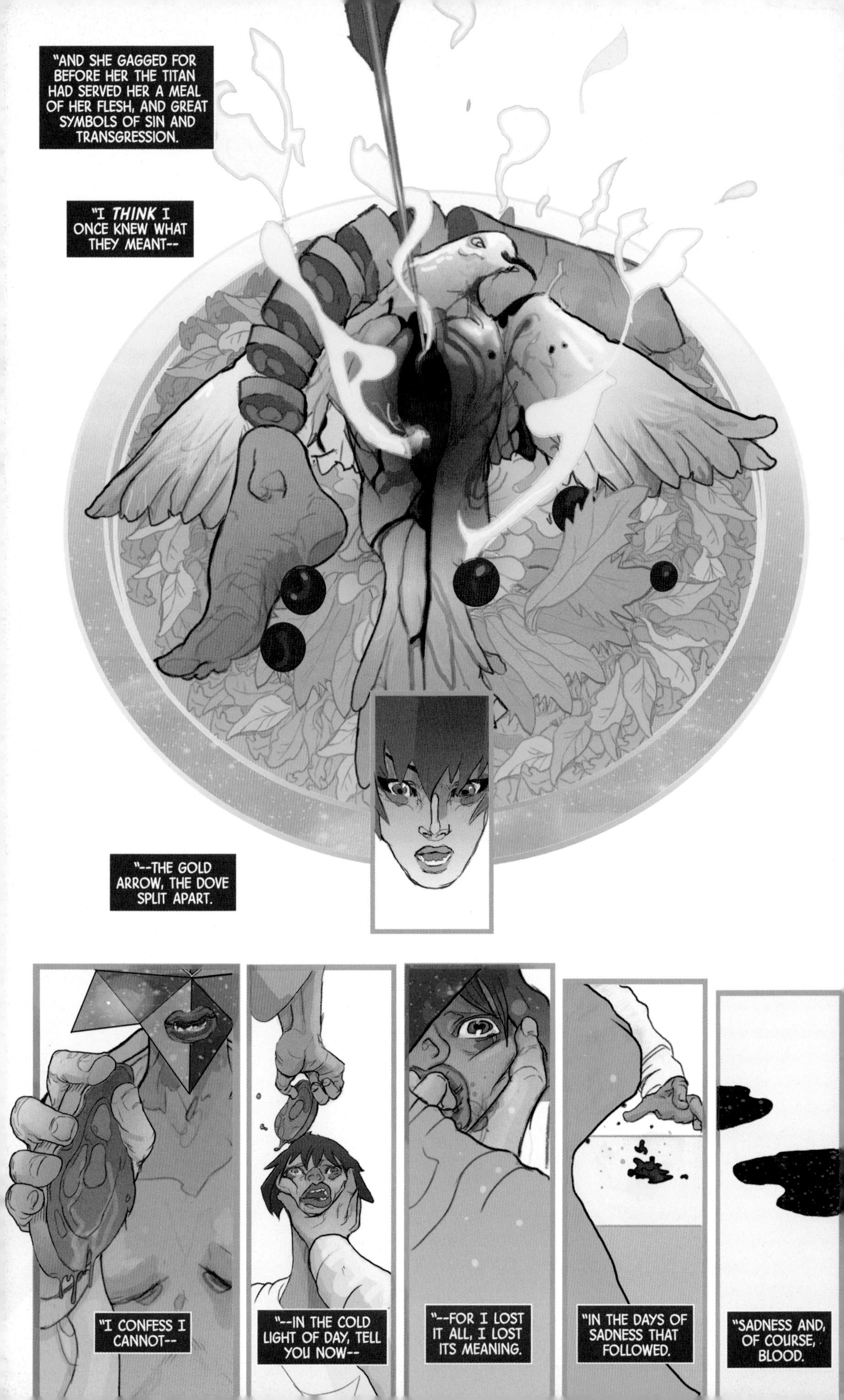
"AND SHE GAGGED FOR BEFORE HER THE TITAN HAD SERVED HER A MEAL OF HER FLESH, AND GREAT SYMBOLS OF SIN AND TRANSGRESSION.
"I *THINK* I ONCE KNEW WHAT THEY MEANT--
"--THE GOLD ARROW, THE DOVE SPLIT APART.
"I CONFESS I CANNOT--
"--IN THE COLD LIGHT OF DAY, TELL YOU NOW--
"--FOR I LOST IT ALL, I LOST ITS MEANING.
"IN THE DAYS OF SADNESS THAT FOLLOWED.
"SADNESS AND, OF COURSE, BLOOD.

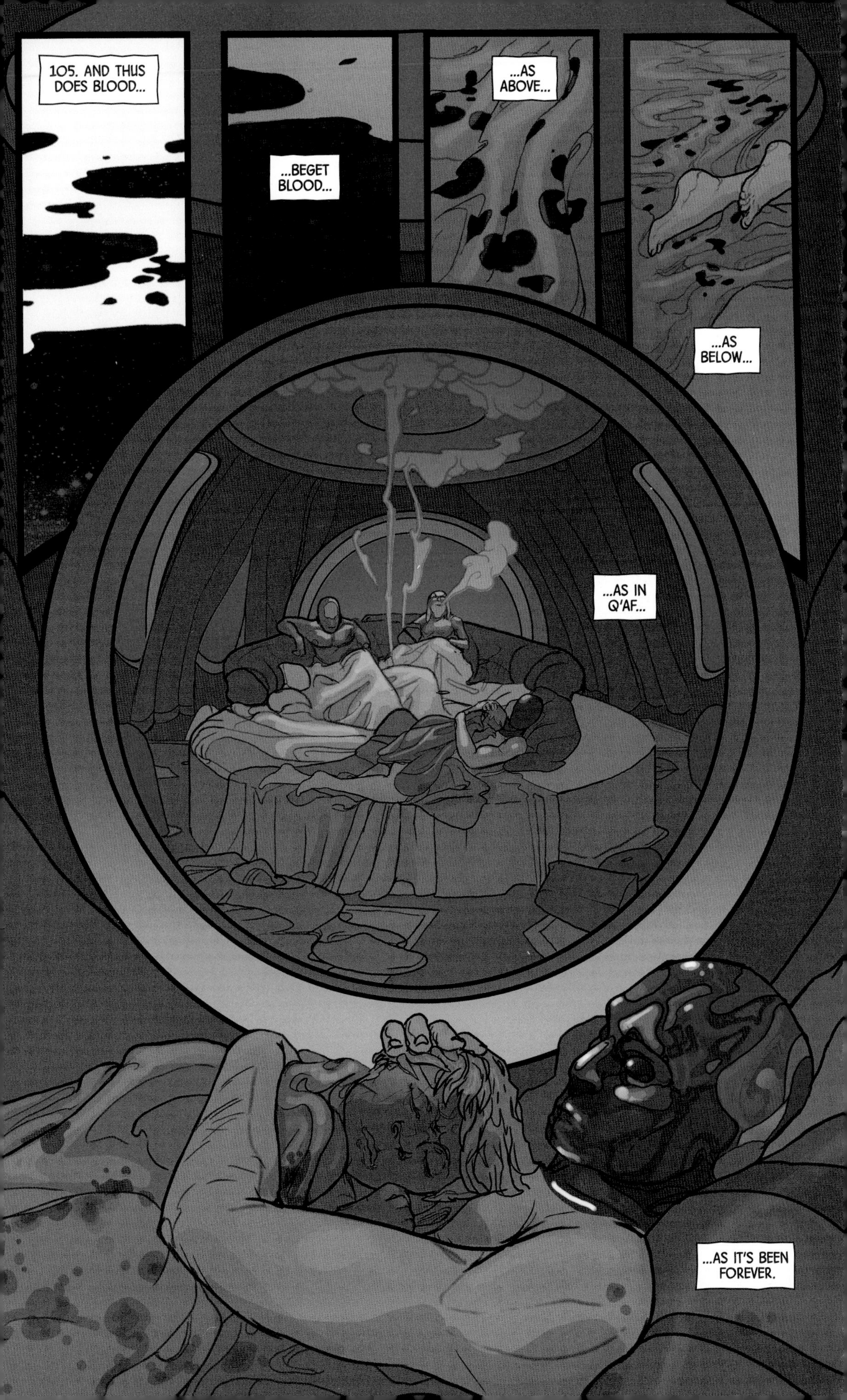
105. AND THUS DOES BLOOD...
...BEGET BLOOD...
...AS ABOVE...
...AS BELOW...
...AS IN Q'AF...
...AS IT'S BEEN FOREVER.

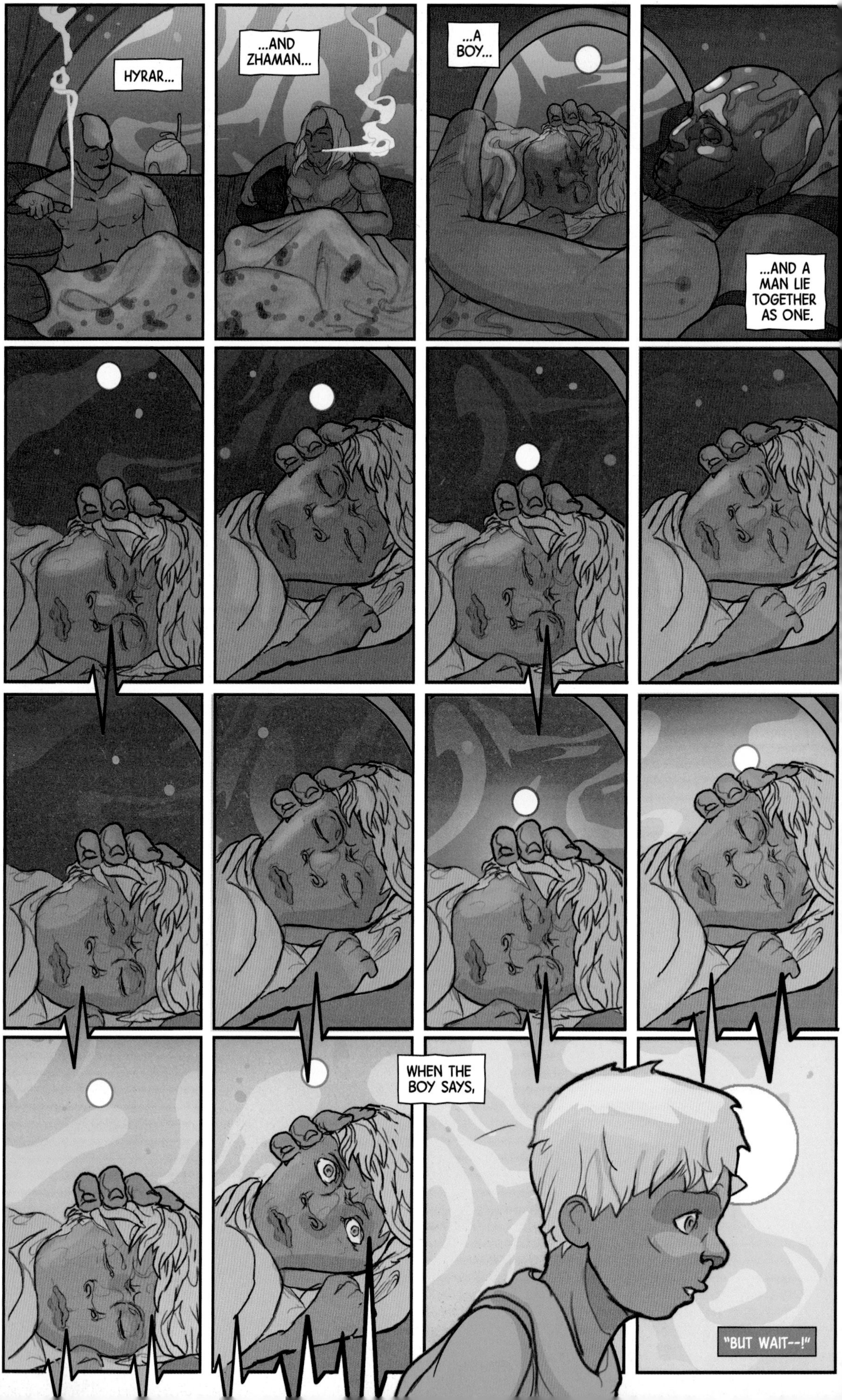
HYRAR...
...AND ZHAMAN...
...A BOY...
...AND A MAN LIE TOGETHER AS ONE.
WHEN THE BOY SAYS,
"BUT WAIT--!"

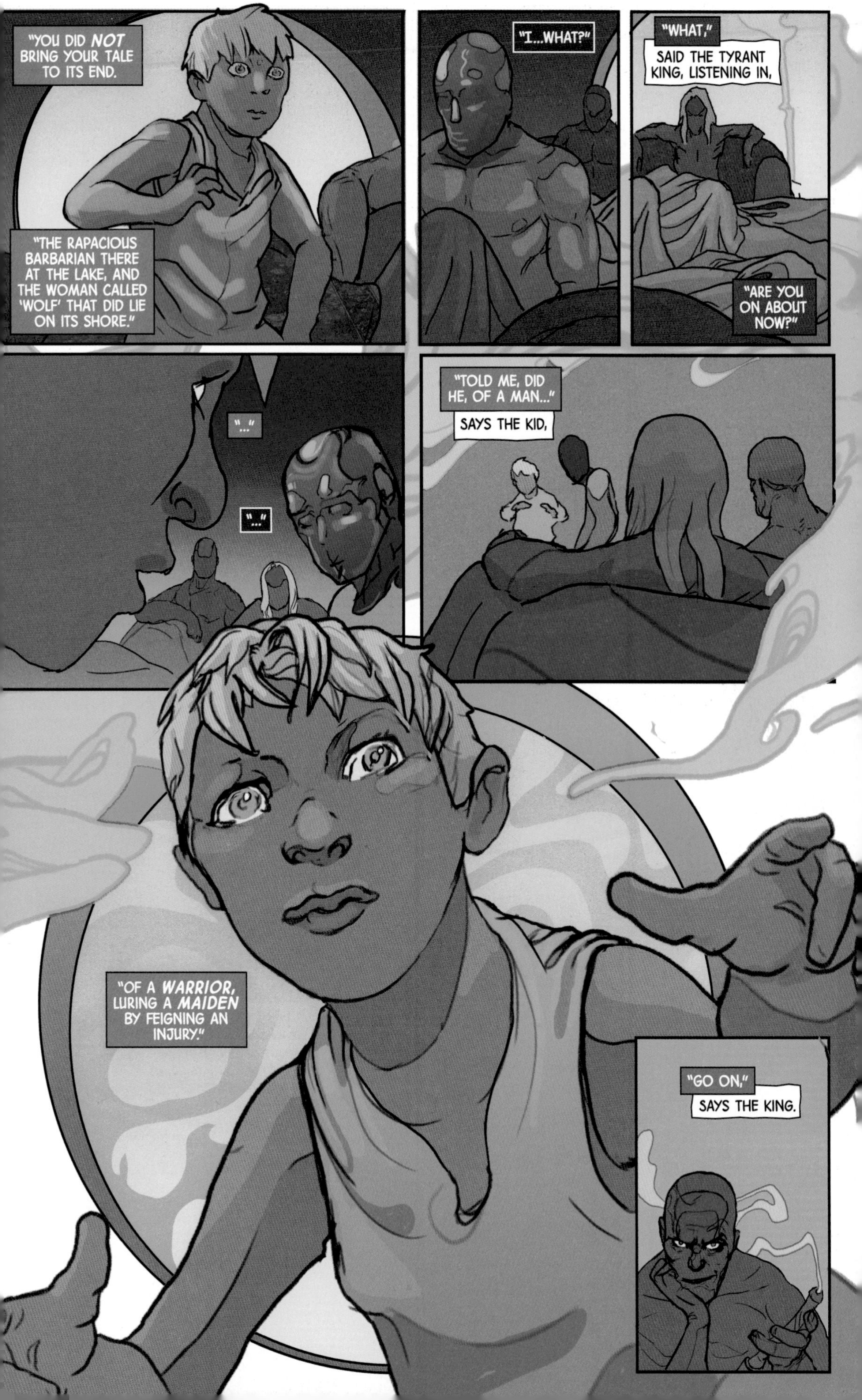
"YOU DID NOT BRING YOUR TALE TO ITS END.
"THE RAPACIOUS BARBARIAN THERE AT THE LAKE, AND THE WOMAN CALLED 'WOLF' THAT DID LIE ON ITS SHORE."
"I...WHAT?"
"WHAT,"
SAID THE TYRANT KING, LISTENING IN,
"ARE YOU ON ABOUT NOW?"
"..."
"..."
"TOLD ME, DID HE, OF A MAN..."
SAYS THE KID,
"OF A WARRIOR, LURING A MAIDEN BY FEIGNING AN INJURY."
"GO ON,"
SAYS THE KING.

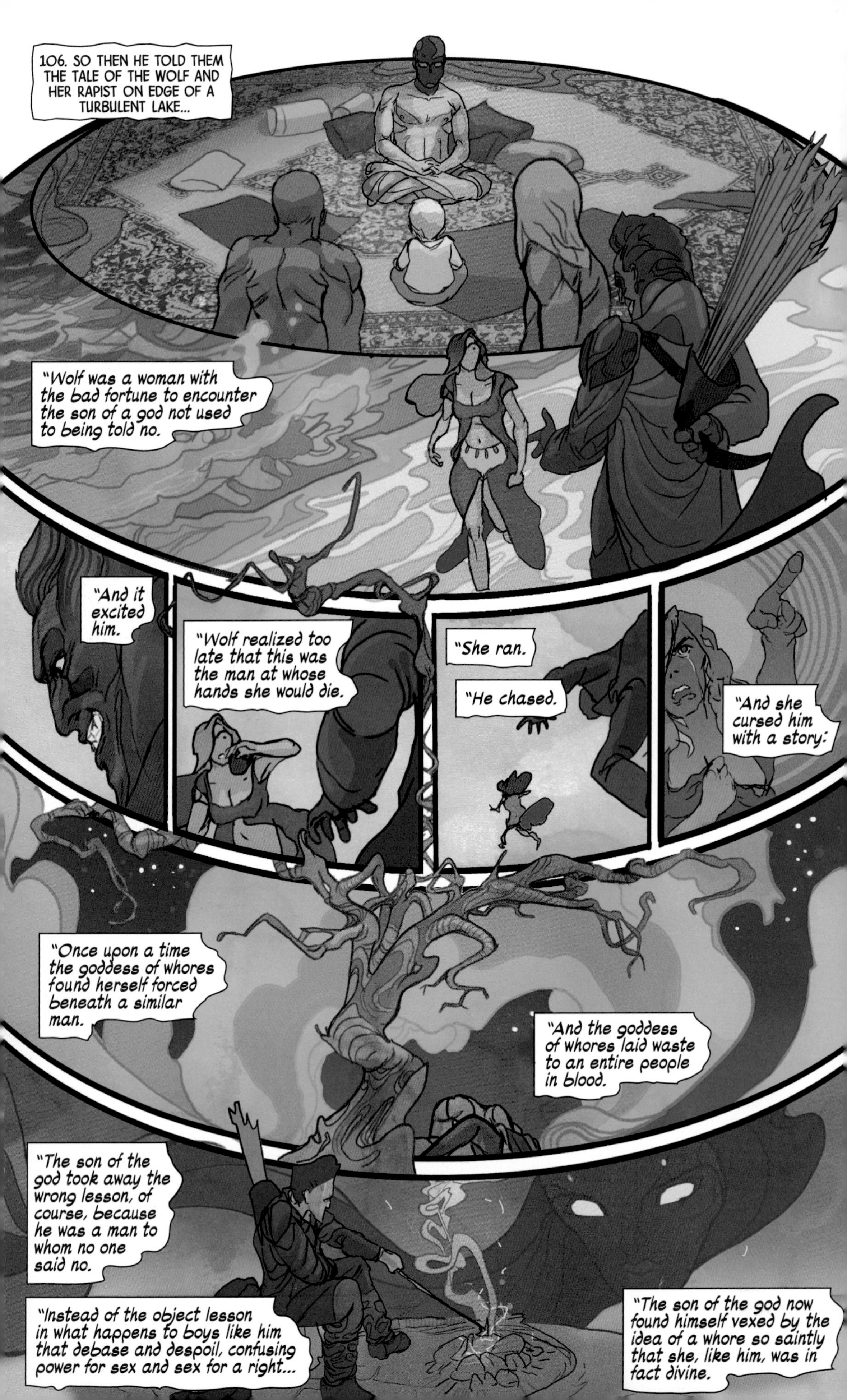
106. SO THEN HE TOLD THEM THE TALE OF THE WOLF AND HER RAPIST ON EDGE OF A TURBULENT LAKE...
"Wolf was a woman with the bad fortune to encounter the son of a god not used to being told no.
"And it excited him.
"Wolf realized too late that this was the man at whose hands she would die.
"She ran.
"He chased.
"And she cursed him with a story:
"Once upon a time the goddess of whores found herself forced beneath a similar man.
"And the goddess of whores laid waste to an entire people in blood.
"The son of the god took away the wrong lesson, of course, because he was a man to whom no one said no.
"Instead of the object lesson in what happens to boys like him that debase and despoil, confusing power for sex and sex for a right...
"The son of the god now found himself vexed by the idea of a whore so saintly that she, like him, was in fact divine.

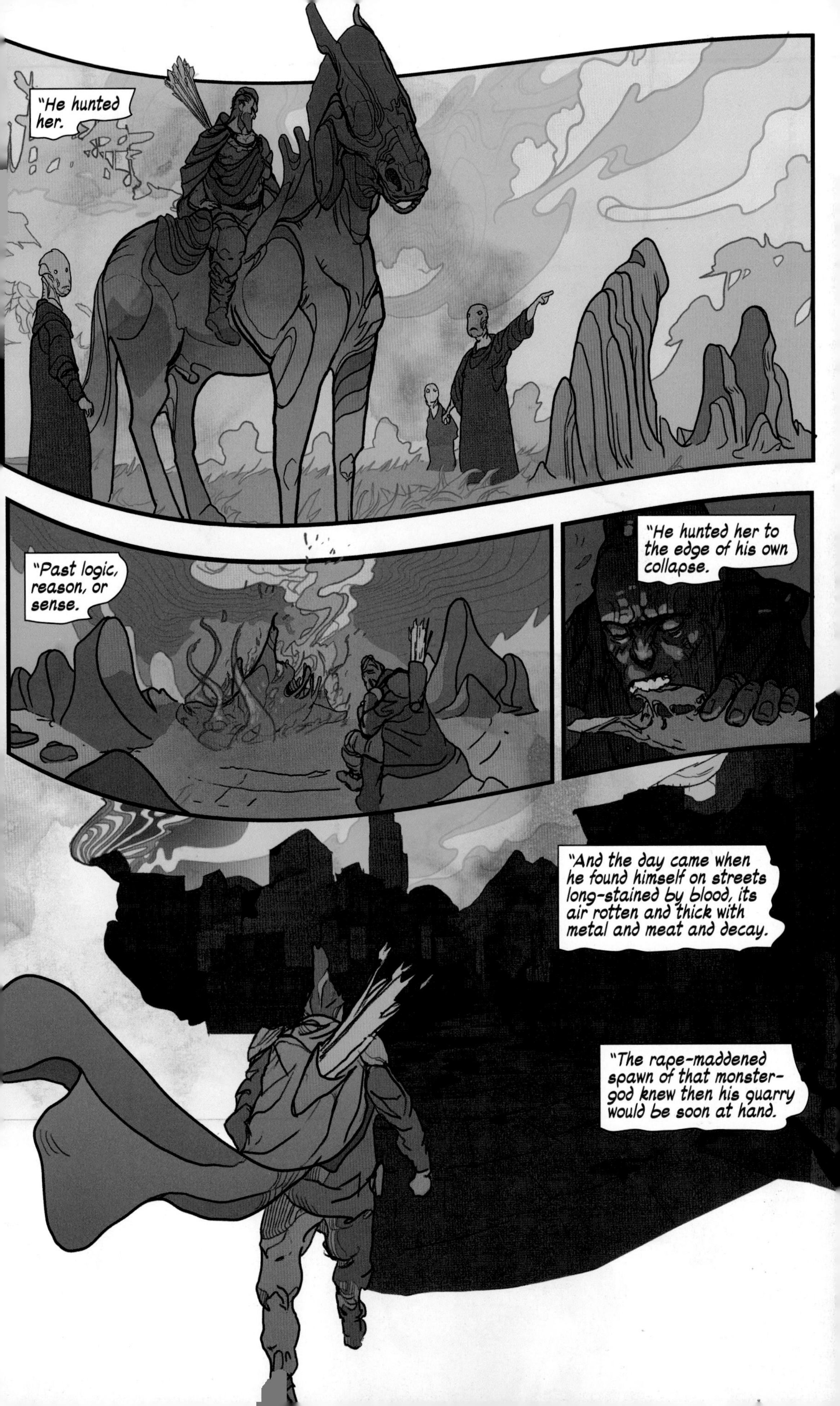
"He hunted her.
"Past logic, reason, or sense.
"He hunted her to the edge of his own collapse.
"And the day came when he found himself on streets long-stained by blood, its air rotten and thick with metal and meat and decay.
"The rape-maddened spawn of that monster-god knew then his quarry would be soon at hand.

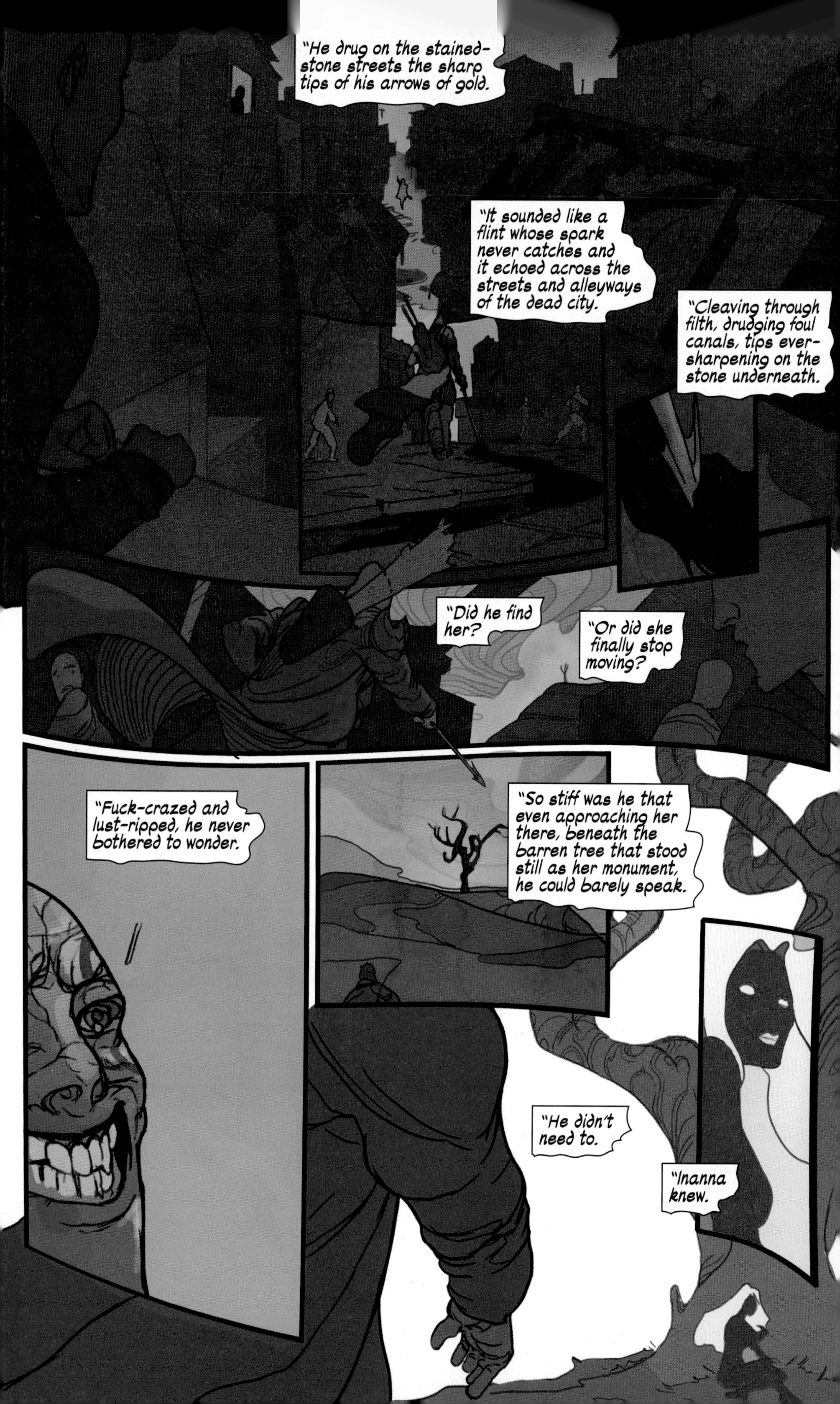
"He drug on the stained-stone streets the sharp tips of his arrows of gold.
"It sounded like a flint whose spark never catches and it echoed across the streets and alleyways of the dead city.
"Cleaving through filth, drudging foul canals, tips ever-sharpening on the stone underneath.
"Did he find her?
"Or did she finally stop moving?
"Fuck-crazed and lust-ripped, he never bothered to wonder.
"So stiff was he that even approaching her there, beneath the barren tree that stood still as her monument, he could barely speak.
"He didn't need to.
"Inanna knew.

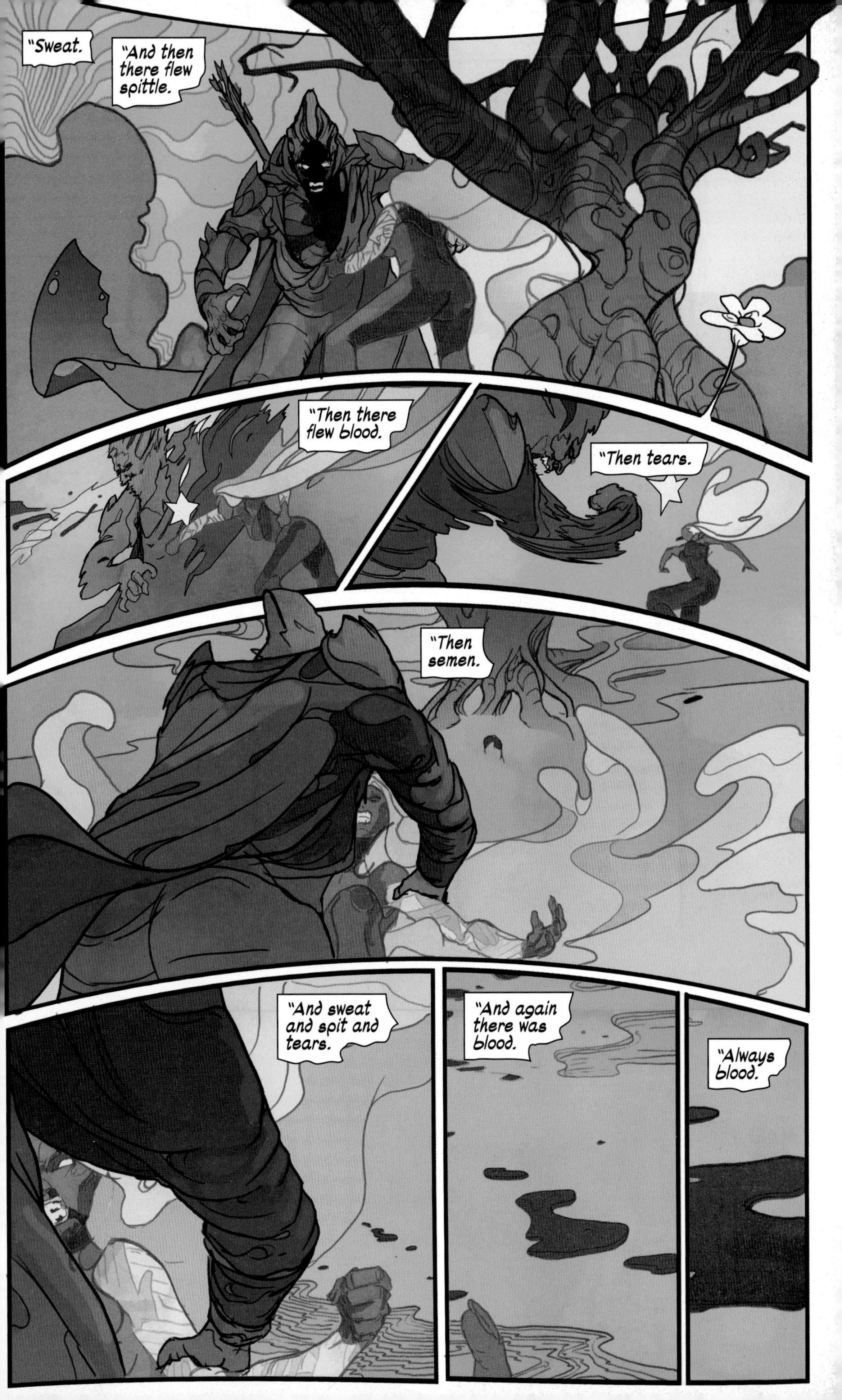
"Sweat.
"And then there flew spittle.
"Then there flew blood.
"Then tears.
"Then semen.
"And sweat and spit and tears.
"And again there was blood.
"Always blood.

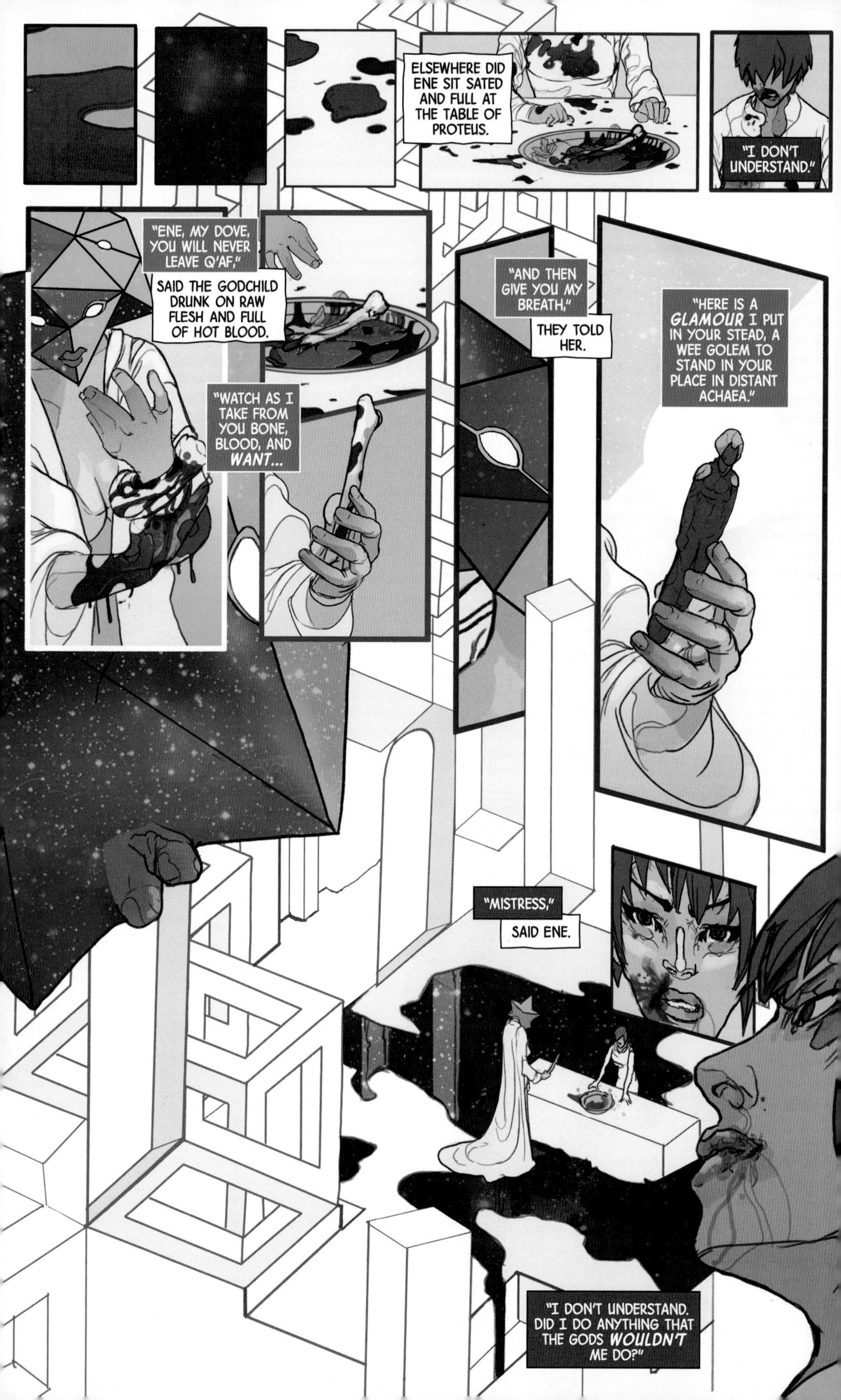
ELSEWHERE DID ENE SIT SATED AND FULL AT THE TABLE OF PROTEUS.
"I DON'T UNDERSTAND."
"ENE, MY DOVE, YOU WILL NEVER LEAVE Q'AF,"
SAID THE GODCHILD DRUNK ON RAW FLESH AND FULL OF HOT BLOOD.
"WATCH AS I TAKE FROM YOU BONE, BLOOD, AND WANT...
"AND THEN GIVE YOU MY BREATH,"
THEY TOLD HER.
"HERE IS A GLAMOUR I PUT IN YOUR STEAD, A WEE GOLEM TO STAND IN YOUR PLACE IN DISTANT ACHAEA."
"MISTRESS,"
SAID ENE.
"I DON'T UNDERSTAND. DID I DO ANYTHING THAT THE GODS WOULDN'T ME DO?"

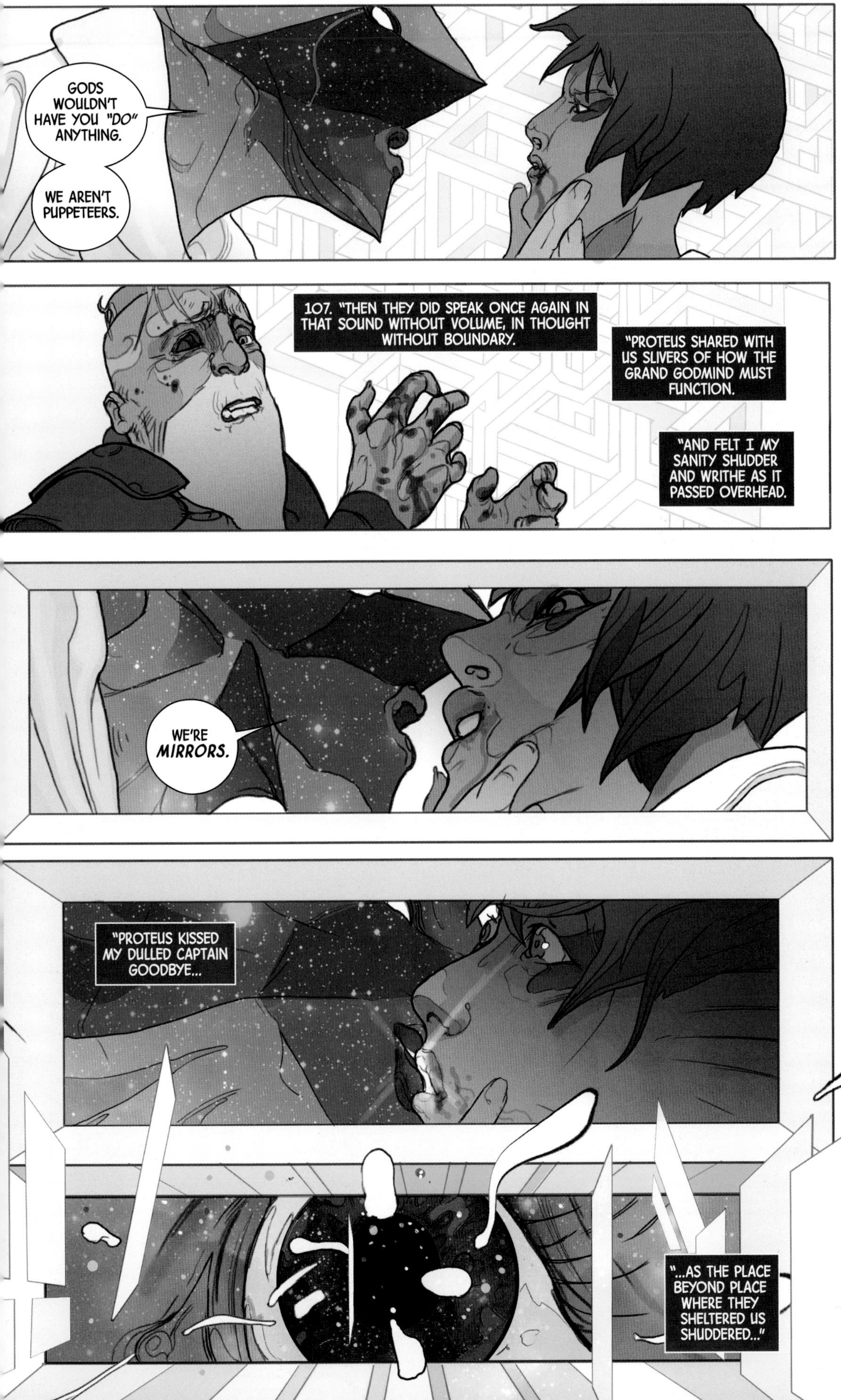
GODS WOULDN'T HAVE YOU "DO" ANYTHING.
WE AREN'T PUPPETEERS.
107. "THEN THEY DID SPEAK ONCE AGAIN IN THAT SOUND WITHOUT VOLUME, IN THOUGHT WITHOUT BOUNDARY.
"PROTEUS SHARED WITH US SLIVERS OF HOW THE GRAND GODMIND MUST FUNCTION.
"AND FELT I MY SANITY SHUDDER AND WRITHE AS IT PASSED OVERHEAD.
WE'RE MIRRORS.
"PROTEUS KISSED MY DULLED CAPTAIN GOODBYE...
"...AS THE PLACE BEYOND PLACE WHERE THEY SHELTERED US SHUDDERED..."

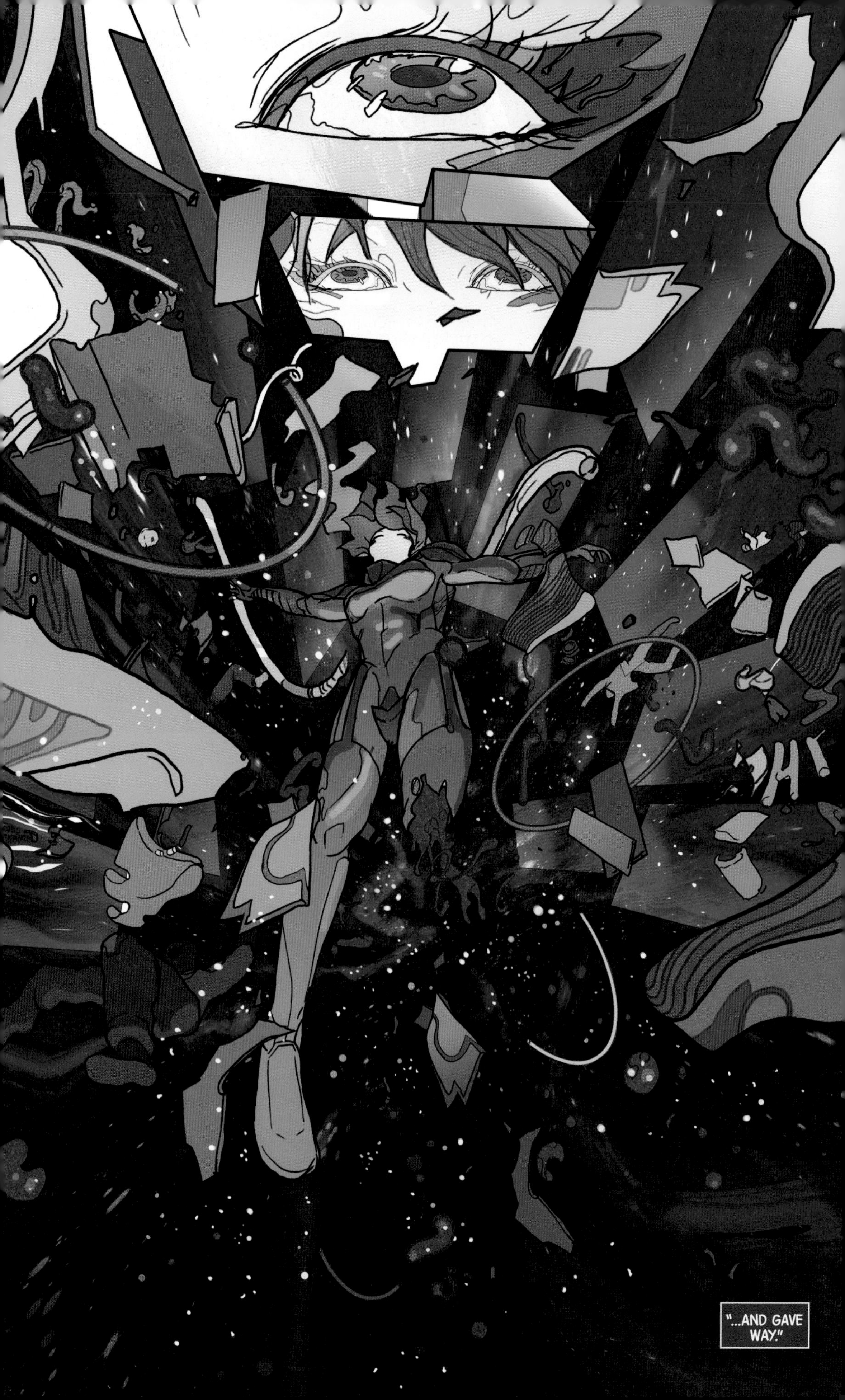
"...AND GAVE WAY."

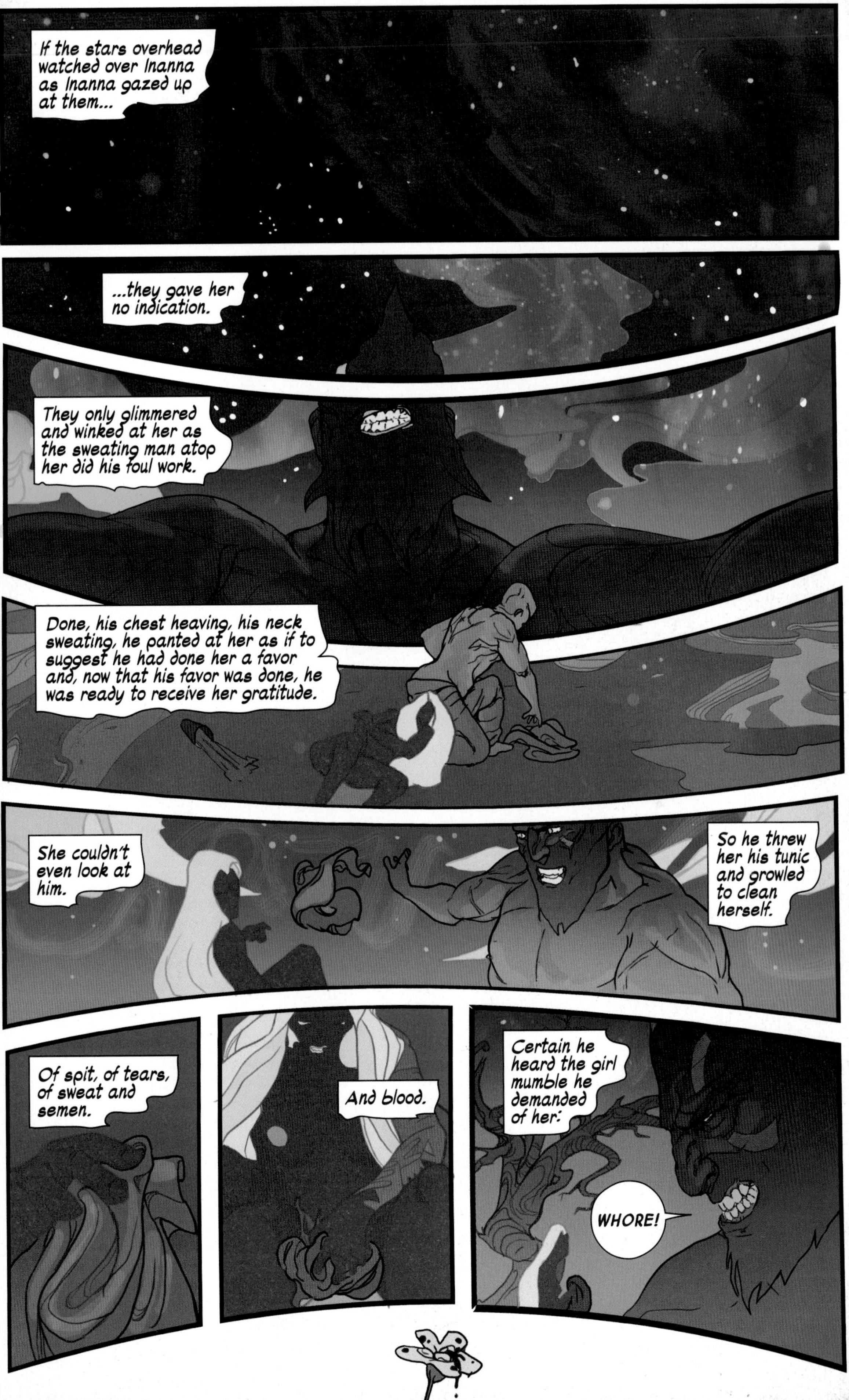
If the stars overhead watched over Inanna as Inanna gazed up at them...
...they gave her no indication.
They only glimmered and winked at her as the sweating man atop her did his foul work.
Done, his chest heaving, his neck sweating, he panted at her as if to suggest he had done her a favor and, now that his favor was done, he was ready to receive her gratitude.
She couldn't even look at him.
So he threw her his tunic and growled to clean herself.
Of spit, of tears, of sweat and semen.
And blood.
Certain he heard the girl mumble he demanded of her:
WHORE!

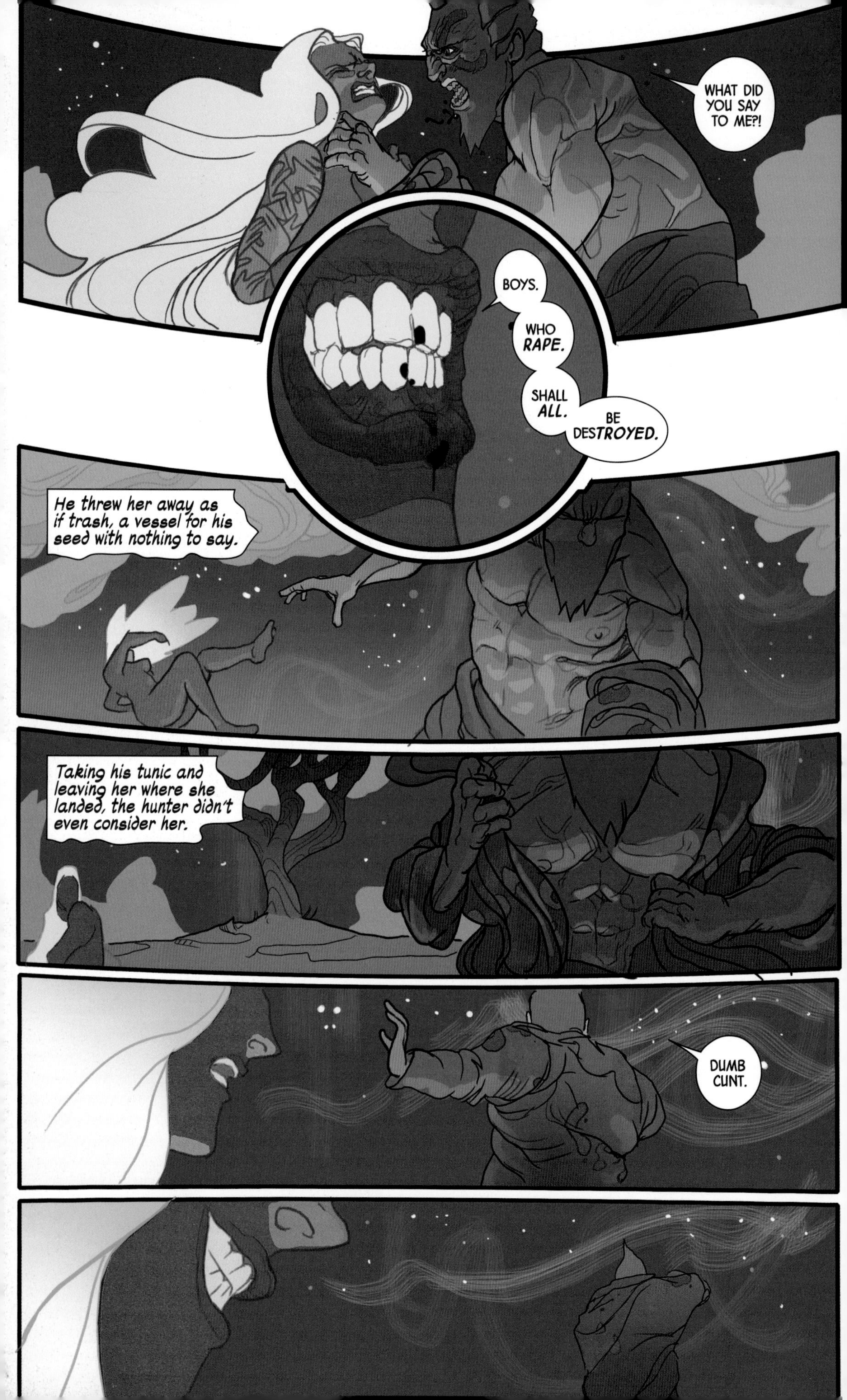
WHAT DID YOU SAY TO ME?!
BOYS.
WHO RAPE.
SHALL ALL.
BE DESTROYED.
He threw her away as if trash, a vessel for his seed with nothing to say.
Taking his tunic and leaving her where she landed, the hunter didn't even consider her.
DUMB CUNT.

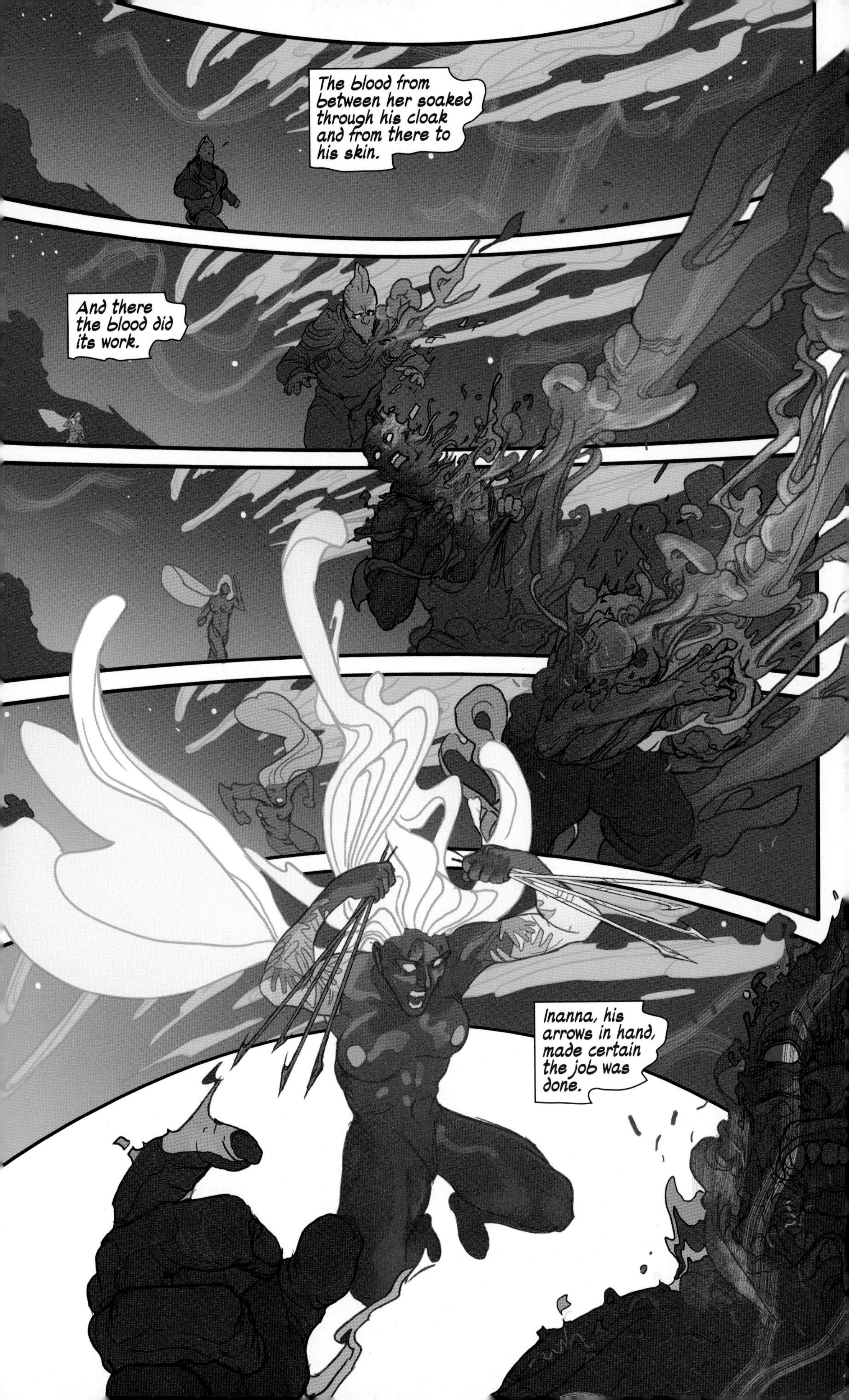
The blood from between her soaked through his cloak and from there to his skin.
And there the blood did its work.
Inanna, his arrows in hand, made certain the job was done.

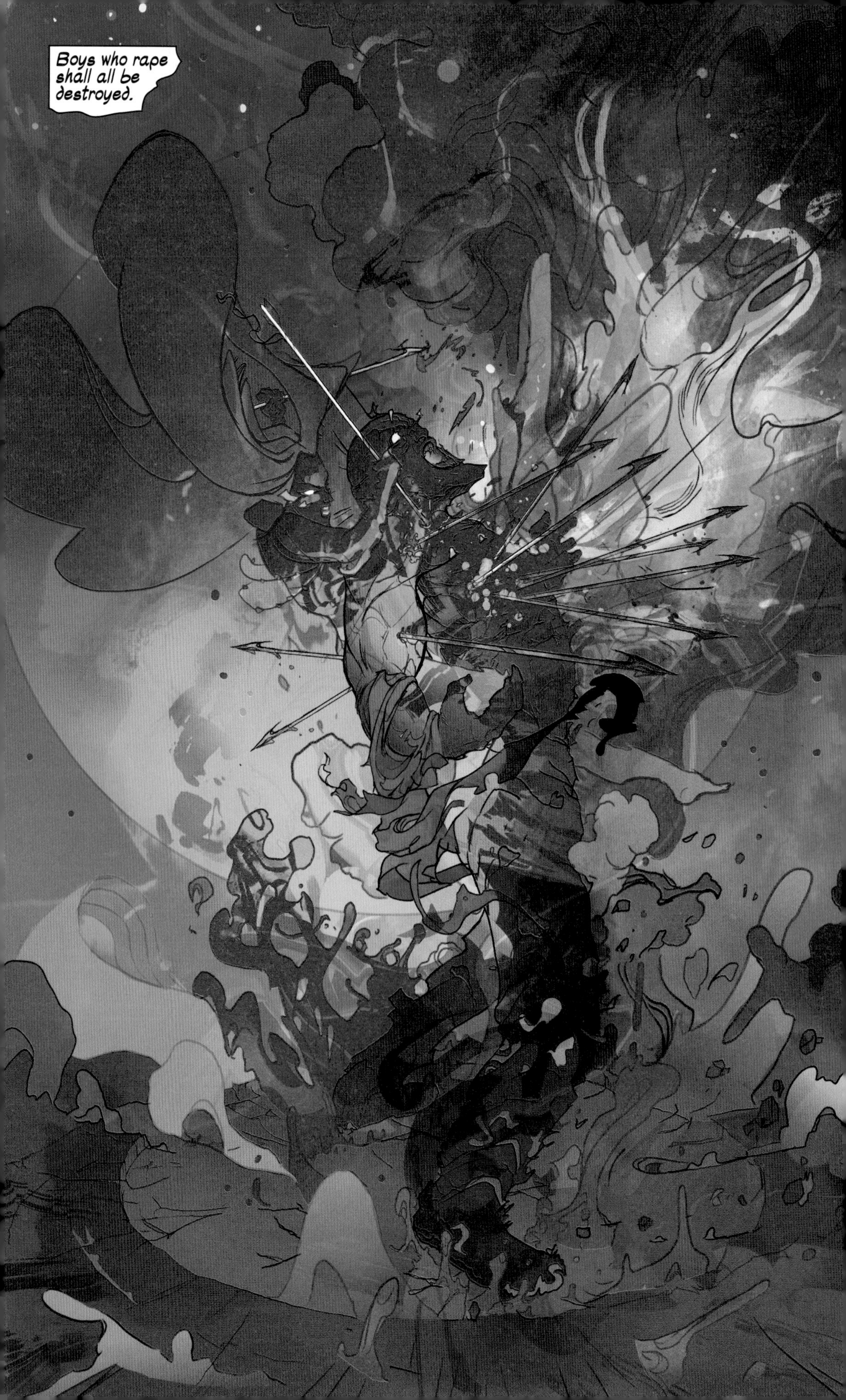
Boys who rape shall all be destroyed.

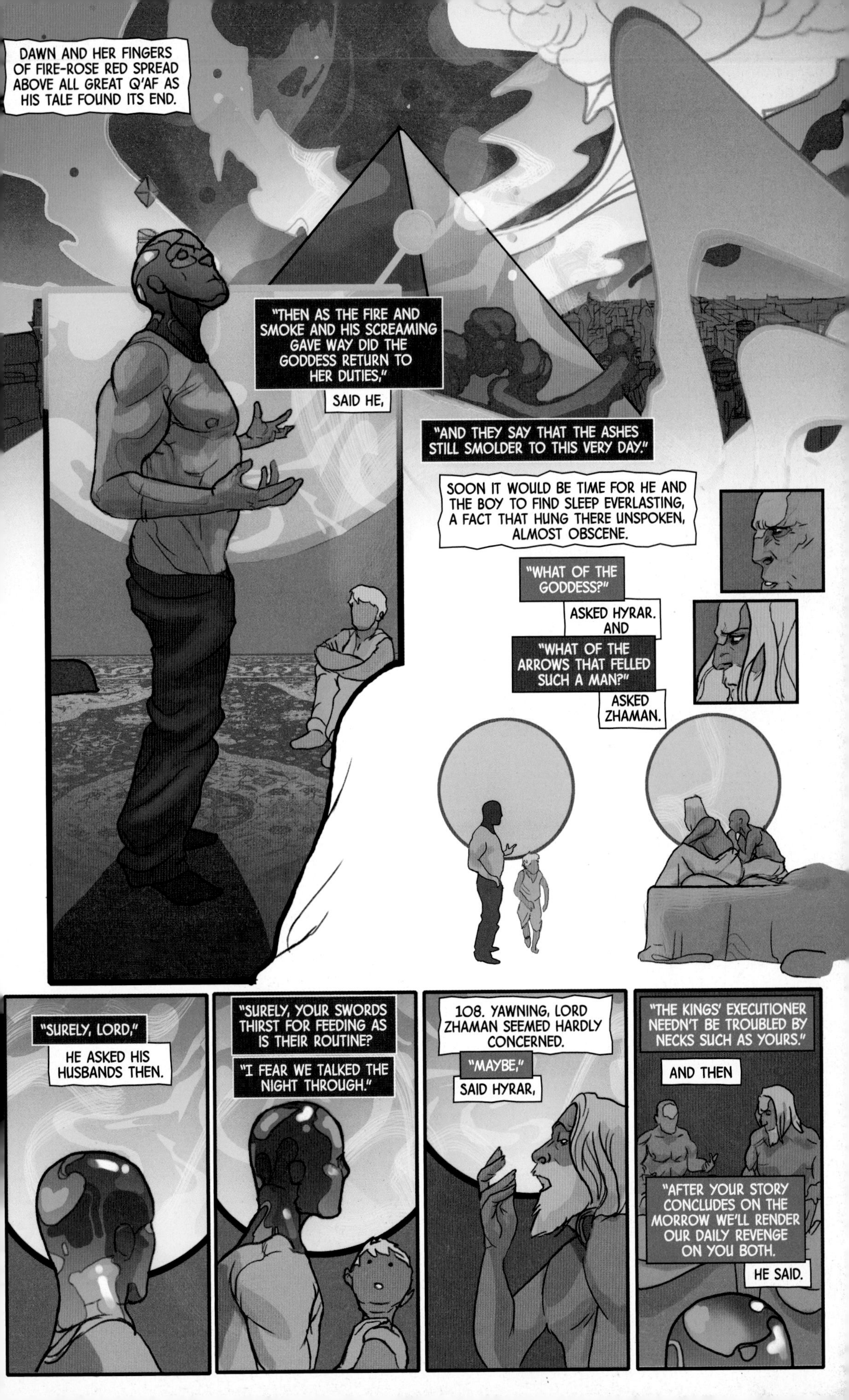
DAWN AND HER FINGERS OF FIRE-ROSE RED SPREAD ABOVE ALL GREAT Q'AF AS HIS TALE FOUND ITS END.
"THEN AS THE FIRE AND SMOKE AND HIS SCREAMING GAVE WAY DID THE GODDESS RETURN TO HER DUTIES,"
SAID HE,
"AND THEY SAY THAT THE ASHES STILL SMOLDER TO THIS VERY DAY."
SOON IT WOULD BE TIME FOR HE AND THE BOY TO FIND SLEEP EVERLASTING, A FACT THAT HUNG THERE UNSPOKEN, ALMOST OBSCENE.
"WHAT OF THE GODDESS?"
ASKED HYRAR. AND
"WHAT OF THE ARROWS THAT FELLED SUCH A MAN?"
ASKED ZHAMAN.
"SURELY, LORD,"
HE ASKED HIS HUSBANDS THEN.
"SURELY, YOUR SWORDS THIRST FOR FEEDING AS IS THEIR ROUTINE?
"I FEAR WE TALKED THE NIGHT THROUGH."
108. YAWNING, LORD ZHAMAN SEEMED HARDLY CONCERNED.
"MAYBE,"
SAID HYRAR,
"THE KINGS' EXECUTIONER NEEDN'T BE TROUBLED BY NECKS SUCH AS YOURS."
AND THEN
"AFTER YOUR STORY CONCLUDES ON THE MORROW WE'LL RENDER OUR DAILY REVENGE ON YOU BOTH.
HE SAID.

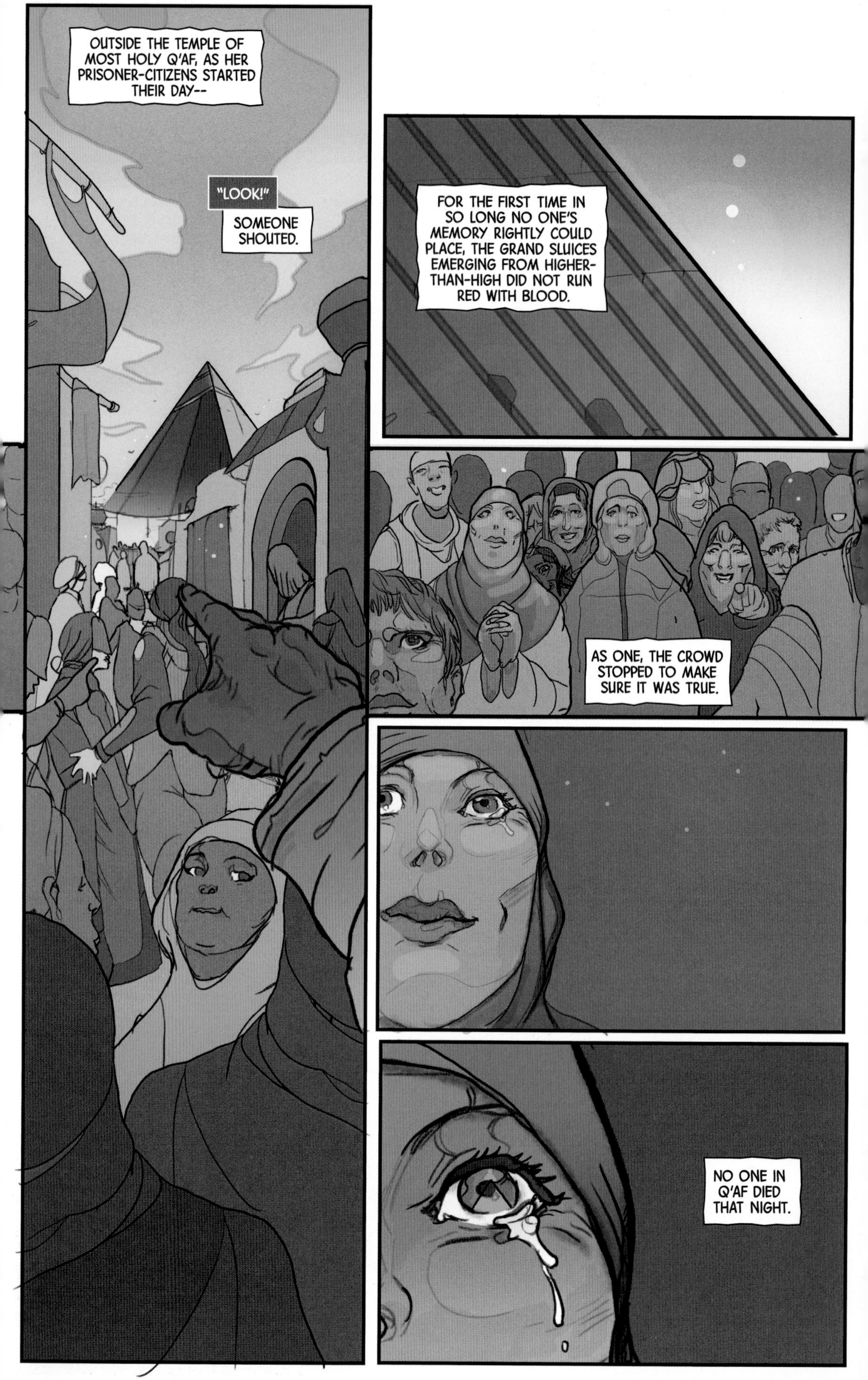
OUTSIDE THE TEMPLE OF MOST HOLY Q'AF, AS HER PRISONER-CITIZENS STARTED THEIR DAY--
"LOOK!"
SOMEONE SHOUTED.
FOR THE FIRST TIME IN SO LONG NO ONE'S MEMORY RIGHTLY COULD PLACE, THE GRAND SLUICES EMERGING FROM HIGHER-THAN-HIGH DID NOT RUN RED WITH BLOOD.
AS ONE, THE CROWD STOPPED TO MAKE SURE IT WAS TRUE.
NO ONE IN Q'AF DIED THAT NIGHT.

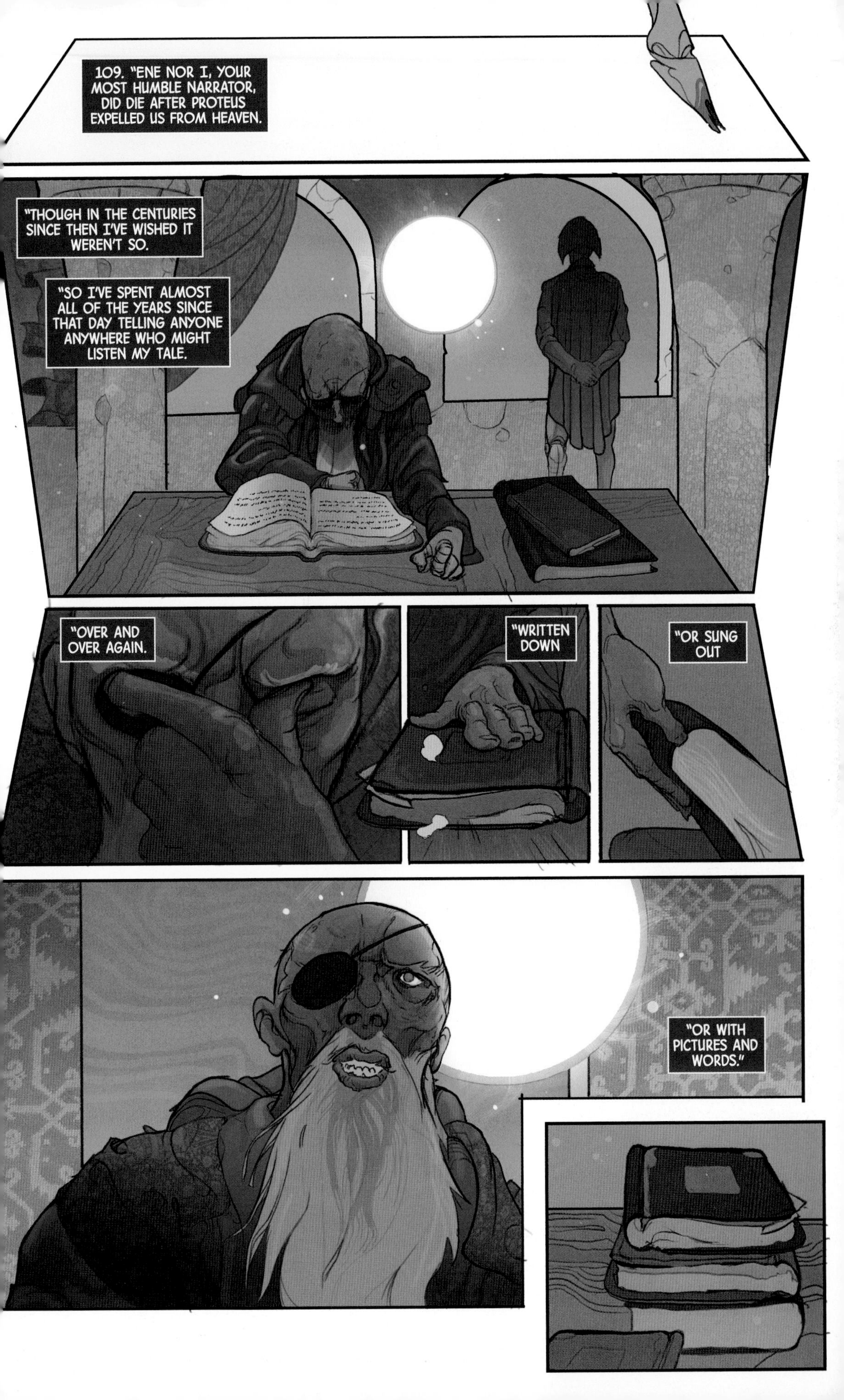
109. "ENE NOR I, YOUR MOST HUMBLE NARRATOR, DID DIE AFTER PROTEUS EXPELLED US FROM HEAVEN.
"THOUGH IN THE CENTURIES SINCE THEN I'VE WISHED IT WEREN'T SO.
"SO I'VE SPENT ALMOST ALL OF THE YEARS SINCE THAT DAY TELLING ANYONE ANYWHERE WHO MIGHT LISTEN MY TALE.
"OVER AND OVER AGAIN.
"WRITTEN DOWN
"OR SUNG OUT
"OR WITH PICTURES AND WORDS."

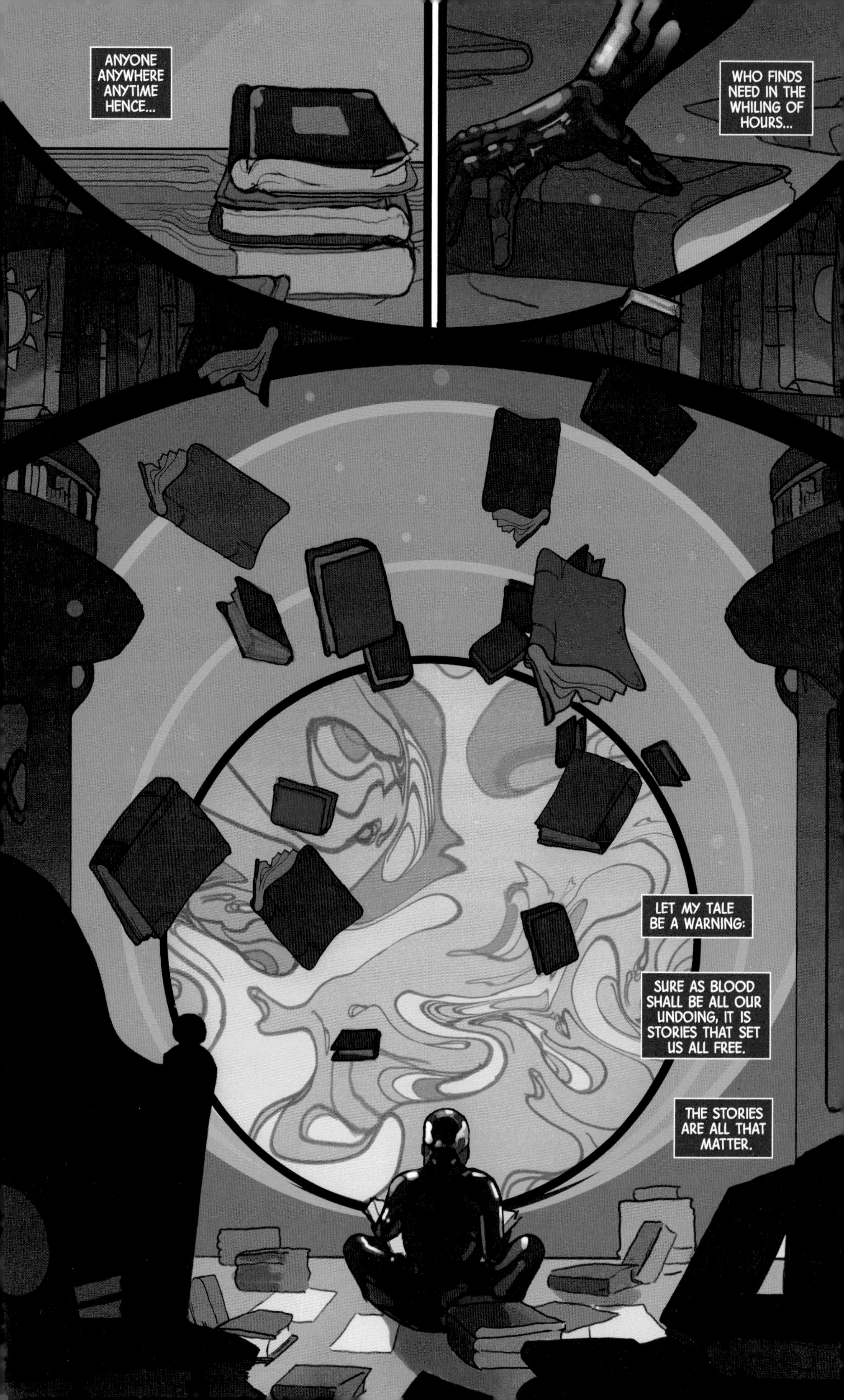
ANYONE ANYWHERE ANYTIME HENCE...
WHO FINDS NEED IN THE WHILING OF HOURS...
LET MY TALE BE A WARNING:
SURE AS BLOOD SHALL BE ALL OUR UNDOING, IT IS STORIES THAT SET US ALL FREE.
THE STORIES ARE ALL THAT MATTER.

PROCESS

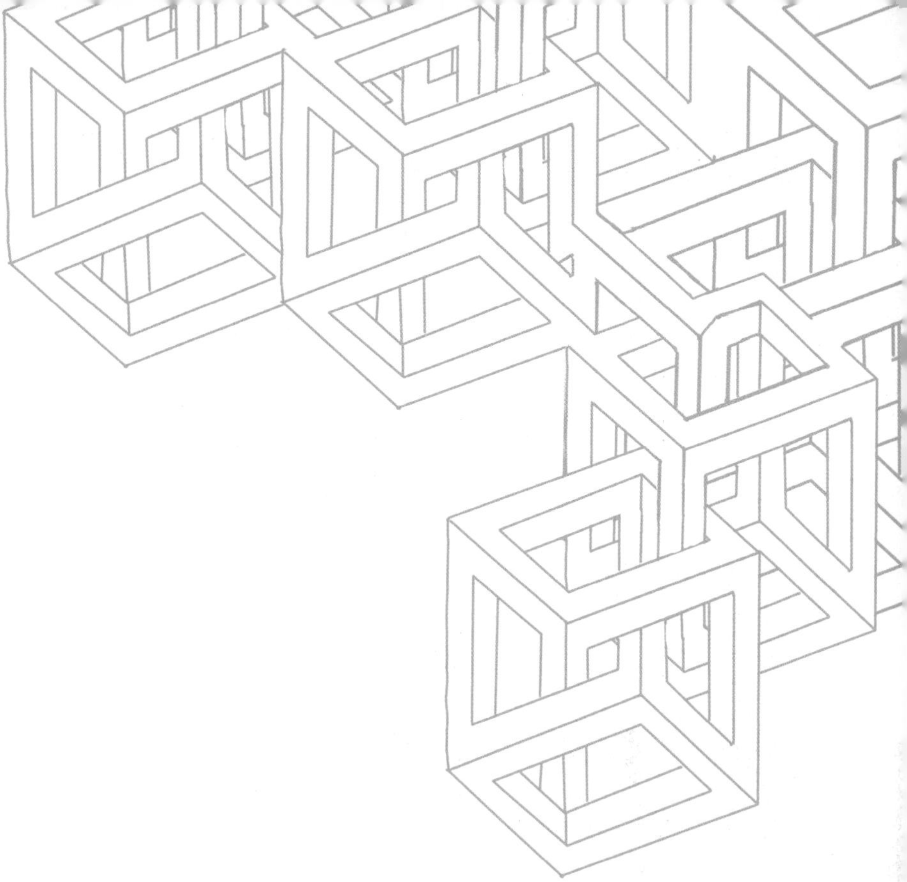

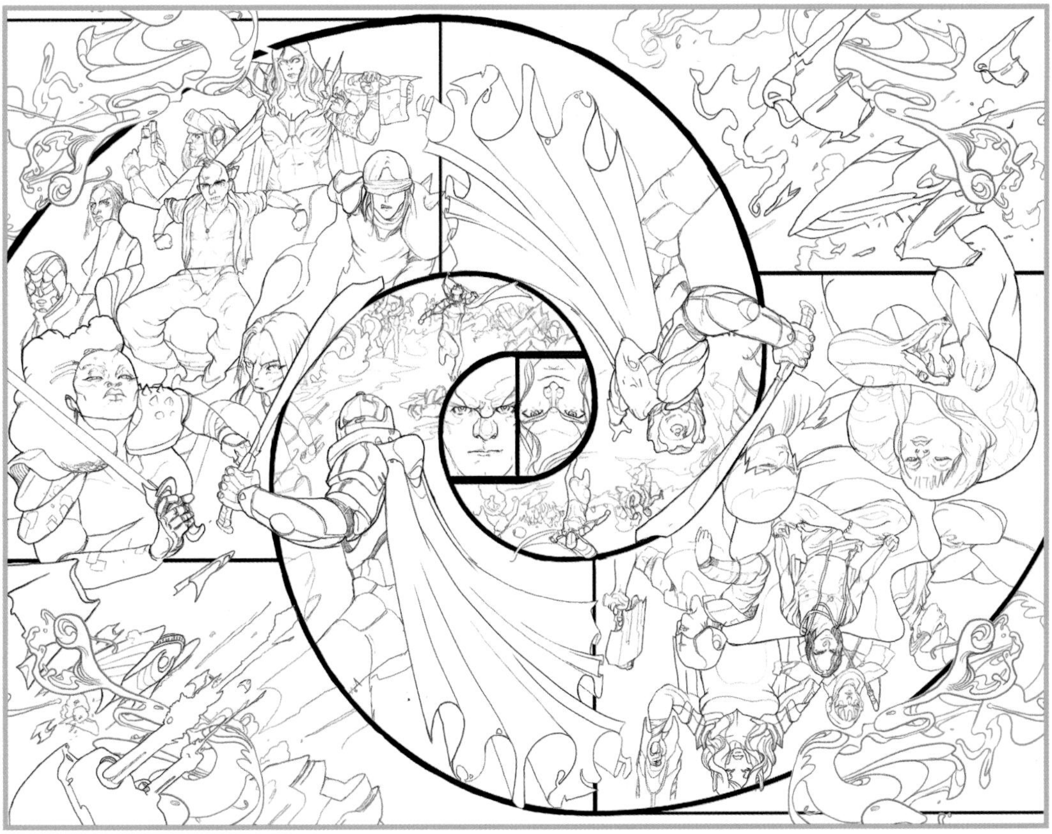

DESIGNS

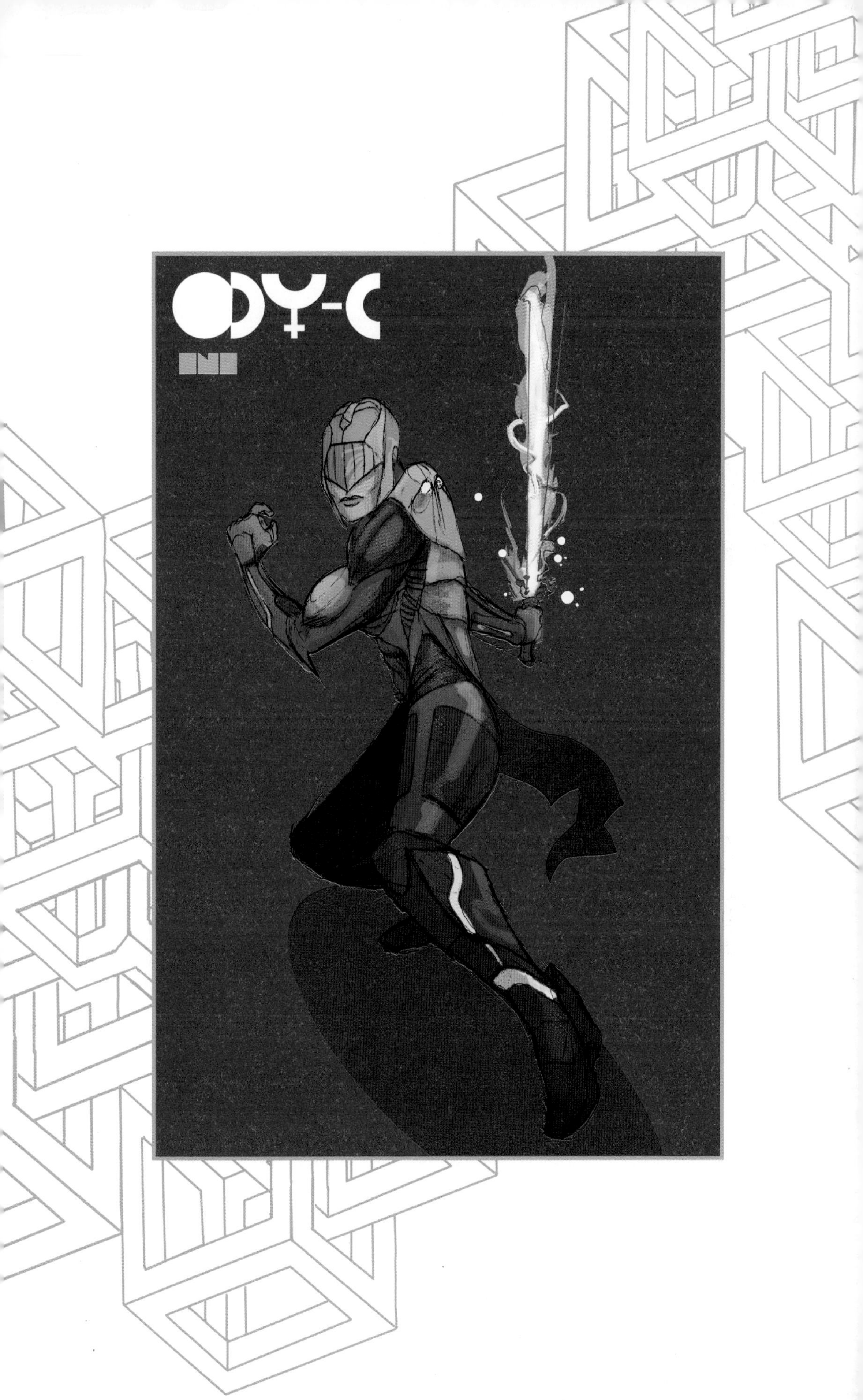
ODY-C

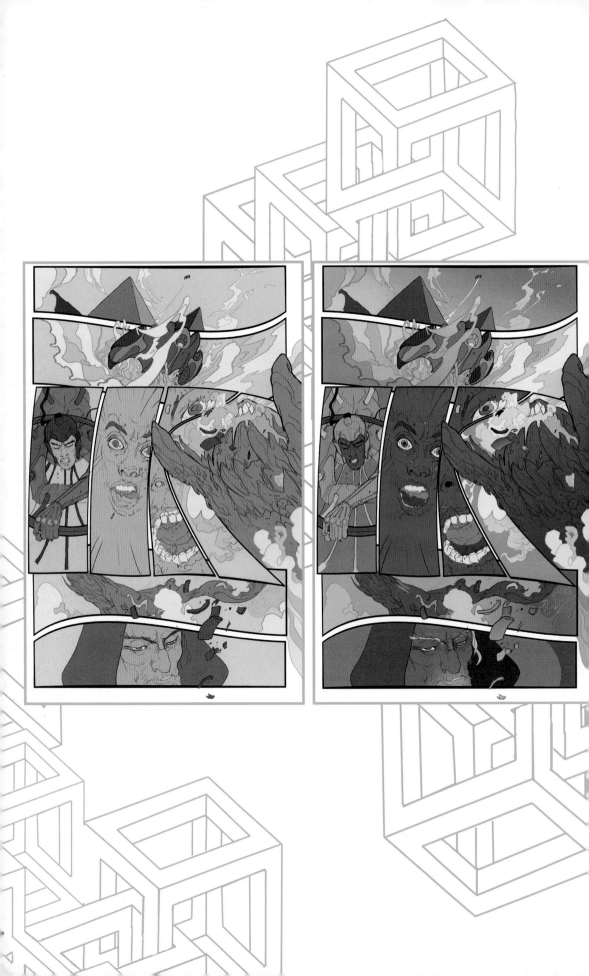

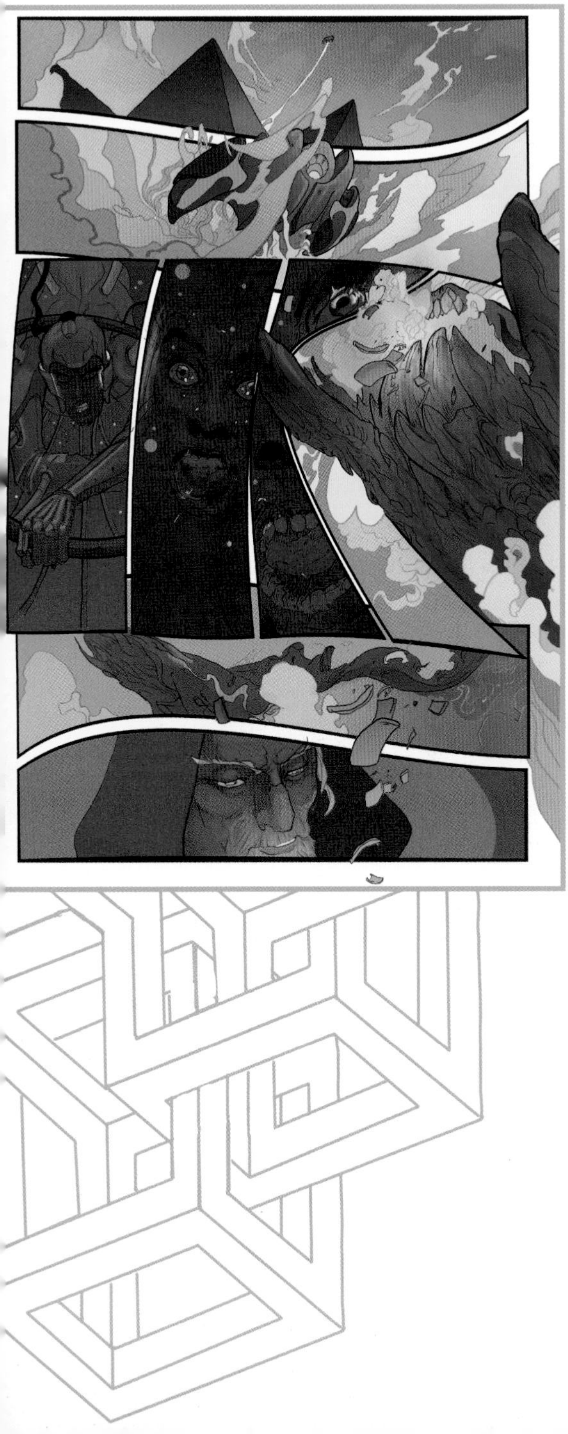

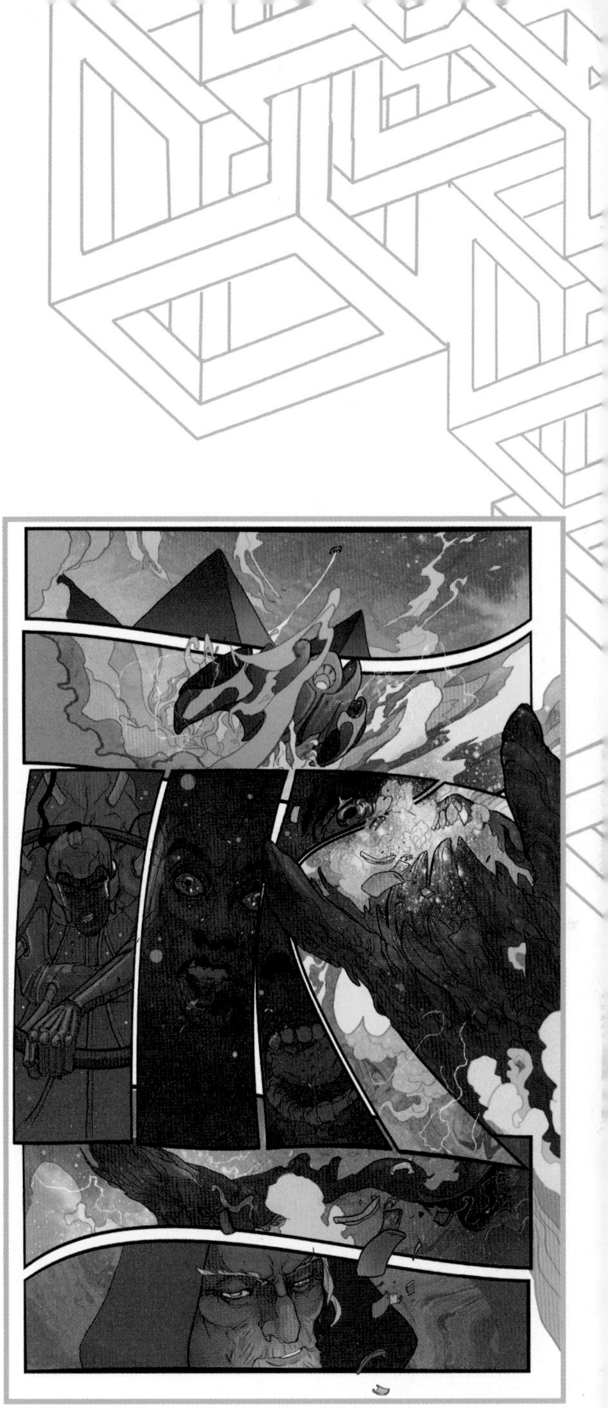

MATT FRACTION LIVES AND WRITES IN THE PACIFIC NORTHWEST WITH HIS FAMILY AND WOODS FULL OF STAGS AND COYOTES AND RAVENS. OR MAYBE CROWS.

HARD TO TELL SOMETIMES.

CHRISTIAN WARD LIVES AND DRAWS (AND OCCASIONALLY WRITES) IN THE UK. HE LIVES WITH HIS WIFE CATHERINE AND, BY THE TIME THIS BOOK COMES OUT, A YOUNG PUG CALLED THOR.